the big book of babycakes®
cupcake maker
recipes

the big book of babycakes® cupcake maker recipes

Homemade Bite-Sized Fun!

Kathy Moore & Roxanne Wyss

Robert
ROSE

The Big Book of Babycakes™ Cupcake Maker Recipes
Text copyright © 2012 Electrified Cooks LLC
Photographs copyright © 2012 Robert Rose Inc.
Cover and text design copyright © 2012 Robert Rose Inc.

For complete cataloguing information, see page 232.

Disclaimer
The recipes in this book have been carefully tested by our kitchen and our tasters. To the best of our knowledge, they are safe and nutritious for ordinary use and users. For those people with food or other allergies, or who have special food requirements or health issues, please read the suggested contents of each recipe carefully and determine whether or not they may create a problem for you. All recipes are used at the risk of the consumer. Consumers should always consult the Babycakes™ manual for recommended procedures and cooking times.

We cannot be responsible for any hazards, loss or damage that may occur as a result of any recipe use.

For those with special needs, allergies, requirements or health problems, in the event of any doubt, please contact your medical adviser prior to the use of any recipe.

Design and production: Daniella Zanchetta/PageWave Graphics Inc.
Editor: Sue Sumeraj
Recipe editor: Jennifer MacKenzie
Copy editor: Kelly Jones
Proofreader: Sheila Wawanash
Indexer: Gillian Watts
Techniques photographer: David Shaughnessy
Techniques stylist: Anne Fisher
Techniques hand model: Shannon Knopke
Recipe photographer: Colin Erricson
Recipe associate photographer: Matt Johannsson
Recipe food stylist: Kathryn Robertson
Recipe prop stylist: Charlene Erricson

Cover image: Lemon Drop Cupcakes (page 28)

We acknowledge the financial support of the Government of Canada through the Book Publishing Industry Development Program (BPIDP) for our publishing activities.

Published by Robert Rose Inc.
120 Eglinton Avenue East, Suite 800, Toronto, Ontario, Canada M4P 1E2
Tel: (416) 322-6552 Fax: (416) 322-6936
www.robertrose.ca

Printed and bound in Canada

1 2 3 4 5 6 7 8 9 TCP 20 19 18 17 16 15 14 13 12

We dedicate this book to the many fans of the
Babycakes™ Cupcake Maker and to our families
for their endless love and support.

....

Contents

Acknowledgments

WE ARE THRILLED and grateful that we were given the opportunity to write this book, and we are thankful for the cooperative spirit and support we received from so many people. A cookbook takes a team, and we are blessed that so many people shared their expertise with us.

First, we want to thank our families. Writing a cookbook takes time, creates endless stacks of dirty dishes and demands lots of late nights at the computer, and we just cannot thank them enough for their endless love and support.

Roxanne's family makes her life complete. Thank you to her husband, Bob Bateman, for his endless reservoir of patience and never-ending support, and for being Roxanne's best friend. Thank you to her daughter, Grace, for sharing her love, soul and spirit and for making Roxanne so proud with her approach to life. Thanks to both for their passion for great food and table-time memories. Roxanne's mom and dad, Kenny and Colleen Wyss, have strengthened her life because of the way they live their lives. Their love, dedication and 62 years of marriage say it all.

Kathy's family is the source of nonstop smiles, and she cannot imagine life without their love and support. Thank you, David, Laura and Amanda, for your patience, joy and encouragement.

Both of us were molded by our families, and the family dinner table is a cherished tradition that continues to center and inspire us. We are so thankful for those memories and for the support our siblings — Kathy's sister, Ellen Ervin, and Roxanne's brother, Mickey Wyss — continue to provide.

We so appreciate Bob Dees and the incredible team at Robert Rose Inc. for all of their work and support. This wonderful team includes our editor, Sue Sumeraj; our recipe editor, Jennifer MacKenzie; our copy editor, Kelly Jones; Martine Quibell, Publicity Manager; and Marian Jarkovich, Director of Sales. And the creative team at PageWave Graphics, including our designer, Daniella Zanchetta, is tops!

Special thanks to the Lisa Ekus Group, including our agents, Lisa Ekus and Sally Ekus, and their entire team for fantastic support and guidance.

Without Select Brands appliances, this book would not be possible. Thanks to Bill Endres, Eric Endres, Wes Endres and the entire worldwide Select Brands team for being so dedicated to designing, manufacturing, marketing, selling and shipping this great line of appliances. You all are great.

When we met Johnna Perry at a Kansas City food bloggers event, we were instantly captivated by both her friendly smile and her tasty gluten-free baking. We are eternally grateful to her for sharing her knowledge of gluten-free and vegan baking with us. She rocks, and we are blessed to now call her a friend!

We are thankful to all of our friends and colleagues who support us each day with helping hands and loving spirits. We are incredibly grateful to Sheri Worrel — truly the most artistic and creative person we know — and love her "think-tank" approach, which she shares so generously with us. We turn so often to Julie Bondank, and so appreciate her being our "right hand." Testing recipes for a collection like this really does take a team, and we are indebted to Mandy

Totoro, Jennifer Parson, Tyson Smith and Shannen Wolverton — an awesome test kitchen team!

Our careers have been based on sharing and networking, and we are grateful to so many people who have encouraged us along the way. A special thanks to colleagues Karen Adler and Judith Fertig, who provide such valuable insights into this journey.

Finally, thanks to all of you who love to bake sweet treats, have enjoyed the Babycakes™ Cupcake Maker and are hungry for more fun!

The Electrified Cooks™

WE ARE PLEASED to share more of our Babycakes™ Cupcake Maker recipes with you. We have to keep pinching ourselves — can the success of the Babycakes™ appliances and the miniature treats still be growing? It is! And we are so blessed to be pioneers in this exciting, tasty culinary category.

We host many events and teach lots of classes, and people always ask us how we got started in this career and how we test recipes. We are happy to share more about our background. Testing food, appliances and recipes means we constantly combine science, careful examination and a critical eye with our passion for cooking. We both are home economists, and we began our careers in the test kitchen of a small appliance company. It was there that we perfected our skills at testing appliances and recipes. We loved what we did. And we loved working together even more. Working with your best friend makes the work so much sweeter.

We absolutely love sharing our newest recipes and cooking methods with you. Whether it is through our cookbooks, articles, blog, cooking classes or consulting work, we are thrilled when we write a new, creative recipe, discover a new use for an appliance, teach a new skill and enable cooks to easily prepare great-tasting meals and treats. That's the premise of the Electrified Cooks. We have always focused on home cooks and helping them answer the question "What's for dinner?"

We have known Bill Endres, owner and president of Select Brands, Inc., for many, many years. What an honor it has been for us to work with him and to test many of Select Brands' newest appliances. When we saw that first prototype of a cupcake baker just a few years ago, we were ecstatic. It was so much fun to use, and we couldn't stop experimenting with it. We wrote the booklet that was packed with the appliance and then wrote *175 Best Babycakes™ Cupcake Maker Recipes* — and still we couldn't stop. We kept dreaming of new cupcake flavors, new appetizers and new ideas for using the Babycakes™ Cupcake Maker, and we just had to share them with you.

Introduction: Nonstop Fun

WE THINK IT'S impossible to bake a batch of small cupcakes in the Babycakes™ Cupcake Maker and not have fun. These moist, perfectly sized bundles are ready in only 5 to 8 minutes. You'll also enjoy preparing delightful two-bite pies, muffins, appetizers and more — perfect for any occasion. You just have to smile: they look so cute, taste so luscious and are so easy to make.

Here are a few times when the Babycakes™ Cupcake Maker can't be beat:

- *Family times:* Kids are captivated by the Babycakes™ Cupcake Maker, and a chapter in this book is devoted to making memories in the kitchen with children. Hungry, excited kids need only wait 5 to 8 minutes to enjoy the rewards of their baking efforts! The Babycakes™ Cupcake Maker is an electric appliance and it gets hot, so children should be closely supervised to avoid getting burnt.

- *Cooking for smaller families:* There's no need to heat up a big oven or make a far-too-large batch to enjoy scrumptious, freshly baked biscuits, muffins, cupcakes, appetizers and more. A special chapter is devoted to baking and cooking for smaller families.

- *Learning to cook:* The Babycakes™ Cupcake Maker enables anyone to bake cupcakes or prepare a quick breakfast, lunch or dinner. The recipes are easy to follow, and they don't require specialty pans or lots of equipment.

- *Your turn to bring the nibbles:* When you hear the plea "Who will bring refreshments?" you can quickly and confidently respond, "I will!" These goodies can be shared with your child's classmates, teammates or club friends, or at your office, church meeting, book club, Bunco game night or anywhere!

- *Bake sales:* These small treats are perfectly sized for quick sales and big profits — with very little in time or ingredient cost to you. It's a win-win for everyone!

- *Celebrations:* Holidays and parties are the time for treats to shine. Whatever the occasion — from tailgate parties, picnics, baby showers or sledding outings to Halloween, Christmas or New Year's — these desserts and appetizers couldn't be more special. Good things really do come in small packages.

Part 1

Getting Started

How to Use the Babycakes™ Cupcake Maker

THE BABYCAKES™ Cupcake Maker is so simple to use.

Preheating

There is no need to preheat the Babycakes™ Cupcake Maker, but once it's hot, you can bake batch after batch. When preparing pies or shaping crusts in the wells, start with a cold appliance and unplug it to cool for about 5 minutes between batches — we don't want you to get burnt!

Paper Liners or Cooking Spray

Paper liners are convenient but not required when you're preparing cupcakes and muffins. They are a must, though, when you're baking brownies and cheesecakes. These freshly baked treats are so hot it is nearly impossible to remove them without the paper liner, and they are so soft they will become misshapen or break apart. Do not use paper liners when baking pies, quiches, phyllo or wonton cups, biscuits or scones. Many of the appetizer recipes also do not require paper liners. The recipes in this book specify when paper liners are required or are optional.

The Babycakes™ Cupcake Maker wells are smaller than standard cupcakes and larger than mini cupcakes. The ideal paper liners to use are those made specifically for the Babycakes™ Cupcake Maker, available through Select Brands at www.thebabycakesshop.com and now sold at some retail stores under the Babycakes™ Cupcake Maker brand.

If you're not using paper liners, spray the wells with nonstick cooking spray as needed before spooning in the batter. Spray again between batches or as needed.

Mixing the Batter

The batters for these recipes are easy to prepare. Many of the recipes suggest beating with an electric mixer. We tested the recipes using a handheld mixer. There is no need to get out a heavy-duty stand mixer; in fact, for many of the recipes the batter does not have enough volume for a stand mixer to perform satisfactorily.

The speeds, power and beater design vary from mixer to mixer, so the speeds suggested in these recipes are to be used as a guide. You may need to adjust the speed a little on your mixer to get the best results.

Filling the Wells

The easiest way to fill the wells is with a small scoop. A variety of scoops is available at most cake and candy decorating shops. The ideal scoop holds just about $1\frac{1}{2}$ tablespoons (22 mL) and has a spring-action "scraper" that pushes the batter out of the scoop.

Of course, if you don't have a small scoop, you can use a small measuring cup to ladle the batter into the wells. Some doughs and batters can be piped into the wells using a pastry bag without a tip; just clip the point off the bag and quickly pipe the batter into the wells.

Fill each of the wells about three-quarters full. If you overfill the wells, the batter will seep out onto the surface area surrounding the wells.

Many of our friends like bigger cupcakes and muffins, while others love dainty, smaller ones. A typical cupcake or muffin baked in the Babycakes™ Cupcake Maker uses about $1\frac{1}{2}$ tablespoons (22 mL) of batter. However, you might use as much as 2 tablespoons (30 mL) or as little as 1 tablespoon (15 mL). Adding or subtracting a teaspoon or two (5 or 10 mL) of batter in each cupcake or muffin can affect the yield by three or four — or even more. No matter what size you choose, it is wise to make all of the treats in a batch the same size. No one wants to take the smallest one, and you want the treats to bake in the same amount of time.

We love to use the Babycakes™ Cupcake Maker at shows and events, and on those occasions, we fill all the wells and make batch after batch after batch. Other times, we want to use just that last bit of batter, and we fill only a well or two. It really doesn't matter if all eight wells or just a well or two are filled with batter.

Baking

Cupcakes and muffins bake quickly — typically in 5 to 8 minutes — so it is best to check their progress and not overbake them. We generally test for doneness at 5 minutes, then keep baking as needed. The closed environment of the Babycakes™ Cupcake Maker tends to keep baked goods especially moist. Many skilled bakers, when using conventional ovens, test for doneness by touching the top of a cupcake or muffin to see if it springs back, but we find the best way to test for doneness is to use a tester, such as a toothpick. If the treats are fully cooked, the tester will come out clean after being inserted into the center, and this method prevents burnt fingers!

We have found that adding an extra teaspoon (5 mL) of batter — or leaving one out —allows some treats to bake faster and others to bake a little slower, so we check several treats in a batch to make sure they are all done.

Removing Treats from the Wells

The freshly baked, hot treats are very tender and need to be carefully removed from the wells so that they don't break apart. Be careful not to burn yourself on the hot surfaces around the wells of the appliance.

There are two ideal tools to help remove baked goods from the wells. One is a small, thin offset spatula with a blade about $4\frac{1}{2}$ inches (11 cm) long. The blade is thinner than a table knife, thin enough to slip between the edge of the treat or paper liner and the well. Be careful not to scratch the surface of the appliance.

(You'll notice that the appliance's instructions caution against using metals on the nonstick coating, so use the offset spatula only to lift the edge of the cupcake or pie.) This little spatula is sold most often in specialty kitchen stores or with the cake- and cookie-decorating supplies at hobby or craft stores or cake decorating shops.

The other tool we love is the fork tool from Select Brands. It is perfectly designed to spear and lift cupcakes, muffins, biscuits and other treats. It can be ordered from their website (www.thebabycakesshop.com).

Once the hot baked items are removed from the wells, set them on a wire rack to cool.

Making Cupcakes

We know that cupcakes are likely the first treat you will make in your cupcake maker. Once you try cupcakes, be sure to explore all of the other different types of treats you can bake.

Do you prefer baking from scratch, or do you use a cake mix? Either is perfect for the Babycakes™ Cupcake Maker, and with this book you can try your hand at both. The types and flavors of cupcakes are nearly endless. The cupcake maker provides a moist cooking environment, so the results will be great. The exception is angel food and chiffon cakes: we do not recommend baking them in the Babycakes™ Cupcake Maker.

Measure carefully when baking. Sure, television chefs appear to just add ingredients, and many of us remember a grandma adding handfuls of flour, but we do not recommend this technique. Baking is a science, and any variation, even slight, will affect the overall results. This is especially true with these recipes because the yields are so small. We recommend using dry measuring cups for flour, sugar and all other dry ingredients. For liquids, use a liquid measuring cup and check the measure at eye level to be sure it is accurate.

Many of the recipes in this book yield fewer cupcakes than other recipes you might have. But if a batch makes more cupcakes than you wish to serve, simply freeze the extras (see page 48).

Cake Mix

The more cupcakes we bake, the more we realize that cake mixes vary by brand, and it may take some experimentation to determine which brand you like the best for each recipe. In general, we use 2 cups (500 mL) of cake mix, which is about half a package. Because of differences among brands — and even among cake mix flavors within brands — there may be a little less than 2 cups (500 mL) of cake mix left over for the next time you prepare a recipe.

Throughout the book, when we call for cake mix, we are referring to dry cake mix. Spoon it out of the box into a measuring cup and level it off. Store leftover cake mix in an airtight container and use by the expiration date stamped on the box.

When preparing batter from a cake mix, use the standard recipe that follows as a guide. This amount of batter will make 24 to 26 cupcakes.

Cake Mix Batter

2 cups	cake mix	500 mL
2	large eggs, at room temperature	2
10 tbsp	water	150 mL
1/4 cup	vegetable oil	60 mL

1. In a medium bowl, using an electric mixer on low speed, beat cake mix, eggs, water and oil for 30 seconds or until moistened. Beat on medium speed for 2 minutes.

Baking Hand Pies and Tarts

The Babycakes™ Cupcake Maker makes perfectly sized hand pies and delightful little tarts. The appliance comes with a two-piece pie crust tool set. The crust cutting tool looks like a double-sided cookie cutter, with one side slightly larger in diameter than the other. Use the large circle (about $3\frac{1}{4}$ inches/8 cm in diameter) to cut the bottom pie crust. Use the small circle (about $2\frac{7}{8}$ inches/7 cm in diameter) to cut the top crust. The other piece in the set is the pie forming tool — or the "pusher" — and it is a handy little device you can use to gently push the crust down into the well. If you have misplaced your crust cutting tool, you can use cookie cutters or biscuit cutters of about the same sizes. See pages 39, 41 and 43 for step-by-step instructions on cutting crusts and baking pies.

Turning Treats

The Babycakes™ Cupcake Maker bakes from both the top and bottom, so cupcakes and pies brown beautifully and bake quickly and evenly. But for certain specialty items, such as scones (pages 131–133) and phyllo bundles (page 155), we recommend turning partway through cooking. These treats don't rise enough to touch the top of the cupcake maker, and turning helps them to cook evenly. To turn a treat, insert the fork tool or a small, thin offset spatula between the well and the edge of the treat and carefully turn the treat over. If turning is required, this will be specified in the recipe.

Cleaning the Babycakes™ Cupcake Maker

Cleanup is simple. Unplug the appliance and let it cool completely. Wipe the surfaces with a damp towel. Use a dry paper towel to absorb any residual oils.

Once in a great while, a damp towel isn't enough for the job. First unplug the appliance, then, while the unit is still warm, wet a kitchen towel or paper towel and place it across the inner surface of the appliance. Close the unit and let it steam for about 5 minutes or until the towel is just cool enough to touch, then wipe the surface clean. Always use caution, and never place the towel in the appliance if it is plugged in.

The plates of the appliance do not come out, and there is nothing to take apart. Do not use soap or abrasive cleaners on it.

Baking Like a Pro!

WE LOVE TO teach cooking classes — and, in fact, we love to take cooking classes because we always learn some fun new tips and ideas! Here are some of our tips and suggestions on the ingredients in a well-stocked Babycakes™ pantry.

Flour

Almost all of the recipes in this book were tested using all-purpose flour. A few recipes call for cake flour, and our gluten-free recipes were tested with specific non-wheat flours. Always use the type of flour specified in the recipe; substituting whole wheat flour for all-purpose flour, for example, will affect the results.

Yes, we use common brands of all-purpose flour, but — given a chance — we love to use Hudson Cream, an artisanal flour by Stafford County Flour Mills Company, an independent midwestern mill. We also often turn to King Arthur flour. Watch for sales, especially before the holidays, so you can stock up. Store flour in a tightly sealed container in a cool, dry place for up to 6 months.

It's important to measure flour carefully. Spoon it from the canister or flour sack into a dry measuring cup and level it off with the straight edge of a knife or spatula. Do not pack it down or tap the measuring cup.

Flour does not need to be sifted for the recipes in this book. We recommend whisking the flour, leavening ingredients and salt together so that they are thoroughly blended before they are added to the batter. If the dry ingredients are not blended thoroughly, your cupcakes may have an uneven texture and leavening.

Sugar

Granulated sugar is a mainstay in baking. Sugar makes baked goods more tender, and reducing the amount of sugar in a recipe will result in a tough texture. We have not tested the recipes using artificial sweeteners, and substitutions of this type will affect both texture and flavor.

For brown sugar, you may use either light or dark; both perform well. Dark brown sugar has a little more molasses flavor. Many times we choose the one we are most familiar with — when Roxanne shops, she chooses dark, while Kathy chooses light. Sometimes an old-fashioned recipe or one specifically reminiscent of Southern cooking will specify dark brown sugar.

Confectioners' (icing) sugar is often used for frostings and glazes, and is very pretty when lightly dusted over cupcakes. We have found that you rarely need to sift confectioners' sugar anymore, as it generally blends into icing smoothly, especially when you are using an electric mixer. If we found it necessary to sift, the recipe will specifically say so; in that case, measure the sugar first, then sift it.

Store sugar in an airtight container at room temperature. Granulated and confectioners' (icing) sugar can be stored indefinitely, as long as they are kept dry. For optimum flavor, brown sugar is best used within 6 months. Watch for sales before the holidays and stock up.

Butter and Dairy

We generally turn to unsalted butter for the optimum flavor it provides in baked goods, and that is what we used when testing the recipes in this book. We have not tested the recipes using margarine. Using whipped and light spreads — often packaged in a tub and marked as diet spreads or with some other similar descriptive name — will affect the results.

We buy butter when it is on sale and keep it frozen. It can be stored in the freezer for up to 6 months. You can also purchase good-quality brands of butter, often at a discount, at warehouse and discount stores.

Dairy products, such as sour cream, half-and-half (10%) cream and heavy or whipping (35%) cream, are common ingredients in many baked goods. If you substitute low-fat or nonfat dairy products for the full-fat options, the flavor and the texture will be affected. Be sure to buy fresh ingredients; read the "sell by" or "best before" date before purchasing dairy products.

Buttermilk adds a delightful tang to baked goods, and — more importantly — its acidity plays an important role in leavening. If you are out of buttermilk, pour 1 tablespoon (15 mL) lemon juice or white vinegar into a 1-cup (250 mL) measure. Add enough milk to equal 1 cup (250 mL), stir and let stand for 5 to 10 minutes or until thickened. There are also dry buttermilk products available — follow the instructions on the label to reconstitute and use the buttermilk.

Vanilla

We choose pure vanilla extract for the best flavor. One of our favorite brands is Nielsen-Massey, available from King Arthur Flour (www.kingarthurflour.com), at gourmet food shops and at some large supermarkets. We watch for sales to save money.

Spices and Dried Herbs

When we teach, we often ask the attendees how long they have stored the herbs and spices in their cabinets — and once they reveal how very old some of those little bottles are, we encourage them to restock. If you open a bottle and cannot tell if it smells of garlic or ginger, it is more than time to purchase a new supply.

Many brands now come with a "use by" date stamped on the bottle or package. Or you can use a marker to date the bottle yourself, as a reminder of when you purchased it. Store spices and dried herbs in a cool, dry spot; do not store them in the freezer. In general, they should be used within a year of opening. If the color or aroma has faded, the flavor will have faded too.

Puff Pastry

We have baked hundreds of two-crust hand pies in the Babycakes™ Cupcake Maker, and we have discovered that puff pastry makes an especially beautiful, golden brown, flaky top crust. Because puff pastry puffs so much, it is not recommended for the bottom crust. Puff pastry is readily available in the freezer section of grocery stores. It is sold as sheets, shells or blocks — choose any of these and thaw according to package directions. Roll out on a lightly floured surface, pressing any perforated seams together, to about $\frac{1}{8}$ inch (3 mm) thick, then cut out crusts using the small circle on the crust cutting tool. If using shells, plan on cutting 2 top crusts from each shell; thaw only the number you need and keep the rest frozen for another use.

Fun with the Babycakes™ Cupcake Maker

TREATS AND CUPCAKES baked in the Babycakes™ Cupcake Maker may be bite-sized, but they are crammed full of fun. Friends and family will ooh and aah over the delightful, freshly baked and unadorned little cakes. Yet the fun is just beginning! Add a swirl of frosting or a decorative garnish, display your treats in a creative setting, and these two-bite bundles are perfect for any party or celebration.

Frosting Cupcakes

A swirl of frosting transforms simple little baked cakes into stunning desserts. Once you use a pastry bag to pipe frosting, you will never go back to simply spreading it on with a knife. It's easy — truly, it is. Even though cake-decorating professionals sometimes make it look complicated, anyone can master the technique. Just give it a try.

First, let the cupcakes cool for at least 30 minutes. If they're frosted while warm, the frosting will melt. When the cupcakes are cool, follow the step-by-step instructions on page 27 to learn how easy it is to fill and use a pastry bag. If children are helping, secure the open end of the bag with a rubber band to help keep the contents from squishing out.

We use disposable pastry bags, which are readily available at cake decorating and craft stores. Shop around; sometimes it's possible to buy rolls of 100 disposable bags for just a few dollars at a wholesale shop. There are reusable bags available as well, but food professionals are now recommending that cooks avoid them because it is nearly impossible to get them really clean and sanitized.

There are lots of decorating tips to choose from, and we are always changing our minds about which are our favorites. Check our blog (www.pluggedintocooking. com) for our latest discoveries. Some of the standards we often turn to are fine writing tips (such as Wilton #1, #2, #3 or #4), open stars (such as Wilton #22, #32 and #1M) and open rounds (such as Wilton #10, #12 or Ateco 805).

How much frosting is ideal? That is a matter of personal preference. We like to leave a small ring of unfrosted cake around the outside edge of each cupcake, only frosting the center. Is that critical? No, but it has become our signature look. Piping frosting only in the center, you can frost about 20 cupcakes with 1 cup (250 mL) of frosting. If you use a knife to spread the frosting, you can frost about 30 cupcakes with 1 cup (250 mL) of frosting. It is fine if you like more — or less — frosting. If you like lots of frosting, you may want to double the recipe.

Leftover frosting is never a problem. Store buttercream frostings in an airtight container in the refrigerator for up to 2 weeks. Store cream cheese frostings in an airtight container in the refrigerator for up to 5 days. Let the frosting come to room temperature before using it.

Tint the frosting to complement the color of the cupcakes or the theme of your party or celebration. Use gels or pastes for the truest, brightest colors. Add the coloring a tiny bit at a time — you can always add more to reach the color you want.

Garnishes and Embellishments

You don't have to stop with frosting — garnishes add the finishing touch. For starters, you could try a contrasting drizzle of chocolate or a colorful sprinkle of sugar, toasted nuts or small candies. But if you haven't browsed the aisles of a cake and candy decorating shop or a craft store lately, you are in for a surprise. The array is inspiring: sugars, colorful candies, glitters and so many more ideas.

An unexpected touch adds so much to these cute little treats. Billowy white frosting, a dusting of cocoa and an inserted soda straw make a cupcake look like a soda fountain favorite. A pirouette cookie sprouting from a blanket of elegant chocolate curls turns a chocolate cupcake into a real showstopper.

Try your hand at some of these classic garnishes! (Tip: Tweezers and food-safe paintbrushes are two of our favorite tools.)

- *Sprinkles:* Sprinkle colored sugars, shimmer dust, pearls, nonpareils, jimmies or colorful sprinkles over the freshly frosted cupcake — or, for a more striking look, dip the cupcake in sprinkles. First, pour the sprinkles into a small bowl. Frost the cupcake as you wish, then turn it upside down into the sprinkles. Gently roll the top of the cupcake through the sprinkles, covering it completely.

- *Chocolate curls:* Using a vegetable peeler, scrape long sweeps down the side of a plain chocolate bar or a bar of baking chocolate. A cool chocolate bar will make shorter curls, while a slightly warmer bar will make longer curls. Experiment with different types of chocolate — dark, milk or white — and with the temperature of the chocolate to achieve the look you want.

- *Chocolate leaves:* Clean and dry a few small mint leaves or other edible leaves. Place the leaves on a tray lined with waxed or parchment paper. In a small microwave-safe glass bowl, microwave chocolate candy melts on High in 30-second intervals, stirring between each, until melted. Using a clean, food-safe paintbrush, paint chocolate evenly over the back of each leaf, covering it completely. Let the chocolate dry, then carefully peel it off the leaf.

- *Chocolate filigree or swirls:* Draw your design (a star, swirls or a lacy decoration) freehand or clip a graphic from a coloring book or other publication. Place the design on the counter and cover it with waxed or parchment paper. Fill a pastry bag or sealable plastic bag with melted chocolate and clip off a small tip. Pipe the design, tracing the original graphic, onto the waxed paper. Let it cool until the chocolate hardens. Carefully peel off the waxed paper.

- *Citrus zest curls:* Use a zester to cut long, curling strips from a citrus fruit. Be sure to get just the colored portion of the fruit: the colored part has the flavor, and the white pith underneath is bitter.

- *Citrus slices:* Cut a thin crosswise slice from a small lemon or lime. Cut the slice in half or into quarters and place one piece on a freshly frosted cupcake. To make a twist, use a sharp knife to cut through the peel on one edge into the fleshy center. Hold the slice so your fingers are on either edge of the cut and twist in opposite directions. If the fruit is small, the twist will look stunning placed on top of a frosted cupcake; if the fruit is a little larger, arrange several twists on the platter around the cupcakes.

- *Fondant:* Purchase prepared fondant at any cake or candy decorating shop. If you don't find the color you want, you can tint white fondant using colored paste or gel food coloring. Before rolling it out, knead the fondant until it is warm and pliable, and any color you've added is evenly distributed. Roll the fondant out on a board lightly coated with confectioners' (icing) sugar or cornstarch. Use a tiny cookie cutter to cut the fondant into the desired shape, or use your fingers to mold the fondant. (It is very similar to working with modeling clay!)

Once opened, fondant dries out quickly. Be sure to keep it covered with plastic wrap and roll out just the amount you need. Store unused fondant in an airtight container and use it within 2 months. For optimum flavor and texture, use unopened packages of fondant within 18 months.

Combining Treats

Combine a treat or two for a fun, dramatic look. Cake pops (see our books *175 Best Babycakes™ Cake Pops Recipes* and *The Big Book of Babycakes™ Cake Pops*) make playful additions to cupcakes. What about a cake pop — without the stick — on top of a cupcake? Or use a cupcake as a "flower pot" and insert a cake pop decorated like a flower into the center. A cake pop decorated as a balloon, smiling face or animal and popping up from a cupcake would make a show-stopping treat!

Displays

Elegant displays make even the simplest cupcakes or appetizers really special. All it takes is a little creativity. Even a plate lined with a paper doily can dress your display up, but cupcake tiers, cake plates and beautiful dessert plates are readily available, and inexpensive options can be found on sales racks and at thrift stores. Decorative boxes and tins are readily available at craft and hobby stores and are perfect for displaying and gifting cupcakes.

One popular trend is to present individual cupcakes in unexpected ways. For example, serve a decorated cupcake in an antique teacup on a saucer. Or place a cupcake in a margarita or martini glass, then surround the cupcake with tiny colored candies; use the same candies on top of the cupcake. It's also fun to set a frosted cupcake on top of an inverted wine glass or footed goblet.

Cupcakes on mirrors make dramatic displays, and a presentation of row upon row of cupcakes on a striking tablecloth is a spectacular sight.

Gifting Treats

Take cues from the fancy bakeries. Your cupcakes taste just as good as the expensive ones, so make them look just as beautiful. Package your cupcakes in an elegant box tied with gorgeous ribbon. Or nestle them in a tin filled with tiny candies — the recipient will be thrilled! We often line a simple plate or cardboard tray with cupcakes and wrap it with cellophane and a big bow, a pretty look that is simple and inexpensive to create.

When making baked goods for gifts, avoid treats that require refrigeration.

Babycakes™ 101

Gingerbread Cupcakes

**Makes
30 to 31 cupcakes**

Kathy has become
quite a legend in her
circle of friends for
her tasty decorated
gingerbread cookies.
It seems only natural
that she should also
become well-known
for these festive
gingerbread treats.

Tip

Molasses is made from
boiling the juice that is
extracted from processing
sugar cane or beets into
sugar. Light (fancy) and dark
(cooking) molasses can be
used interchangeably in this
recipe, but dark (cooking)
molasses will give your
cupcakes a more robust
flavor.

- Paper liners (optional)

½ cup	water	125 mL
½ tsp	baking soda	2 mL
½ cup	dark (cooking) molasses	125 mL
¼ cup	cold water	60 mL
1 cup + 2 tbsp	all-purpose flour	280 mL
1½ tsp	baking powder	7 mL
1 tsp	ground cinnamon	5 mL
1 tsp	ground ginger	5 mL
¼ tsp	salt	1 mL
¼ tsp	ground cloves	1 mL
½ cup	packed brown sugar	125 mL
¼ cup	unsalted butter, softened	60 mL
1	large egg, at room temperature	1
2 tbsp	finely chopped crystallized ginger	30 mL

1. In a small saucepan, bring ½ cup (125 mL) water
   to a boil over high heat. Remove from heat and stir
   in baking soda and molasses. When mixture stops
   foaming, stir in ¼ cup (60 mL) cold water. Set aside
   to cool.

2. In a small bowl, whisk together flour, baking powder,
   cinnamon, ground ginger, salt and cloves. Set aside.

3. In a medium bowl, using an electric mixer on
   medium-high speed, beat brown sugar and butter
   for 1 to 2 minutes or until fluffy. Beat in egg until
   blended. Add flour mixture alternately with molasses
   mixture, making three additions of flour and two of
   molasses and beating on low speed until smooth.
   Fold in crystallized ginger.

4. If desired, place paper liners in wells. Fill each well
   with about 1½ tbsp (22 mL) batter. Bake for 6 to
   8 minutes or until a tester inserted in the center of
   a cupcake comes out clean. Transfer cupcakes to a
   wire rack to cool. Repeat with the remaining batter.

See the step-by-step photographs on photo page A. ▶

Tips

Paper liners are convenient but not required when you're preparing cupcakes and muffins. They are a must, though, when you're baking brownies and cheesecakes.

Look for a scoop with a spring-action "scraper" that pushes the batter out of the scoop.

If you don't have a small scoop, you can use a small measuring cup to ladle the batter into the wells.

Filling Wells and Baking Cupcakes

1. If desired, place paper liners in the wells.

2. To easily fill the wells, use a scoop that holds about $1\frac{1}{2}$ tbsp (22 mL) batter. Fill each of the wells with about $1\frac{1}{2}$ tbsp (22 mL) batter. The wells will be about two-thirds to three-quarters full.

3. Bake for 6 to 8 minutes. After 6 minutes, check the doneness by inserting a tester in the center of a cupcake. If it comes out moist, continue baking for 1 to 2 minutes more. The cupcakes are done when the tester comes out clean. Test several cupcakes to be sure they are all done.

4. Use a small offset spatula with a thin blade to carefully lift the edge of each cupcake out of its well, allowing you to pull it out. (Or use the fork tool to spear the cupcake and lift it out.)

5. Place the cupcakes on a wire rack to cool.

Pumpkin Maple Cupcakes

Makes
16 to 18 cupcakes

When driving through Vermont one summer, Kathy and her family crested a hill and she spotted a sign at the next farm inviting visitors to stop and taste the maple syrup. The farmers had tapped the trees for generations and were passionate about the syrup they made. What a fun side trip — and these cupcakes are a tasty reminder of that special day.

Tips

If desired, frost these cupcakes with Maple Frosting (page 112).

Leftover canned pumpkin purée? Refrigerate it in an airtight container for up to 1 week, or freeze it for up to 3 months. To use from frozen, thaw the pumpkin overnight in the refrigerator, then stir well and use it to bake another batch of cupcakes.

- Paper liners (optional)

1⅓ cups	all-purpose flour	325 mL
1 tsp	baking powder	5 mL
1 tsp	ground cinnamon	5 mL
½ tsp	ground nutmeg	2 mL
¼ tsp	baking soda	1 mL
¼ tsp	salt	1 mL
1	large egg, at room temperature	1
½ cup	canned pumpkin purée (not pie filling)	125 mL
½ cup	pure maple syrup	125 mL
¼ cup	vegetable oil	60 mL
1 tsp	vanilla extract	5 mL
⅓ cup	chopped pecans, toasted (see tip, page 65)	75 mL

1. In a small bowl, whisk together flour, baking powder, cinnamon, nutmeg, baking soda and salt. Set aside.

2. In a large bowl, using an electric mixer on medium-high speed, beat egg, pumpkin, maple syrup, oil and vanilla for 1 minute. Stir in flour mixture. Stir in pecans.

3. If desired, place paper liners in wells. Fill each well with about 1½ tbsp (22 mL) batter. Bake for 6 to 8 minutes or until a tester inserted in the center of a cupcake comes out clean. Transfer cupcakes to a wire rack to cool. Repeat with the remaining batter.

See the step-by-step photographs on photo page B. ▶

Tips

We use disposable pastry bags, which are readily available at cake decorating and craft stores. Shop around; sometimes it's possible to buy rolls of 100 disposable bags for just a few dollars at a wholesale shop.

Professional cake decorators often use a coupler and ring to attach the decorating tip, but if you're using a disposable pastry bag, that's rarely necessary for these little cupcakes. If you're using a reusable bag — or if you plan to change decorating tips while frosting — slip the coupler inside the bag, then use the ring to fasten the decorating tip onto the coupler.

Filling a Pastry Bag

1. A pastry bag makes frosting and decorating cupcakes quick and easy. First, fold 2 to 3 inches (5 to 7.5 cm) of the top edge of the bag down, like a sleeve cuff.

2. Snip off the tip of the bag.

3. Place the decorating tip inside the bag and slide it down to the new opening.

4. Spoon frosting into the bag, filling it about half full.

5. Roll up the collar of the bag and twist the top shut directly above the frosting.

6. Gently push from the top down, squeezing the bag where it is twisted so that frosting flows out of the tip.

Lemon Drop Cupcakes

We work a lot of public events and we love doing it because we meet so many great people. But this means we talk a lot and sometimes a drink of ice water is just not possible. Roxanne always tries to keep lemon drop candies in our booth, because the refreshing lemon flavor is the little pickup we need. We capture that vibrant lemon flavor in these lemon cupcakes.

Tip

If desired, garnish the top of each frosted cupcake with a lemon drop candy.

- Paper liners (optional)

2 cups	lemon cake mix	500 mL
3½ tbsp	vanilla instant pudding mix (half of a 3.4 oz/96 g box)	52 mL
2	large eggs, at room temperature	2
⅓ cup	freshly squeezed lemon juice	75 mL
⅓ cup	water	75 mL
¼ cup	vegetable oil	60 mL
	Lemon Glaze (page 118)	
	Lemon Frosting (page 109)	

1. In a large bowl, whisk together cake mix and pudding. Add eggs, lemon juice, water and oil. Using an electric mixer on low speed, beat for 30 seconds or until moistened. Beat on medium speed for 2 minutes.

2. If desired, place paper liners in wells. Fill each well with about 1½ tbsp (22 mL) batter. Bake for 6 to 8 minutes or until a tester inserted in the center of a cupcake comes out clean. Transfer cupcakes to a wire rack to cool for 10 minutes or until just barely warm. Repeat with the remaining batter.

3. Using a toothpick, prick the top of each cupcake two or three times. Slowly drizzle about ¼ tsp (1 mL) of the Lemon Glaze over the top of each cupcake. Use the back of the measuring spoon to lightly spread the glaze. Let cool completely.

4. Frost with Lemon Frosting.

See the step-by-step photographs on photo page C. ▶

Tip
Let cupcakes cool for at least 30 minutes before frosting.

Piping a Frosting Swirl

1. Select a medium to large open star tip and place the tip on the pastry bag.

2. Fill the pastry bag with frosting (see page 27) and twist the bag shut.

3. Hold the pastry bag at the twist with one hand, and a cupcake in the other hand. Place the tip of the pastry bag close to the surface of the cupcake.

4. Starting near the edge of the cupcake (but leaving a ring of unfrosted cake), pipe frosting in a circle on top of the cupcake.

5. Without stopping, pipe in a spiral fashion a slightly smaller circle of frosting just inside the first. Continue to the center of the cupcake, allowing each smaller circle to overlap slightly so it perches on the one before it.

6. When you reach the center, lift the piping bag straight up to make a small point of frosting.

Golden Yellow Cupcakes

There is nothing plain
or ordinary about these
yellow cupcakes. They
are truly a favorite and
make perfect canvases
for decorating.

Tip
No buttermilk on hand? Stir
2 tsp (10 mL) lemon juice or
white vinegar into ⅔ cup
(150 mL) milk. Let stand
for 5 to 10 minutes or until
thickened. Proceed with
the recipe.

• Paper liners (optional)

1⅓ cups	all-purpose flour	325 mL
1½ tsp	baking powder	7 mL
½ tsp	baking soda	2 mL
⅛ tsp	salt	0.5 mL
1 cup	granulated sugar	250 mL
½ cup	unsalted butter, softened	125 mL
2	large eggs, at room temperature	2
⅔ cup	buttermilk	150 mL
1 tsp	vanilla extract	5 mL

1. In a small bowl, whisk together flour, baking powder, baking soda and salt. Set aside.

2. In a large bowl, using an electric mixer on medium-high speed, beat sugar and butter for 1 to 2 minutes or until fluffy. Add eggs, one at a time, beating well after each addition. Add flour mixture alternately with buttermilk, making three additions of flour and two of buttermilk and beating on low speed until smooth. Beat in vanilla.

3. If desired, place paper liners in wells. Fill each well with about 1½ tbsp (22 mL) batter. Bake for 6 to 8 minutes or until a tester inserted in the center of a cupcake comes out clean. Transfer cupcakes to a wire rack to cool. Repeat with the remaining batter.

See the step-by-step photographs on photo page D. ▶

Tips

Knead fondant until it's warm and pliable before rolling it out. Fondant dries quickly, so keep it covered with plastic wrap until you're ready to use it.

When attaching fondant to fondant, use a dampened food-safe paintbrush to lightly moisten the pieces of fondant before pressing them together.

Making a Simple Fondant Bow

1. Lightly dust a cutting board with confectioners' (icing) sugar. Place a piece of prepared fondant on the cutting board and use a rolling pin to roll it out to 1/8- to 1/4-inch (3 to 5 mm) thickness.

2. Use the large circle of the pie cutting tool to cut out a circle from the fondant. Place the circle on top of a lightly frosted cupcake.

3. Roll out a piece of fondant in a contrasting color. Use a knife and a straight edge to cut three 1/4-inch (5 mm) wide strips. Lay one of the strips across the center of the cupcake, like a ribbon across a package. Trim the edges of the strip to match the edges of the fondant circle.

4. Cut the other two fondant strips into 1 1/2-inch (4 cm) lengths. Fold each in half to make a loop, pinching the ends to secure.

5. Place the ends of the loops together, then wrap a 3/4- to 1-inch (2 to 2.5 cm) long piece of fondant around the ends to make a "knot" in the center of the loops.

6. Place the fondant bow on top of the fondant ribbon.

All-American Chocolate Cupcakes

**Makes
35 to 37 cupcakes**

Almost every
birthday at Roxanne's
house is celebrated
with chocolate
cake. Roxanne is
a chocoholic —
Kathy, not so much.
Friendship prevails,
and Kathy developed
this recipe for her
friend and business
partner of more than
30 years!

Tip

For a more intense flavor,
substitute steaming hot
coffee for the boiling water.

* Paper liners (optional)

½ cup	unsweetened cocoa powder	125 mL
1 cup	boiling water	250 mL
1⅓ cups	all-purpose flour	325 mL
1 tsp	baking soda	5 mL
½ tsp	baking powder	2 mL
¼ tsp	salt	1 mL
1¼ cups	granulated sugar	300 mL
½ cup	unsalted butter, softened	125 mL
2	large eggs, at room temperature	2
1 tsp	vanilla extract	5 mL

1. In a small bowl, whisk together cocoa and water. Set aside to cool completely.

2. In another small bowl, whisk together flour, baking soda, baking powder and salt. Set aside.

3. In a large bowl, using an electric mixer on medium-high speed, beat sugar and butter for 1 to 2 minutes or until fluffy. Add eggs, one at a time, beating well after each addition. Add flour mixture alternately with cocoa mixture, making three additions of flour and two of cocoa and beating on low speed until smooth. Beat in vanilla.

4. If desired, place paper liners in wells. Fill each well with about 1½ tbsp (22 mL) batter. Bake for 6 to 8 minutes or until a tester inserted in the center of a cupcake comes out clean. Transfer cupcakes to a wire rack to cool. Repeat with the remaining batter.

See the step-by-step photographs on photo page E. ▶

Tips

Knead fondant until it's warm and pliable before rolling it out. Fondant dries quickly, so keep it covered with plastic wrap until you're ready to use it.

After a bit of practice, your roses will look beautiful, but you may not be happy with your first attempt. Don't give up: simply knead the fondant again, roll it out and reshape it before letting the rose dry. Experiment to find the size and shape of rose you like best.

For a stunning presentation, decorate some of your cupcakes with rosebuds and some with open roses. Add leaves in a variety of sizes — just as you would find in nature — and vary the number of leaves on each cupcake.

Making a Fondant Rose

1. Lightly dust a cutting board with confectioners' (icing) sugar. Place a piece of prepared fondant on the cutting board and use a rolling pin to roll it out to $\frac{1}{8}$- to $\frac{1}{4}$-inch (3 to 5 mm) thickness. Cut out a strip about $1\frac{1}{2}$ inches (4 cm) wide and 5 inches (12.5 cm) long. (If you're making a rosebud, you won't need as long a strip as you would to make an open rose, but it's a good idea to be generous with the length, as you can always trim off the excess once the rose is the desired size.) Trim both ends so they are straight. Fold the strip in half lengthwise.

2. With the folded edge at the top, start at one narrow end and tightly roll the strip continuously around itself in a coil. Pinch the bottom (cut) edge tightly as you roll and allow the top (folded) edge to remain slightly loose.

3. Roll the strip until your rose is the desired shape, stopping when it looks like a tight rosebud or continuing to roll along the entire strip for an open rose. Use a knife to trim off the end of the strip, if necessary, then press the end to the side of the rose to hold it closed. (If necessary, lightly moisten the end with a dampened food-safe paintbrush before pressing to help it stick.)

4. Pinch the bottom edge of the rose into a slightly elongated triangle. Gently set the rose aside on your work surface and let it dry for 1 to 2 hours, until the fondant feels a little dry to the touch.

5. Roll a piece of green fondant into a tiny ball ($\frac{1}{4}$ to $\frac{1}{2}$ inch/0.5 to 1 cm in diameter), then press it gently into a leaf shape. Using the tip of a toothpick or the blunt end of a tiny food-safe paintbrush, draw simple veins in the leaf. (If making a larger leaf, you'll only need one per rose for these little cupcakes. If making smaller leaves, position three around each rose.)

6. Pipe frosting onto a cupcake in a decorative swirl, as shown on photo page C. Nestle the rose and leaf on top of the swirl.

Old-Fashioned White Cupcakes

**Makes
30 to 32 cupcakes**

A cupcake store opened up within walking distance of Roxanne's house. The bakers there prepare a white cake with chocolate icing that Roxanne could not resist. After many months, she drew a line in the sand and said, "No more," refusing to pay $3 for a cupcake she could bake at home. This recipe is a result of many tests, and we think you will agree that it could compete on a Food Network challenge — and win!

Tips

Cake flour has a fine texture that makes it perfect for cakes. Look for boxes of cake flour wherever flour is sold. Store it in an airtight container at room temperature for up to 6 months, or freeze it for up to 1 year.

If desired, frost with Classic Chocolate Buttercream Frosting (page 106).

• Paper liners (optional)

1⅓ cups	cake flour	325 mL
1 tsp	baking powder	5 mL
¼ tsp	salt	1 mL
½ cup	shortening	125 mL
¼ cup	unsalted butter, softened	60 mL
1 cup	granulated sugar	250 mL
2	large eggs, at room temperature	2
½ cup	buttermilk	125 mL
1 tsp	vanilla extract	5 mL
½ tsp	almond extract	2 mL

1. In a small bowl, whisk together cake flour, baking powder and salt. Set aside.

2. In a medium bowl, using an electric mixer on medium-high speed, beat shortening and butter for 2 minutes or until creamy. Gradually add sugar, beating well. Add eggs, one at a time, beating well after each addition. Add flour mixture alternately with buttermilk, making three additions of flour and two of buttermilk and beating on low speed until smooth. Beat in vanilla and almond extract.

3. If desired, place paper liners in wells. Fill each well with about 1½ tbsp (22 mL) batter. Bake for 6 to 8 minutes or until a tester inserted in the center of a cupcake comes out clean. Transfer cupcakes to a wire rack to cool. Repeat with the remaining batter.

Variation
Fold ½ cup (125 mL) mini semisweet chocolate chips into the batter.

See the step-by-step photographs on photo page F. ▶

Tips

If your marshmallows are quite fresh and sticky, chill them by placing them in the freezer for about 10 to 15 minutes. They will cut more easily.

For the eyes, try using miniature candy-covered chocolate candies (such as mini M&Ms) or any other tiny candies. Give different bunnies different eye colors!

Creating a Bunny Decoration

1. Frost each cupcake with Vanilla Buttercream Frosting (page 105) or your favorite white frosting, using a small offset spatula to spread it evenly, making it smooth.

2. Dip the cupcake in sweetened flaked coconut, covering the frosting completely.

3. Use scissors to cut a large marshmallow in half crosswise. Gently pull each half into an oval. Dip the cut edge of each oval in pink decorating sugar. Place the ovals on the cupcake so that they resemble bunny ears.

4. Cut a pink jelly bean in half. Place one half in the center of the cupcake for the nose. Add two tiny candies for eyes.

5. Cut a miniature marshmallow in half crosswise for the bunny's cheeks.

6. Use a tube of pink decorating gel to draw whiskers.

Classic Waldorf Astoria Cupcakes

Makes 24 to 26 cupcakes

Red velvet or Waldorf Astoria? Whatever you call this popular cake, it's as beautiful as it is tasty. When we tried to research the origin of this cake, we realized it is simply timeless — every family seems to have a favorite recipe. Here's ours.

Tip

No buttermilk on hand? Stir 1½ tsp (7 mL) lemon juice or white vinegar into ½ cup (125 mL) milk. Let stand for 5 to 10 minutes or until thickened. Proceed with the recipe.

• Paper liners (optional)

1¼ cups	all-purpose flour	300 mL
¼ tsp	salt	1 mL
½ cup	unsalted butter, softened	125 mL
1 cup	granulated sugar	250 mL
1	large egg, at room temperature	1
1 tsp	vanilla extract	5 mL
1½ tbsp	unsweetened cocoa powder	22 mL
1 tbsp	red food coloring	15 mL
½ cup	buttermilk	125 mL
¾ tsp	baking soda	3 mL
1½ tsp	white vinegar	7 mL

1. In a small bowl, whisk together flour and salt. Set aside.

2. In a large bowl, using an electric mixer on medium-high speed, beat butter for 1 minute or until creamy. Add sugar and beat for 1 minute. Beat in egg and vanilla. Beat in cocoa and food coloring until well blended. Add flour mixture alternately with buttermilk, making three additions of flour and two of buttermilk and beating on low speed until smooth.

3. In a small bowl, stir together baking soda and vinegar until completely dissolved. Beat into the batter until well blended.

4. If desired, place paper liners in wells. Fill each well with about 1½ tbsp (22 mL) batter. Bake for 6 to 8 minutes or until a tester inserted in the center of a cupcake comes out clean. Transfer cupcakes to a wire rack to cool. Repeat with the remaining batter.

See the step-by-step photographs on photo page G. ▶

Tips

In place of the candies, you could also use miniature chocolate chips for the eyes and nose.

If your marshmallows are quite fresh and sticky, chill them by placing them in the freezer for about 10 to 15 minutes. They will cut more easily.

Making a Simple Santa

1. Frost each cupcake with Vanilla Buttercream Frosting (page 105) or your favorite white frosting, using a small offset spatula to spread it evenly, making it smooth.

2. To make Santa's hat, sprinkle the top third of the cupcake with red sanding sugar, then sprinkle it along the outer edge of one side of the cupcake.

3. Place miniature candy-covered chocolate candies for the eyes and nose.

4. Cut two miniature marshmallows in half crosswise. Arrange three of the halves, cut side down, across the edge of the red sugar to make a furry hat brim.

5. Place the remaining marshmallow half at the bottom of the red sugar on the side of the cupcake to make a tassel on the hat.

6. Cut several more miniature marshmallows in half and arrange them as the beard.

Favorite Buttery Pie Crust

This classic, flaky pie crust is sure to be a winner. Shortening makes the crust easy to work with, and butter adds a hit of flavor.

Tips

Wrap leftover dough tightly in plastic wrap and refrigerate; use within 3 days or freeze for up to 2 months. Let thaw overnight in the refrigerator, then roll out and use as desired.

For a flakier crust, substitute pastry flour for all-purpose flour.

- Pastry blender or blending fork

1½ cups	all-purpose flour	375 mL
½ tsp	salt	2 mL
⅓ cup	cold unsalted butter, cut into small pieces	75 mL
¼ cup	shortening	60 mL
1	cold large egg yolk	1
4 to 5 tbsp	ice water	60 to 75 mL

1. In a large bowl, whisk together flour and salt. Using a pastry blender or blending fork, cut in butter and shortening until mixture is crumbly.

2. In a small bowl, using a fork, whisk together egg yolk and 4 tbsp (60 mL) ice water. Sprinkle evenly over flour mixture and let stand for 30 seconds. Blend with a fork until dough holds together and cleans the sides of the bowl, adding more ice water, if needed. Form dough into a disk, wrap in plastic wrap and refrigerate for at least 30 minutes, until chilled, or for up to 24 hours.

3. If firmly chilled, let dough stand at room temperature for 10 minutes. On a lightly floured surface, lightly dust top of dough with flour. Roll out gently, picking dough up after each roll, dusting underneath with flour as necessary and rotating it from 12 o'clock to 3 o'clock. (This keeps the dough from sticking.) Roll and rotate until dough is about ⅛ inch (3 mm) thick.

4. Use as directed in the recipe or, to bake single crusts blind (empty), see page 39. To bake single-crust mini pies, see page 41. To bake two-crust hand pies, see page 43.

See the step-by-step photographs on photo page H. ▶

Tips

Fill the cooled pie crusts with any of the fillings in this book, or, for a quick filling, spoon in prepared pudding, mousse, fruit, jam or ice cream.

If you have misplaced the crust cutting tool, you can use a cookie cutter or biscuit cutter of about the same size. The large circle of the crust cutting tool is about $3\frac{1}{4}$ inches (8 cm) in diameter.

Baking Single Crusts Blind

1. Use the large circle of the crust cutting tool to cut 6 to 8 crusts from Favorite Buttery Pie Crust (page 38) or a store-bought refrigerated pie crust (see tip, page 40).

2. Place crusts evenly on top of wells and gently press into wells with the pie forming tool.

3. If desired, crimp the edges.

4. Evenly prick the bottom and around the sides of each crust with the tines of a fork, being careful not to scratch the surface of the wells. Bake for 8 to 10 minutes or until the crusts are golden and crisp.

5. Use a small, thin offset spatula to carefully lift the crusts out of the wells.

6. Transfer the crusts to a wire rack to cool. Let the appliance cool for 5 minutes between batches.

Southern-Style Pecan Mini Pies

A distinct chocolate flare and a hint of bourbon transform traditional pecan pie into a gourmet delight. These are perfect for any dessert buffet.

Tip

If using a store-bought refrigerated pie crust, let come to room temperature, then unroll according to package directions and proceed with the recipe. You can cut 14 Babycakes™ single crusts from one packaged pie crust (half a 14-oz/400 g package) by rerolling the scraps.

Crusts

	Favorite Buttery Pie Crust (page 38) or store-bought refrigerated pie crust (see tip, at left)	

Filling

¼ cup	granulated sugar	60 mL
1	large egg, at room temperature	1
2 tbsp	unsalted butter, melted	30 mL
¼ cup	light (white or golden) corn syrup	60 mL
1½ tsp	bourbon	7 mL
¼ cup	chopped pecans	60 mL
2 tbsp	mini semisweet chocolate chips	30 mL

1. *Crusts:* Use the large circle of the crust cutting tool to cut 8 crusts from the pie crust. Place crusts evenly on top of wells and gently press into wells with the pie forming tool. If desired, crimp the edges.

2. *Filling:* In a medium bowl, whisk together sugar, egg, butter, corn syrup and bourbon. Stir in pecans and chocolate chips.

3. Spoon 1½ to 2 tbsp (22 to 30 mL) filling into each crust. Bake for 10 to 12 minutes or until filling is set and crusts are golden. Transfer pies to a wire rack to cool.

See the step-by-step photographs on photo page I. ▶

Tips

If you have misplaced the crust cutting tool, you can use a cookie cutter or biscuit cutter of about the same size. The large circle of the crust cutting tool is about 3¼ inches (8 cm) in diameter.

Wrap leftover dough tightly in plastic wrap and refrigerate; use within 3 days or freeze for up to 2 months. Let thaw overnight in the refrigerator, then roll out and use as desired.

Baking Single-Crust Mini Pies

1. Use the large circle of the crust cutting tool to cut 6 to 8 crusts from Favorite Buttery Pie Crust (page 38) or a store-bought refrigerated pie crust (see tip, page 40).

2. Place crusts evenly on top of wells and gently press into wells with the pie forming tool.

3. If desired, crimp the edges.

4. Spoon 1 to 2 tbsp (15 to 30 mL) filling into each crust. Bake for 10 to 12 minutes or until the filling is cooked according to the recipe directions and the crusts are golden brown.

5. Use a small, thin offset spatula to carefully lift the pies out of the wells.

6. Transfer the pies to a wire rack to cool. Let the appliance cool for 5 minutes between batches.

Rhubarb Berry Hand Pies

When we travel together and visit restaurants, it is a sure bet that Roxanne will order any item from the menu that has rhubarb in it. She loves rhubarb and even went so far as to grow it in her backyard, where it was prolific for many years. Neighbors enjoyed her rhubarb jam and now are equally pleased when these rhubarb-stuffed hand pies are delivered to their doorsteps.

Tips

Go ahead, take the plunge and be a purist. Omit the strawberries and substitute rhubarb. Increase the granulated sugar by 3 tbsp (45 mL).

Because puff pastry puffs so much, it is not recommended for the bottom crust of a two-crust hand pie.

Crusts

Favorite Buttery Pie Crust (page 38) or store-bought refrigerated pie crust (see tip, page 40)
Puff pastry (see tip, page 94)

Filling

1/3 cup	granulated sugar	75 mL
2 tsp	quick-cooking tapioca	10 mL
1 cup	sliced rhubarb (fresh or thawed frozen)	250 mL
3/4 cup	sliced strawberries	175 mL
1 tsp	grated orange zest	5 mL
1 tbsp	freshly squeezed orange juice	15 mL

Egg Wash

1	large egg, at room temperature	1
1 tbsp	water	15 mL

1. *Crusts:* Use the large circle of the crust cutting tool to cut 12 bottom crusts from the pie crust, rerolling scraps as necessary. Place 8 crusts evenly on top of wells and gently press into wells with the pie forming tool. Cover the remaining crusts with plastic wrap and set aside.

2. On a lightly floured surface, roll out puff pastry to about 1/8 inch (3 mm) thick, pressing any perforated seams together. Use the small circle of the crust cutting tool to cut 12 top crusts. Cover with plastic wrap and set aside.

3. *Filling:* In a medium bowl, combine sugar and tapioca. Add rhubarb and strawberries, tossing to coat. Stir in orange zest and orange juice. Let stand for 15 minutes.

4. Spoon about 1 1/2 tbsp (22 mL) filling into each bottom crust; do not overfill. Place a top crust directly over the center of each filled shell.

5. *Egg Wash:* In a small bowl, whisk together egg and water. Brush lightly over top crusts.

6. Bake for 10 to 12 minutes or until crusts are browned and crisp. Transfer pies to a wire rack to cool. Let appliance cool for 5 minutes. Repeat with the remaining crusts and filling.

See the step-by-step photographs on photo page J. ▶

Tip
If you have misplaced the crust cutting tool, you can use cookie cutters or biscuit cutters of about the same sizes. The large circle of the crust cutting tool is about 3¼ inches (8 cm) in diameter, and the small circle is about 2⅞ inches (7 cm) in diameter.

Baking Double-Crust Hand Pies

1. Use the large circle of the crust cutting tool to cut 6 to 8 bottom crusts from Favorite Buttery Pie Crust (page 38) or a store-bought refrigerated pie crust (see tip, page 40).

2. Use the small circle to cut 6 to 8 top crusts, rerolling scraps as necessary.

3. Place bottom crusts evenly on top of wells and gently press into wells with the pie forming tool.

4. Spoon filling into each bottom crust until about half full.

5. Place a top crust directly over the center of each filled shell. For added browning and sheen, lightly whisk together 1 egg and 1 tbsp (15 mL) water and brush lightly over top crusts. Bake for 12 to 15 minutes or until top crusts are golden brown and crisp.

6. Use a small, thin offset spatula to carefully lift the pies out of the wells and transfer the pies to a wire rack to cool. Let the appliance cool for 5 minutes between batches.

Phyllo Cups

**Makes
8 cups**

We just shared this recipe at a cooking class and everyone was thrilled to learn how easy it is to use the Babycakes™ Cupcake Maker to make crisp, fresh phyllo cups — without butter! We bet you will make these again and again.

Tips

Fill baked phyllo cups with dip, fruit, mousse or another favorite filling.

Store cooled baked phyllo cups in an airtight container at room temperature for 1 to 2 days.

Bake the entire roll of phyllo dough, seal any extra cups in an airtight container and freeze for up to 2 months.

| 8 | sheets frozen phyllo dough (see tip, page 45), thawed
Nonstick baking spray | 8 |

1. Form phyllo dough into cups as directed on page 45.

2. Spray the inside of each cup lightly with baking spray.

3. Bake for 5 to 7 minutes or until phyllo cups are golden brown and crisp. Transfer cups to a wire rack to cool slightly.

See the step-by-step photographs on photo page K. ▶

Tips

Different brands of phyllo come in different-size sheets. We used sheets that are 14 by 9 inches (35 by 23 cm), which is about half of a 16-oz (454 g) package. Some sheets are larger (17 by 12 inches/43 by 30 cm or 18 by 14 inches/ 45 by 35 cm), so use 4 and cut them in half crosswise before folding as directed.

Thaw phyllo dough in the refrigerator according to the package directions. If extra sheets remain, wrap them tightly in plastic wrap and refrigerate for up to 2 weeks or refreeze and use within 9 months.

Forming Phyllo Cups

1. Place one sheet of thawed frozen phyllo dough on a cutting board. Immediately cover the remaining phyllo sheets with plastic wrap and then a lightly dampened towel, keeping them covered to prevent them from drying out.

2. Fold the sheet into thirds, making a 9- by 4½-inch (23 by 11 cm) rectangle.

3. Fold the rectangle in half, making a 4½-inch (11 cm) square.

4. Using the large circle of the crust cutting tool, imprint a circle on the phyllo, pressing firmly.

5. Use kitchen shears to cut out the circle. Discard scraps.

6. Place the circle (there will be 6 layers) on top of a well and very gently press into the well with the pie forming tool, making a cup. Repeat with 7 more sheets of phyllo until all 8 wells are covered. Bake as directed on page 44, or fill and bake as directed on page 47.

Phyllo Cups Filled with Artichoke Dip

**Makes
16 filled cups**

Each Christmas Eve, Roxanne's brother and his family fly from Florida to spend Christmas in his hometown of Kansas City. These treats are always on the buffet table for all to enjoy while celebrating the special season and cherishing family ties.

Tip

For a less acidic flavor, omit lemon juice.

16	sheets frozen phyllo dough (see tip, page 45), thawed	16
1	clove garlic, minced	1
1	can (14 oz/425 mL) quartered artichoke hearts, drained and finely chopped	1
2/3 cup	freshly grated Parmesan cheese	150 mL
1/4 cup	dry bread crumbs with Italian seasoning	60 mL
1/2 cup	mayonnaise	125 mL
1 tbsp	freshly squeezed lemon juice	15 mL

1. Form 8 sheets of phyllo dough into cups as directed on page 45.

2. In a medium bowl, combine garlic, artichokes, Parmesan, bread crumbs, mayonnaise and lemon juice. Spoon about 2 tbsp (30 mL) filling into each phyllo cup.

3. Bake for 10 to 12 minutes or until cups are crisp and filling is hot. Carefully transfer cups to a wire rack to cool slightly.

4. Let appliance cool for 5 minutes. Repeat with the remaining phyllo dough and filling. Serve warm.

See the step-by-step photographs on photo page L. ▶

Tips

Phyllo sheets dry out very quickly. Work with one sheet at a time and be sure to keep the rest covered with plastic wrap and a lightly dampened towel. As you gently lift off each sheet, recover the remaining sheets immediately.

Wrap any leftover phyllo sheets tightly in plastic wrap and store in the refrigerator for up to 2 weeks.

Baking Filled Phyllo Cups

1. Form 8 sheets of thawed frozen phyllo dough into cups as directed on page 45.

2. Spoon about 2 tbsp (30 mL) filling into each phyllo cup. Bake for 10 to 12 minutes or until the cups are crisp and the filling is hot.

3. Use a small, thin offset spatula to carefully lift the baked cups out of the wells.

4. Transfer the cups to a wire rack to cool.

Storing Your Baked Goods

BAKED GOODS TASTE best when freshly baked, but occasionally you may need to store them for another day. Always let the treats cool completely, then store them in an airtight container and label it with the date. Remember that typical sealable food bags are not freezer-safe.

Store unfrosted cupcakes layered between parchment or waxed paper in an airtight container at room temperature for up to 3 days or in the freezer for up to 3 months. If frozen, thaw at room temperature for about an hour, then frost and serve.

Cheesecakes, cream-filled cupcakes and cupcakes frosted with cream cheese or whipped cream must be stored in the refrigerator and should not sit out at room temperature for more than 2 hours. If you are planning a buffet that includes these treats, set out only those that will be eaten right away, then replenish as needed. Cheesecakes freeze beautifully — just refrigerate until firm, then seal them in an airtight container or freezer bag, separating the layers with parchment or waxed paper, and freeze for up to 2 months. Let them thaw overnight in the refrigerator before serving.

Cream-filled pies can be stored in the refrigerator for up to 2 days. Do not freeze cream-filled pies. Pies with a meat filling can be stored in the refrigerator for up to 4 days or in the freezer for up to 2 months.

Muffins, biscuits and scones are best served fresh and warm. We do not recommend storing them.

Filling Wells and Baking Cupcakes

(see page 25 for detailed step-by-step instructions)

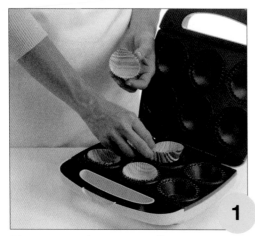

Place paper liners in wells.

Use a scoop to fill wells.

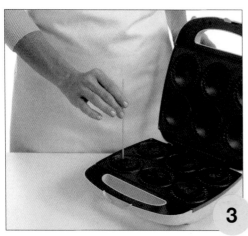

Bake cupcakes and test for doneness.

Use an offset spatula to lift the edge of each cupcake.

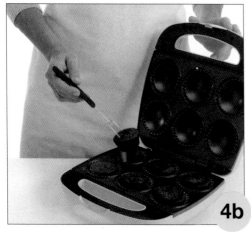

Or use the fork tool to spear the cupcake.

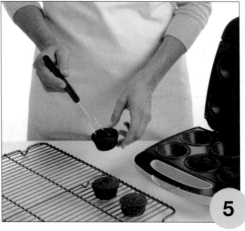

Place the cupcakes on a wire rack to cool.

A.

Filling a Pastry Bag

(see page 27 for detailed step-by-step instructions)

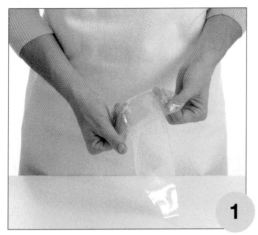

1

Fold top edge of pastry bag down to make a collar.

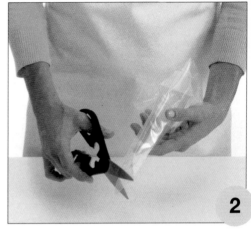

2

Snip the tip of the bag off.

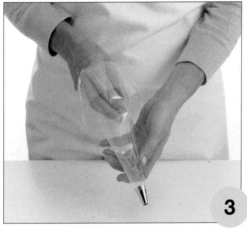

3

Slide the decorating tip into the bag.

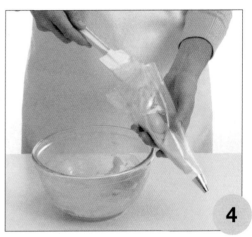

4

Spoon frosting into the bag.

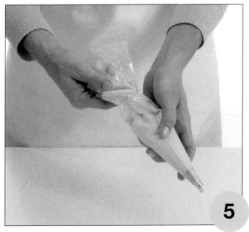

5

Roll up the collar and twist the top shut.

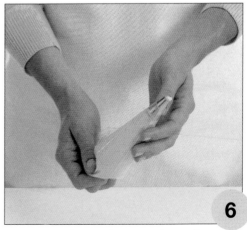

6

Gently push out frosting from the top down.

B.

Piping a Frosting Swirl

(see page 29 for detailed step-by-step instructions)

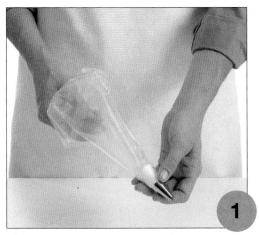

Place an open star tip on the pastry bag.

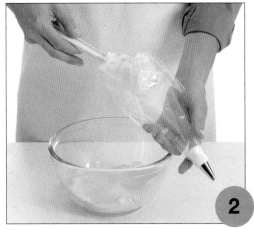

Fill the pastry bag with frosting.

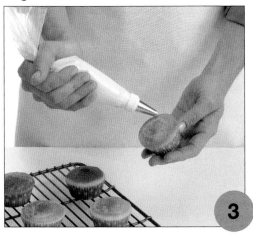

Place the tip of the pastry bag close to the surface of the cupcake.

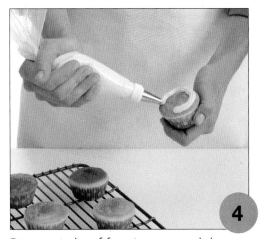

Pipe a circle of frosting around the edge of the cupcake.

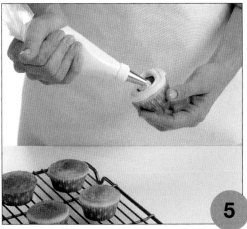

Continue to pipe circles in a spiral fashion toward the center.

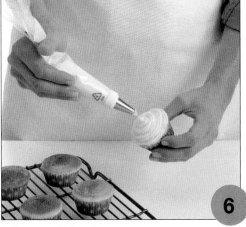

Lift the piping bag straight up to make a small point of frosting.

C.

Making a Simple Fondant Bow

(see page 31 for detailed step-by-step instructions)

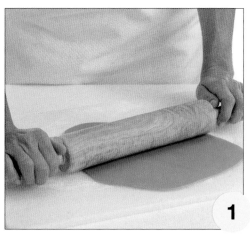

Roll out fondant on a cutting board.

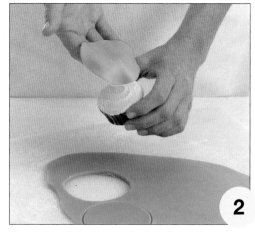

Cut out a circle and place it on a lightly frosted cupcake.

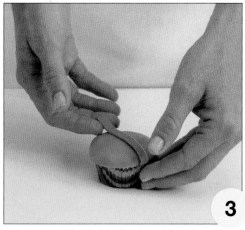

Lay a fondant strip in a contrasting color across the circle.

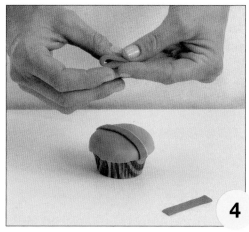

Fold two more fondant strips into loops.

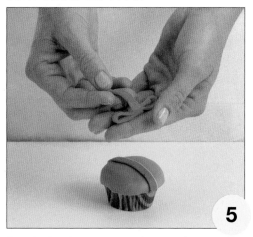

Pinch the loops together and wrap the center with a fondant strip.

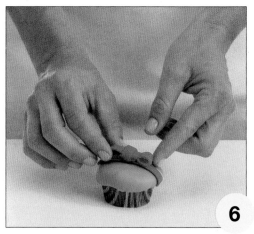

Place the bow on top of the fondant ribbon.

D.

Making a Fondant Rose

(see page 33 for detailed step-by-step instructions)

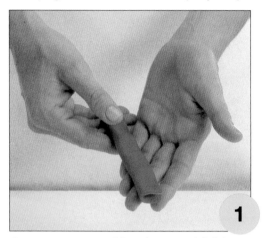

1

Cut out a strip of fondant and fold it in half lengthwise.

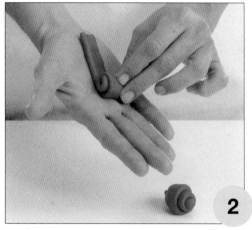

2

Tightly roll the folded strip around itself in a coil.

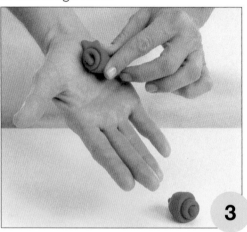

3

Roll the strip into a tight rosebud or an open rose.

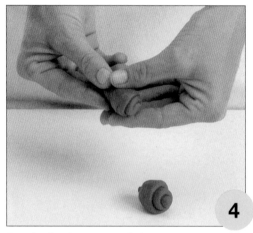

4

Pinch the bottom of the rose into a triangle.

5

Form leaves from green fondant and draw simple veins.

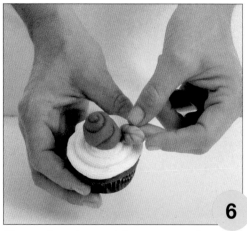

6

Pipe a frosting swirl on a cupcake and nestle the rose and leaf on top.

E.

Creating a Bunny Decoration

(see page 35 for detailed step-by-step instructions)

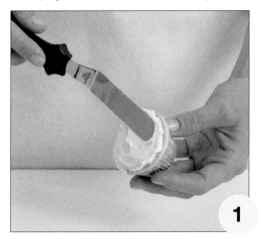

1

Frost a cupcake with white frosting.

2

Dip the frosting in flaked coconut.

3

Create bunny ears from the halves of a large marshmallow.

4

Place half a pink jelly bean for the nose and tiny candies for eyes.

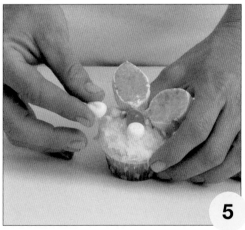

5

Cut a mini marshmallow in half for the cheeks.

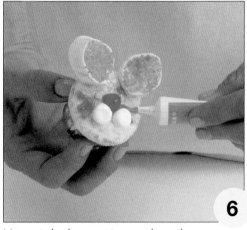

6

Use pink decorating gel to draw whiskers.

F.

Making a Simple Santa

(see page 37 for detailed step-by-step instructions)

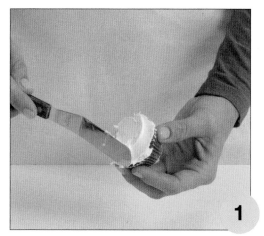

1

Frost a cupcake with white frosting.

2

Sprinkle red sanding sugar for Santa's hat.

3

Place mini candies for the eyes and nose.

4

Arrange mini marshmallow halves as the hat brim.

5

Place a mini marshmallow half as a tassel.

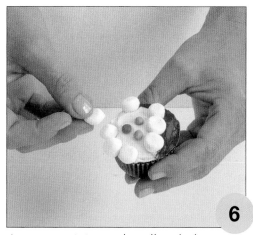

6

Arrange mini marshmallow halves as a beard.

G.

Baking Single Crusts Blind

(see page 39 for detailed step-by-step instructions)

Use the large circle of the crust cutting tool to cut 6 to 8 crusts.

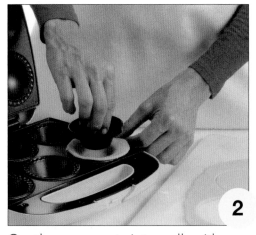

Gently press crusts into wells with the pie forming tool.

If desired, crimp the edges.

Prick the crust with a fork and bake for 8 to 10 minutes.

Carefully lift the crusts out of the wells.

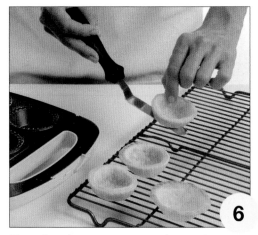

Transfer the crusts to a wire rack to cool.

H.

Baking Single-Crust Mini Pies

(see page 41 for detailed step-by-step instructions)

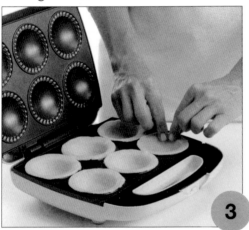

1

Use the large circle of the crust cutting tool to cut 6 to 8 crusts.

2

Gently press crusts into wells with the pie forming tool.

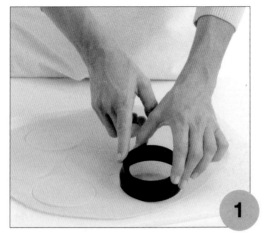

3

If desired, crimp the edges.

4

Spoon filling into the crusts and bake for 10 to 12 minutes.

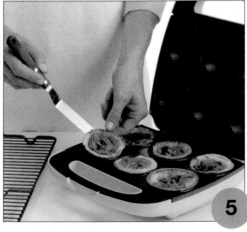

5

Carefully lift the pies out of the wells.

6

Transfer the pies to a wire rack to cool.

Baking Double-Crust Hand Pies

(see page 43 for detailed step-by-step instructions)

Use the large circle of the crust cutting tool to cut 6 to 8 bottom crusts.

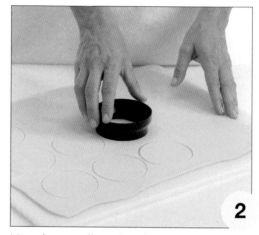

Use the small circle of the crust cutting tool to cut 6 to 8 top crusts.

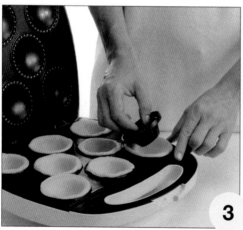

Gently press bottom crusts into wells with the pie forming tool.

Spoon filling into crusts until about half full.

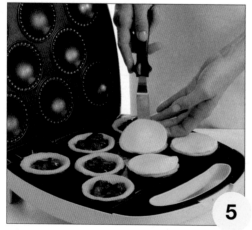

Place top crusts over filling, brush with egg wash and bake.

Lift the pies out of the wells and transfer to a wire rack to cool.

J.

Forming Phyllo Cups

(see page 45 for detailed step-by-step instructions)

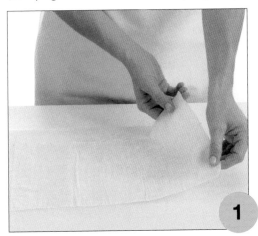

Place one sheet of phyllo on a cutting board.

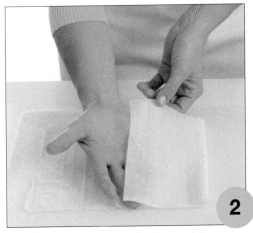

Fold the sheet into thirds, making a rectangle.

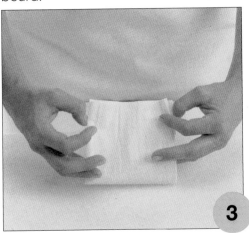

Fold the rectangle in half, making a square.

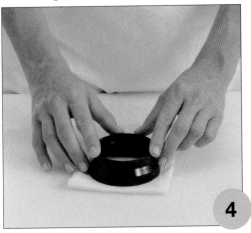

Imprint a circle on the phyllo.

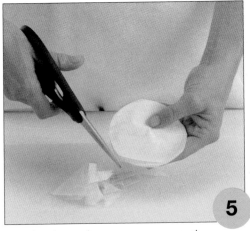

Use kitchen shears to cut out the circle.

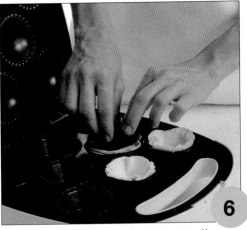

Gently press the circle into a well. Repeat to cover all wells.

K.

Baking Filled Phyllo Cups

(see page 47 for detailed step-by-step instructions)

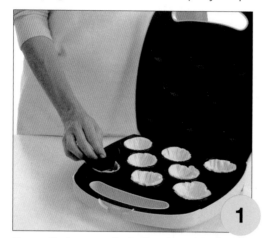

Form 8 sheets of phyllo dough into cups.

Spoon filling into cups and bake for 10 to 12 minutes.

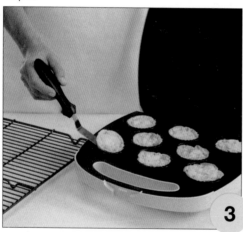

Carefully lift the baked cups out of the wells.

Transfer the cups to a wire rack to cool.

L.

Part 2

Sweet Treats

Bake Shop Cupcakes

Marbled Swirl Cupcakes

**Makes
24 to 26 cupcakes**

Can't decide if you
like chocolate or
vanilla best? Now you
won't have to choose!
Both classic flavors
are captured in these
cupcakes — plus, the
color contrast makes
them absolutely
gorgeous.

· ·

Tips

Do not swirl the two colors
of the batter too much —
once or twice is enough.
As you scoop the batter
into the wells, the batter
will naturally swirl more.

For a different look, keep
the batters separate.
Fill one pastry bag with
chocolate batter and
another with white batter.
Pipe the batters into the
wells simultaneously, so
that half of each cupcake is
chocolate and half is white.
Bake as directed.

- Paper liners (optional)

2 oz	unsweetened chocolate, coarsely chopped	60 g
1½ cups	all-purpose flour	375 mL
1½ tsp	baking powder	7 mL
½ tsp	baking soda	2 mL
¼ tsp	salt	1 mL
1 cup	granulated sugar	250 mL
⅓ cup	unsalted butter, softened	75 mL
2	large eggs, at room temperature	2
¼ cup	sour cream	60 mL
1 tsp	vanilla extract	5 mL
½ cup	milk	125 mL

Vanilla Buttercream Frosting
(page 105)
Chocolate Drizzle (page 119)

1. Place chocolate in a medium microwave-safe glass
   bowl. Microwave on High in 30-second intervals,
   stirring after each, until melted. Stir until smooth.
   Let cool to room temperature.

2. In a small bowl, whisk together flour, baking powder,
   baking soda and salt. Set aside.

3. In a large bowl, using an electric mixer on medium-high
   speed, beat sugar and butter for 1 to 2 minutes or until
   fluffy. Add eggs, one at a time, beating well after each
   addition. Beat in sour cream and vanilla. Add flour mixture
   alternately with milk, making three additions of flour
   and two of milk and beating on low speed until smooth.

4. Spoon 1 cup (250 mL) batter into melted chocolate. Stir
   until blended. Using a spoon, drop dollops of chocolate
   batter on top of the white batter. Swirl with the tip of a
   knife just once or twice; do not swirl completely or blend.

5. If desired, place paper liners in wells. Fill each well
   with about 1½ tbsp (22 mL) batter. Bake for 6 to
   8 minutes or until a tester inserted in the center of
   a cupcake comes out clean. Transfer cupcakes to a
   wire rack to cool. Repeat with the remaining batter.

6. Frost with Vanilla Buttercream Frosting, then drizzle
   with Chocolate Drizzle.

Italian Cream Cake Bites

Makes
28 to 30 cupcakes

Classic Italian cream cake — light with egg whites and rich with coconut and pecans — is captured in these delightful bite-size cupcakes.

Tips

Frost with Cream Cheese Frosting (page 114) and garnish, if desired, with additional toasted finely chopped pecans.

No buttermilk on hand? Stir 1½ tsp (7 mL) lemon juice or white vinegar into ½ cup (125 mL) milk. Let stand for 5 to 10 minutes or until thickened. Proceed with the recipe.

• Paper liners (optional)

1 cup	all-purpose flour	250 mL
½ tsp	baking soda	2 mL
¼ tsp	salt	1 mL
1 cup	granulated sugar	250 mL
¼ cup	shortening	60 mL
¼ cup	unsalted butter, softened	60 mL
3	large eggs, separated, at room temperature	3
1 tsp	vanilla extract	5 mL
½ cup	buttermilk	125 mL
1 cup	sweetened shredded coconut	250 mL
½ cup	finely chopped pecans, toasted (see tip, page 65)	125 mL

1. In a small bowl, whisk together flour, baking soda and salt. Set aside.

2. In a medium bowl, using an electric mixer on medium speed, beat sugar, shortening and butter for 1 to 2 minutes or until fluffy. Add egg yolks, one at a time, beating well after each addition. Beat in vanilla. Add flour mixture alternately with buttermilk, making three additions of flour and two of buttermilk and beating on low speed until smooth.

3. In another medium bowl, using an electric mixer with clean beaters, beat egg whites on high speed until stiff peaks form. Gently fold into batter. Fold in coconut and pecans.

4. If desired, place paper liners in well. Fill each well with about 1½ tbsp (22 mL) batter. Bake for 6 to 8 minutes or until a tester inserted in the center of a cupcake comes out clean. Transfer cupcakes to a wire rack to cool. Repeat with the remaining batter.

Cream-Filled Chocolate-Glazed Cupcakes

· ·

**Makes
24 to 26 cupcakes**

These little cakes bear a strong resemblance to a brand-name childhood favorite. Roxanne and her husband, Bob Bateman, loved them so much, they chose them for a cupcake tier on their wedding day.

· ·

Tips

To fill a cupcake, fit a pastry bag with a medium writing tip, such as a Wilton #3, and spoon the filling into the bag. Insert the tip of the bag into the top of the cooled cupcake and gently squeeze the bag. The filling will flow into the cupcake, swelling it slightly. Do not overfill.

To really replicate that childhood favorite, drizzle a white chocolate swirl on top of each glazed cupcake.

Running short of time? Omit the filling and simply glaze these cupcakes for a quick chocolate dessert.

- Paper liners (optional)
- Pastry bag fitted with medium writing tip

2 cups	chocolate cake mix	500 mL
2 tbsp	unsweetened cocoa powder	30 mL
2	large eggs, at room temperature	2
$\frac{2}{3}$ cup	buttermilk	150 mL
$\frac{1}{4}$ cup	vegetable oil	60 mL
	Vanilla Cream Filling (page 119)	
	Chocolate Glaze (page 117)	

1. In a medium bowl, using an electric mixer on low speed, beat cake mix, cocoa, eggs, buttermilk and oil for 30 seconds or until moistened. Beat on medium speed for 2 minutes.

2. If desired, place paper liners in wells. Fill each well with about $1\frac{1}{2}$ tbsp (22 mL) batter. Bake for 6 to 8 minutes or until a tester inserted in the center of a cupcake comes out clean. Transfer cupcakes to a wire rack to cool. Repeat with the remaining batter.

3. Fill the pastry bag with Vanilla Cream Filling. Pipe filling into the cupcakes (see tip, at left), making sure not to overfill. Spoon Chocolate Glaze over the cupcakes, then smooth it with the back of the spoon.

Orange-Glazed Citrus Poppy Seed Cakes

The scent of oranges growing in the Floridian groves is unforgettable, just like these orange-flavored cakes.

Tip

When grating citrus zest, be sure to grate only the colored portion of the peel. The colored part is packed with flavor, but the white pith underneath is bitter.

- Paper liners (optional)

2 cups	lemon cake mix	500 mL
1	large egg, at room temperature	1
1	large egg white, at room temperature	1
1½ tsp	grated orange zest	7 mL
⅔ cup	freshly squeezed orange juice	150 mL
¼ cup	vegetable oil	60 mL
1 tbsp	poppy seeds	15 mL
	Orange Glaze (page 118)	

1. In a medium bowl, using an electric mixer on low speed, beat cake mix, egg, egg white, orange juice and oil for 30 seconds or until moistened. Beat on medium speed for 2 minutes. Fold in poppy seeds and orange zest.

2. If desired, place paper liners in wells. Fill each well with about 1½ tbsp (22 mL) batter. Bake for 6 to 8 minutes or until a tester inserted in the center of a cupcake comes out clean. Transfer cupcakes to a wire rack to cool slightly. Repeat with the remaining batter.

3. Drizzle Orange Glaze over warm cupcakes.

Apple Cider Cupcakes

The flavors of fall explode with each bite of these delightful cupcakes. Why not visit a local apple cider mill with your family to purchase the cider? That's what Roxanne did — and the memories will last forever.

Tips

When frosting over a filling, as with the apple butter here, it is easiest and neatest to pipe the frosting, covering the filling and the cupcake.

Reserve the cake you cut from the tops of these cupcakes for other uses. Try layering the pieces with fresh fruit for a parfait, or crumbling them over ice cream. They also make great lunch box treats. Freeze leftover cake pieces in a freezer bag for up to 2 months.

• Paper liners (optional)

1 cup + 2 tbsp	all-purpose flour	280 mL
$\frac{1}{2}$ tsp	baking soda	2 mL
$\frac{1}{2}$ tsp	ground cinnamon	2 mL
$\frac{1}{8}$ tsp	ground cloves	0.5 mL
$\frac{3}{4}$ cup	granulated sugar	175 mL
$\frac{1}{3}$ cup	unsalted butter, softened	75 mL
1	large egg, at room temperature	1
$\frac{3}{4}$ cup	unsweetened apple cider	175 mL
$\frac{1}{4}$ cup	apple butter	60 mL
	Apple Cider Frosting (page 113)	
	Toasted chopped walnuts (optional)	

1. In a small bowl, whisk together flour, baking soda, cinnamon and cloves. Set aside.

2. In a medium bowl, using an electric mixer on medium speed, beat sugar and butter for 1 to 2 minutes or until fluffy. Beat in egg. Add flour mixture alternately with cider, making three additions of flour and two of cider and beating on low speed until smooth.

3. If desired, place paper liners in wells. Fill each well with about $1\frac{1}{2}$ tbsp (22 mL) batter. Bake for 6 to 8 minutes or until a tester inserted in the center of a cupcake comes out clean. Transfer cupcakes to a wire rack to cool. Repeat with the remaining batter.

4. Using a serrated knife, cut a $\frac{1}{2}$-inch (1 cm) circle out of the top of each cupcake. Fill each circle with about $\frac{1}{2}$ tsp (2 mL) apple butter. Frost with Apple Cider Frosting (see tips, at left). If desired, garnish with walnuts.

Strawberry Smoothie Cupcakes

Roxanne's daughter, Grace, prefers these fruit-filled delights over a smoothie any day.

Tip

It's fun to split these cupcakes in half and fill them with sliced strawberries, then dollop with whipped cream before serving.

- Blender
- Paper liners (optional)

1	package (10 oz/300 g) frozen sliced strawberries in syrup, thawed	1
1½ cups	all-purpose flour	375 mL
1¼ tsp	baking powder	6 mL
¼ tsp	baking soda	1 mL
Pinch	salt	Pinch
¾ cup	granulated sugar	175 mL
½ cup	unsalted butter, softened	125 mL
2	large eggs, at room temperature	2
1 tsp	strawberry extract	5 mL
2 to 4	drops red food coloring	2 to 4

1. In blender, process strawberries and their syrup until smooth. Set aside.

2. In a small bowl, whisk together flour, baking powder, baking soda and salt. Set aside.

3. In a medium bowl, using an electric mixer on medium speed, beat sugar and butter for 1 to 2 minutes or until fluffy. Beat in strawberry purée. Add eggs, one at a time, beating well after each addition. Add flour mixture and beat on low speed until smooth. Beat in strawberry extract and food coloring.

4. If desired, place paper liners in wells. Fill each well with about 1½ tbsp (22 mL) batter. Bake for 6 to 8 minutes or until a tester inserted in the center of a cupcake comes out clean. Transfer cupcakes to a wire rack to cool. Repeat with the remaining batter.

Raspberry Lemonade Cupcakes

Makes 28 to 30 cupcakes

If a perfect summer day was captured in a cupcake, it might just taste like these treats. They make a delightful dessert to serve after a cookout on a beautiful summer evening — but you might find they're so good you'll serve them year-round.

Tips

This batter may appear a little thin at first, but it thickens to a nice consistency as you finish adding all of the ingredients.

If desired, garnish with fresh raspberries and lime zest curls (see page 20).

Variation

Pink Lemonade Cupcakes: Substitute frozen pink lemonade concentrate for the raspberry lemonade concentrate in both the cupcakes and the frosting.

• Paper liners (optional)		
1½ cups	all-purpose flour	375 mL
1 tsp	baking soda	5 mL
½ tsp	baking powder	2 mL
¼ tsp	salt	1 mL
¾ cup	granulated sugar	175 mL
⅓ cup	vegetable oil	75 mL
3	large egg whites, at room temperature	3
½ cup	thawed frozen raspberry lemonade concentrate	125 mL
⅓ cup	buttermilk	75 mL
2 to 3	drops red food coloring	2 to 3
	Raspberry Lemonade Frosting (page 110)	

1. In a small bowl, whisk together flour, baking soda, baking powder and salt. Set aside.

2. In a large bowl, using an electric mixer on medium-high speed, beat sugar and oil for 2 minutes or until fluffy. Add egg whites, one at a time, beating well after each addition. Beat in raspberry lemonade concentrate. Add flour mixture alternately with buttermilk, making three additions of flour and two of buttermilk and beating on low speed until smooth. Beat in food coloring.

3. If desired, place paper liners in wells. Fill each well with about 1½ tbsp (22 mL) batter. Bake for 6 to 8 minutes or until a tester inserted in the center of a cupcake comes out clean. Transfer cupcakes to a wire rack to cool. Repeat with the remaining batter.

4. Frost with Raspberry Lemonade Frosting.

Creamy Coconut Cupcakes

Who can resist a snow white coconut cupcake? It is definitely worth keeping a supply of cream of coconut in the pantry. The addition of Creamy Coconut Frosting (page 112) makes these treats absolutely delectable.

Tips

Canned cream of coconut is commonly sold for cocktails and can be found in the mixed drink section of your grocery store. It should not be confused with coconut milk.

If desired, toast the coconut. Spread flaked coconut in a thin layer on a baking sheet. Bake at 300°F (150°C) for about 20 minutes, stirring every 5 minutes, until coconut is evenly browned.

• Paper liners (optional)

2 cups	white cake mix	500 mL
2	large egg whites, at room temperature	2
½ cup	water	125 mL
⅓ cup	cream of coconut	75 mL
	Creamy Coconut Frosting (page 112)	
½ cup	sweetened flaked coconut	125 mL

1. In a medium bowl, using an electric mixer on low speed, beat cake mix, egg whites, water and cream of coconut for 30 seconds or until moistened. Beat on medium speed for 2 minutes.

2. If desired, place paper liners in wells. Fill each well with about 1½ tbsp (22 mL) batter. Bake for 6 to 8 minutes or until a tester inserted in the center of a cupcake comes out clean. Transfer cupcakes to a wire rack to cool. Repeat with the remaining batter.

3. Frost cupcakes with Creamy Coconut Frosting, then sprinkle with flaked coconut.

Carrot, Coconut and Walnut Cupcakes

Kathy loves carrot cake. This cupcake version is rich, moist and packed with flavor, and the cream cheese frosting gives it the ultimate in great flavor.

Tips

Toasting walnuts intensifies their flavor. Spread chopped walnuts in a single layer on a baking sheet. Bake at 350°F (180°C) for 5 to 7 minutes or until lightly toasted. Let cool, then measure.

To shred the carrots, use a box grater or a food processor equipped with a shredding attachment. Packaged shredded carrots are also sold in the produce section of the grocery store — or check the salad bar and purchase just the amount you need.

- Paper liners (optional)

1 cup	all-purpose flour	250 mL
1 tsp	ground cinnamon	5 mL
1 tsp	baking powder	5 mL
1/2 tsp	ground nutmeg	2 mL
1/2 tsp	baking soda	2 mL
1/4 tsp	salt	1 mL
3/4 cup	granulated sugar	175 mL
1/2 cup	vegetable oil	125 mL
2	large eggs, at room temperature	2
1 tsp	vanilla extract	5 mL
1 cup	shredded carrots (about 3 medium)	250 mL
1/2 cup	chopped walnuts, toasted (see tip, at left)	125 mL
1/4 cup	sweetened flaked coconut	60 mL
	Cream Cheese Frosting (page 114)	
	Toasted sweetened flaked coconut (optional; see tip, page 58)	

1. In a medium bowl, whisk together flour, cinnamon, baking powder, nutmeg, baking soda and salt. Set aside.

2. In a large bowl, using an electric mixer on medium-high speed, beat sugar and oil for 2 minutes or until creamy. Add eggs, one at a time, beating well after each addition. Beat in vanilla. Add flour mixture and beat on low speed until smooth. Gently stir in carrots, walnuts and coconut.

3. If desired, place paper liners in wells. Fill each well with about 1 1/2 tbsp (22 mL) batter. Bake for 6 to 8 minutes or until a tester inserted in the center of a cupcake comes out clean. Transfer cupcakes to a wire rack to cool. Repeat with the remaining batter.

4. Frost with Cream Cheese Frosting. Garnish with toasted coconut, if desired.

Chocolate Velvet Cupcakes

You have to love a recipe that has the word "velvet" in the title. The texture and incredible chocolate flavor of these little delights rival any version of velvet cupcakes, even red ones.

Variation

Dissolve ½ tsp (2 mL) espresso powder in ½ cup (125 mL) hot water and substitute for the coffee.

• Paper liners (optional)

¾ cup	semisweet chocolate chips	175 mL
1 cup	all-purpose flour	250 mL
½ tsp	baking soda	2 mL
¼ tsp	salt	1 mL
1 cup	packed brown sugar	250 mL
¼ cup	unsalted butter, softened	60 mL
1	large egg, at room temperature	1
1	large egg yolk, at room temperature	1
1 tsp	vanilla extract	5 mL
½ cup	sour cream	125 mL
½ cup	hot coffee or hot water	125 mL

1. Place chocolate chips in a small microwave-safe glass bowl. Microwave on High in 30-second intervals, stirring after each, until melted. Stir until smooth. Set aside.

2. In a small bowl, whisk together flour, baking soda and salt. Set aside.

3. In a medium bowl, using an electric mixer on medium-high speed, beat brown sugar and butter for 1 to 2 minutes or until fluffy. Add egg, then egg yolk, beating well after each addition. Beat in vanilla. Beat in melted chocolate just until blended. Add flour mixture alternately with sour cream, making three additions of flour and two of sour cream and beating on low speed until blended. Gradually add coffee, beating until blended.

4. If desired, place paper liners in wells. Fill each well with about 1½ tbsp (22 mL) batter. Bake for 6 to 8 minutes or until a tester inserted in the center of a cupcake comes out clean. Transfer cupcakes to a wire rack to cool. Repeat with the remaining batter.

Mocha Fudge Cupcakes

There's no need to get in the car and drive to the coffee shop when you can easily prepare these gratifying bites in the comfort of your home.

Variation

Dissolve ½ tsp (2 mL) espresso powder in ⅓ cup (75 mL) hot water and substitute for the coffee.

• Paper liners (optional)

2 cups	devil's food cake mix	500 mL
2	large eggs, at room temperature	2
½ cup	sour cream	125 mL
⅓ cup	strong brewed coffee	75 mL
2 tbsp	vegetable oil	30 mL
⅓ cup	miniature semisweet chocolate chips	75 mL

1. In a medium bowl, using an electric mixer on medium speed, beat cake mix, eggs, sour cream, coffee and oil for 30 seconds or until moistened. Beat on medium speed for 2 minutes. Stir in chocolate chips.

2. If desired, place paper liners in wells. Fill each well with about 1½ tbsp (22 mL) batter. Bake for 6 to 8 minutes or until a tester inserted in the center of a cupcake comes out clean. Transfer cupcakes to a wire rack to cool. Repeat with the remaining batter.

Southern Caramel Chocolate Chip Cakes

Can you picture the magnolia blossoms on those gargantuan, gorgeous trees from the old South? Any time Roxanne can sneak away to enjoy Southern charm, she is gone in a minute. No doubt she would take along this Southern-inspired recipe.

Tip
Garnish each cupcake with a pecan half.

Variation
Stir in ½ cup (125 mL) toasted chopped pecans along with the miniature semisweet chocolate chips.

• Paper liners (optional)

2 cups	white cake mix	500 mL
½ tsp	baking soda	2 mL
¼ tsp	baking powder	1 mL
2	large egg whites, at room temperature	2
¾ cup	vanilla-flavored yogurt	175 mL
½ cup	miniature semisweet chocolate chips	125 mL
	Southern Praline Frosting (page 113)	
	Chocolate Drizzle (page 119)	

1. In a medium bowl, using an electric mixer on low speed, beat cake mix, baking soda, baking powder, egg whites and yogurt for 30 seconds or until moistened. Beat on medium speed for 2 minutes. Stir in chocolate chips.

2. If desired, place paper liners in wells. Fill each well with about 1½ tbsp (22 mL) batter. Bake for 6 to 8 minutes or until a tester inserted in the center of a cupcake comes out clean. Transfer cupcakes to a wire rack to cool. Repeat with the remaining batter.

3. Frost with Southern Praline Frosting, then drizzle with Chocolate Drizzle.

Praline Cupcakes

Kathy and Roxanne do not always share the same food tastes; in fact, they usually prefer opposite flavors! The exception to this rule is pralines, which they both adore. When they attend culinary conferences in New Orleans, their idea of a fun afternoon is "praline tasting" in the French Quarter.

Tips

No buttermilk on hand? Stir 2 tsp (10 mL) lemon juice or white vinegar into ⅔ cup (150 mL) milk. Let stand for 5 to 10 minutes or until thickened. Proceed with the recipe.

Garnish each cupcake with a pecan half.

• Paper liners (optional)		
1½ cups	all-purpose flour	375 mL
1 tsp	baking powder	5 mL
¼ tsp	baking soda	1 mL
¼ tsp	salt	1 mL
½ cup	unsalted butter, softened	125 mL
¾ cup	granulated sugar	175 mL
½ cup	packed brown sugar	125 mL
2	large eggs, at room temperature	2
2 tsp	vanilla extract	10 mL
⅔ cup	buttermilk	150 mL
	Southern Praline Frosting (page 113)	

1. In a small bowl, whisk together flour, baking powder, baking soda and salt. Set aside.

2. In a medium bowl, using an electric mixer on medium-high speed, beat butter for about 2 minutes or until fluffy. Add granulated sugar and brown sugar; beat for 1 to 2 minutes or until light and fluffy. Add eggs, one at a time, beating well after each addition. Beat in vanilla. Add flour mixture alternately with buttermilk, making three additions of flour and two of buttermilk and beating on low speed until blended.

3. If desired, place paper liners in wells. Fill each well with about 1½ tbsp (22 mL) batter. Bake for 6 to 8 minutes or until a tester inserted in the center of a cupcake comes out clean. Transfer cupcakes to a wire rack to cool completely. Repeat with the remaining batter.

4. Frost with Southern Praline Frosting.

Hazelnut Cupcakes

Kathy's daughters both enjoyed chocolate hazelnut spread while studying in Italy. We captured the flavor of that famous spread in these cupcakes.

Tips

Hazelnuts may also be labeled "filberts."

If you purchase chopped hazelnuts, they're ready to use. If you buy whole hazelnuts, you'll need to remove the bitter skin. To do so, soak the nuts in cold water for 1 minute. Drain, then spread the nuts in a single layer on a baking sheet. Bake at 400°F (200°C) for 5 to 7 minutes or until the skin begins to flake. Use a kitchen towel to rub the skin off.

- Paper liners (optional)

2 cups	yellow cake mix	500 mL
1	large egg, at room temperature	1
1	large egg yolk, at room temperature	1
2/3 cup	water	150 mL
3 tbsp	chocolate hazelnut spread (such as Nutella)	45 mL
3 tbsp	vegetable oil	45 mL
	Hazelnut Buttercream Frosting (page 108)	
	Toasted chopped hazelnuts (optional)	

1. In a medium bowl, using an electric mixer on low speed, beat cake mix, egg, egg yolk, water, chocolate hazelnut spread and oil for 30 seconds or until moistened. Beat on medium speed for 2 minutes.

2. If desired, place paper liners in wells. Fill each well with about $1\frac{1}{2}$ tbsp (22 mL) batter. Bake for 6 to 8 minutes or until a tester inserted in the center of a cupcake comes out clean. Transfer cupcakes to a wire rack to cool. Repeat with the remaining batter.

3. Frost cupcakes with Hazelnut Buttercream Frosting. Garnish with hazelnuts, if desired.

Cola Cupcakes

Roxanne's mother, Colleen Wyss, made a version of this recipe in sheet cake form. These cupcakes are a tribute to her. Thanks, Colleen, for passing your love of cooking on to your daughter!

Tip

Toasting pecans intensifies their flavor. Spread chopped pecans in a single layer on a baking sheet. Bake at 350°F (180°C) for 5 to 7 minutes or until lightly browned. Let cool, then measure.

- Paper liners (optional)

½ cup	unsweetened cocoa powder	125 mL
1 cup	cola	250 mL
¼ cup	unsalted butter	60 mL
⅔ cup	granulated sugar	150 mL
¼ cup	packed brown sugar	60 mL
1 cup	all-purpose flour	250 mL
¾ tsp	baking soda	3 mL
½ tsp	salt	2 mL
1	large egg, at room temperature	1
	Cola Frosting (page 114)	
⅓ cup	chopped pecans, toasted (see tip, at left)	75 mL

1. In a small saucepan, combine cocoa, cola and butter. Heat over medium heat until butter is melted. Remove from heat and whisk in granulated sugar and brown sugar until dissolved. Let cool for 5 to 10 minutes or until no longer steaming.

2. Meanwhile, in a small bowl, whisk together flour, baking soda and salt. Set aside.

3. Whisk egg into cola mixture. Fold in flour mixture (batter may be slightly lumpy).

4. If desired, place paper liners in wells. Fill each well with about 1½ tbsp (22 mL) batter. Bake for 6 to 8 minutes or until a tester inserted in the center of a cupcake comes out clean. Transfer cupcakes to a wire rack to cool slightly. Repeat with the remaining batter.

5. Glaze warm cupcakes with Cola Frosting, then sprinkle with pecans.

Brownie Bites

Traditional Brownie Bites

**Makes
16 to 18 brownies**

Classic brownies are traditional for a reason, and they'll never go out of style. Roxanne's husband, Bob Bateman, can never get enough of these.

Tips

Brownies should be slightly firm on the outer edges and softly set in the center, and the surface will appear slightly dry. A toothpick inserted in the center will have moist crumbs attached; if it comes out clean, the brownie is overbaked and, once cool, will be very crisp.

Check brownies for doneness at the earliest time specified in the recipe. If they're too soft, continue baking for another 2 minutes, but do not overbake. Brownies are still quite soft even when fully baked, but will become firmer as they come to room temperature, so allow plenty of cooling time.

Variation

Stir in ½ cup (125 mL) toasted chopped pecans or walnuts before baking.

• Paper liners

1 cup	granulated sugar	250 mL
¾ cup	all-purpose flour	175 mL
⅓ cup	unsweetened cocoa powder	75 mL
¼ tsp	salt	1 mL
2	large eggs, at room temperature	2
½ cup	vegetable oil	125 mL
1 tsp	vanilla extract	5 mL
	Nonstick baking spray	

1. In a medium bowl, using an electric mixer on medium speed, beat sugar, flour, cocoa, salt, eggs, oil and vanilla until blended.

2. Place paper liners in wells. Spray inside of liners with baking spray. Fill each well with about 1½ tbsp (22 mL) batter. Bake for 12 to 14 minutes or until set (see tips, at left). Using a small offset spatula, carefully transfer brownies to a wire rack to cool completely. Repeat with the remaining batter.

Blonde Brownies

If you like chocolate chip cookies, you will adore this "blonde" version of a traditional favorite.

Tips

You can substitute mini semisweet chocolate chips for the full-size chocolate chips.

If desired, drizzle Chocolate Drizzle (page 119) over cooled brownies.

• Paper liners

6 tbsp	unsalted butter	90 mL
¾ cup	packed brown sugar	175 mL
1 tbsp	light (white or golden) corn syrup	15 mL
2 tsp	espresso powder	10 mL
1 tsp	vanilla extract	5 mL
¾ cup	all-purpose flour	175 mL
½ tsp	baking powder	2 mL
¼ tsp	salt	1 mL
1	large egg, at room temperature	1
½ cup	semisweet chocolate chips	125 mL
½ cup	chopped pecans or walnuts, toasted (see tip, page 65)	125 mL

1. In a medium saucepan, melt butter over medium heat. Whisk in brown sugar and corn syrup until mixture is smooth and emulsified. Remove from heat and whisk in espresso powder and vanilla. Let cool for 5 minutes.

2. In a small bowl, whisk together flour, baking powder and salt. Set aside.

3. Add egg to brown sugar mixture and whisk until well blended. Stir in flour mixture until well blended. Fold in chocolate chips and nuts.

4. Place paper liners in wells. Fill each well with about 1½ tbsp (22 mL) batter. Bake for 10 to 12 minutes or until set (see tips, page 67). Using a small offset spatula, carefully transfer brownies to a wire rack to cool completely. Repeat with the remaining batter.

Cheesecake Brownies

**Makes
24 to 26 brownies**

Kathy has become
quite famous for
the cheesecakes
she prepares in her
slow cooker. These
delectable morsels also
receive a blue ribbon
rating from her friends
and family.

Tip

For even richer brownies,
frost with Classic Chocolate
Buttercream Frosting
(page 106).

• Paper liners

Brownie Batter

2 oz	unsweetened chocolate, chopped	60 g
1/3 cup	vegetable oil	75 mL
3/4 cup	all-purpose flour	175 mL
1/2 tsp	baking powder	2 mL
1/2 tsp	salt	2 mL
1 cup	granulated sugar	250 mL
2	large eggs, at room temperature	2
1/2 tsp	vanilla extract	2 mL

Cheesecake Batter

1/4 cup	granulated sugar	60 mL
1 tbsp	all-purpose flour	15 mL
3 oz	cream cheese, softened	90 g
3 tbsp	unsalted butter, softened	45 mL
1/2 tsp	vanilla extract	2 mL
1	large egg, at room temperature	1
	Nonstick baking spray	

1. *Brownie Batter:* In a medium saucepan, combine chocolate and oil. Heat over low heat, stirring often, until chocolate is melted. Let cool for 5 minutes.

2. In a small bowl, whisk together flour, baking powder and salt. Set aside.

3. Using a strong, heavy-duty spoon, beat sugar into cooled chocolate mixture, stirring until well blended. Add eggs, one at a time, beating well after each addition. Stir in flour mixture until blended. Stir in vanilla. Set aside.

4. *Cheesecake Batter:* In a medium bowl, using an electric mixer on medium-high speed, beat sugar, flour, cream cheese, butter and vanilla until smooth. Add egg and beat on low speed until blended.

5. Place paper liners in wells. Spray inside of liners with baking spray. Fill each well with about 1 tbsp (15 mL) brownie batter, then dollop each with about 1 1/2 tsp (7 mL) cream cheese batter. Using a small spatula, swirl cream cheese batter into brownie batter. Bake for 10 to 12 minutes or until set (see tips, page 67). Using a small offset spatula, carefully transfer brownies to a wire rack to cool completely. Repeat with the remaining batter.

Cranberry Orange Blondies

Why not offer
your friends and
family a new take
on brownies? The
cranberries and fresh
orange complement
each other to form a
mouthwatering delight.

Tip

If desired, drizzle cooled
brownies with Vanilla Glaze
(page 117).

• Paper liners

1¼ cups	all-purpose flour	300 mL
¼ tsp	baking soda	1 mL
¼ tsp	salt	1 mL
½ cup	packed brown sugar	125 mL
½ cup	granulated sugar	125 mL
½ cup	unsalted butter, melted	125 mL
1	large egg, at room temperature	1
2 tsp	grated orange zest	10 mL
1 tbsp	freshly squeezed orange juice	15 mL
1 tsp	vanilla extract	5 mL
½ cup	sweetened dried cranberries	125 mL
¼ cup	chopped pecans, toasted (see tip, page 74)	60 mL

1. In a small bowl, whisk together flour, baking soda and salt. Set aside.

2. In a large bowl, using an electric mixer on medium speed, beat brown sugar, granulated sugar and butter for 1 to 2 minutes or until fluffy. Beat in egg. Beat in orange juice and vanilla. Add flour mixture, one-third at a time, beating well after each addition. Stir in cranberries, pecans and orange zest.

3. Place paper liners in wells. Fill each well with about 1½ tbsp (22 mL) batter. Bake for 10 to 12 minutes or until set (see tips, page 67). Using a small offset spatula, carefully transfer brownies to a wire rack to cool completely. Repeat with the remaining batter.

Peppermint Brownies

Makes 10 to 12 brownies

This is Roxanne's go-to brownie recipe when she wants to serve simple but impressive treats. The swirl of frosting and glaze creates an elegant presentation.

Variation

Stir ½ cup (125 mL) toasted chopped pecans or walnuts into the batter.

• Paper liners

1	package (10.5 oz/298 g) brownie mix	1
	Ingredients listed on brownie package	
	Nonstick baking spray	
	Peppermint Frosting (page 111)	
	Chocolate Drizzle (page 119)	

1. Prepare brownie batter as directed on package.

2. Place paper liners in wells. Spray inside of liners with baking spray. Fill each well with about 1½ tbsp (22 mL) batter. Bake for 12 to 14 minutes or until set (see tips, page 67). Using a small offset spatula, carefully transfer brownies to a wire rack to cool completely. Repeat with the remaining batter.

3. Frost with Peppermint Frosting, then drizzle with Chocolate Drizzle. Create a decorative swirl by dragging the point of a wooden toothpick through the chocolate.

Peanut Butter Brownies

We adore recipes that create decadent results from pantry ingredients. This one is a great way to revisit childhood memories.

Tips

When frosting over a filling, as with the fruit jelly here, it is easiest and neatest to pipe the frosting, covering the filling and the cupcake.

Reserve the cake you cut from the tops of these cupcakes for other uses. Try layering the pieces with fresh fruit for a parfait, or crumbling them over ice cream. They also make great lunch box treats. Freeze leftover cake pieces in a freezer bag for up to 2 months.

Variation

Stir ½ cup (125 mL) mini semisweet chocolate chips into the batter. Omit the jelly. Frost with Peanut Butter Cream Cheese Frosting, then drizzle with Chocolate Drizzle (page 119).

• Paper liners

1¼ cups	all-purpose flour	300 mL
1 tsp	baking powder	5 mL
½ tsp	salt	2 mL
½ cup	creamy peanut butter	125 mL
⅓ cup	vegetable oil	75 mL
1 cup	granulated sugar	250 mL
2	large eggs, at room temperature	2
1 tsp	vanilla extract	5 mL
	Nonstick baking spray	
6 tbsp	fruit jelly (such as grape or strawberry)	90 mL
	Peanut Butter Cream Cheese Frosting (page 115)	

1. In a small bowl, whisk together flour, baking powder and salt. Set aside.

2. In a medium bowl, using an electric mixer on medium speed, beat peanut butter and oil until smooth. Add sugar and beat until smooth. Add eggs, one at a time, beating well after each addition. Beat in vanilla. Gradually add flour mixture, beating until smooth.

3. Place paper liners in wells. Spray inside of liners with baking spray. Fill each well with about 1½ tbsp (22 mL) batter. Bake for 12 to 14 minutes or until set (see tips, page 67). Using a small offset spatula, carefully transfer brownies to a wire rack to cool completely. Repeat with the remaining batter.

4. Using a serrated knife, cut a ½-inch (1 cm) circle out of the top of each brownie. Fill each circle with about 1 tsp (5 mL) jelly (see tips, at left). Frost with Peanut Butter Cream Cheese Frosting.

Caramel Brownies

The day Roxanne brought these treats home from the test kitchen, her daughter, Grace, clamored for more. They received Grace's highest rating.

Tip

If you have a larger can of evaporated milk, measure $\frac{2}{3}$ cup (150 mL) for this recipe. Cover and refrigerate the remaining milk and use within 3 days.

• Paper liners

1	package (15.25 oz/432 g) yellow cake mix	1
1	can (5 oz/142 mL) evaporated milk (see tip, at left)	1
$\frac{1}{2}$ cup	chopped pecans, toasted (see tip, page 74)	125 mL
$\frac{1}{4}$ cup	unsalted butter, softened	60 mL
12 to 13	chocolate-covered caramel candies (such as Rolo), cut in half	12 to 13

1. In a large bowl, combine cake mix, evaporated milk, pecans and butter until well blended. Set aside.

2. Place paper liners in wells. Fill each well with about $1\frac{1}{2}$ tsp (7 mL) batter (the well should be about half full). Place one candy half, cut side down, in each well and cover with 1 tbsp (15 mL) batter. Bake for 6 to 8 minutes or until golden. Using a small offset spatula, carefully transfer brownies to a wire rack to cool completely. Repeat with the remaining batter and candies.

Turtle Brownies

**Makes
16 to 18 brownies**

Expect a crowd in your kitchen when you serve these caramel-frosted, chocolatey delights.

Tips

Garnish each brownie with a pecan half, if desired.

Toasting pecans intensifies their flavor. Spread chopped pecans in a single layer on a baking sheet. Bake at 350°F (180°C) for 5 to 7 minutes or until lightly browned. Let cool, then measure.

- Paper liners

½ cup	all-purpose flour	125 mL
3 tbsp	unsweetened cocoa powder	45 mL
¼ tsp	salt	1 mL
½ cup	unsalted butter, softened	125 mL
½ cup	granulated sugar	125 mL
½ cup	packed brown sugar	125 mL
2	large eggs, at room temperature	2
1 tsp	vanilla extract	5 mL
⅓ cup	chopped pecans, toasted (see tip, at left)	75 mL
	Nonstick baking spray	
½	recipe Caramel Cream Cheese Frosting (page 115)	½
	Chocolate Drizzle (page 119)	

1. In a small bowl, whisk together flour, cocoa and salt. Set aside.

2. In a medium bowl, using an electric mixer on medium-high speed, beat butter for 1 to 2 minutes or until fluffy. Reduce mixer speed to medium and beat in granulated sugar and brown sugar. Add eggs, one at a time, beating well after each addition. Beat in vanilla. Beat in flour mixture until well blended. Stir in pecans.

3. Place paper liners in wells. Spray inside of liners with baking spray. Fill each well with about 1½ tbsp (22 mL) batter. Bake for 10 to 12 minutes or until set (see tips, page 67). Using a small offset spatula, carefully transfer brownies to a wire rack to cool completely. Repeat with the remaining batter.

4. Frost with Caramel Cream Cheese Frosting, then drizzle with Chocolate Drizzle.

Toffee Crunch Brownies

A version of these brownies sealed the deal on Kathy and Roxanne's longtime business partnership. Roxanne's mom and daughter loved Paula Deen and never missed her early television program. Kathy and Roxanne were at a meeting filled with foodies, discussing Paula's upcoming visit to Kansas City. Roxanne impulsively volunteered to bake 1,400 brownies — if Kathy would help her and if Roxanne's daughter could meet Paula Deen. Many hundreds of hours later, all was accomplished, and a wonderful evening was had by all. We have pictures to prove it!

Tip

Using paper liners makes it easier to remove the brownies from the wells. You'll find it easier to remove the paper liners from the brownies if you let the brownies cool completely first.

• Paper liners

1	package (about 18 oz/550 g) brownie mix	1
1 tsp	espresso powder	5 mL
2	large eggs, at room temperature	2
½ cup	vegetable oil	125 mL
2 tbsp	water	30 mL
4	chocolate-covered toffee candy bars, such as Skor or Heath (each 1.4 oz/39 g), crushed Nonstick baking spray	4

1. In a large bowl, combine brownie mix, espresso powder, eggs, oil and water. Fold in crushed candy.

2. Place paper liners in wells. Spray inside of liners with baking spray. Fill each well with about 1½ tbsp (22 mL) batter. Bake for 12 to 14 minutes or until set (see tips, page 67). Using a small offset spatula, carefully transfer brownies to a wire rack to cool completely. Repeat with the remaining batter.

Caramel Toffee Brownie Trifle

**Makes
16 to 20 servings**

Roxanne's daughter, Grace, sings in the youth choir at their church. The choir director, Joyce Blakesley, hosts an annual Christmas party for the choir, complete with her chocolate trifle. Roxanne adapted the recipe and created this version for her family, using brownies in lieu of chocolate cake. It received rave reviews when served to the entire family on Christmas Eve.

Variation

Create a chocoholic's delight by substituting chocolate ice cream topping for the caramel ice cream topping.

- Paper liners
- 12-cup (3 L) trifle bowl

1	package (about 18 oz/550 g) brownie mix	1
	Ingredients listed on brownie package	
	Nonstick baking spray	
2	packages (each 3.9 oz/102 g) instant chocolate pudding mix	2
3 cups	milk	750 mL
1	container (8 oz or 500 mL) frozen whipped topping, thawed	1
1	jar (12.25 oz/347 mL) caramel ice cream topping	1
1	package (8 oz/227 g) chocolate-covered toffee bits (about 1⅓ cups/325 mL)	1

1. Prepare brownie batter as directed on package.

2. Place paper liners in wells. Spray inside of liners with baking spray. Fill each well with about 1½ tbsp (22 mL) batter. Bake for 10 to 12 minutes or until set (see tips, page 67). Using a small offset spatula, carefully transfer brownies to a wire rack to cool completely. Repeat with the remaining batter.

3. Prepare pudding as directed on package, using 3 cups (750 mL) milk. Cover and refrigerate for 30 minutes.

4. Place half the brownie bites in a single layer in trifle bowl, breaking some into smaller pieces to fill any gaps. Layer half the whipped topping, half the pudding, half the caramel ice cream topping and half the toffee bits over brownie bites. Repeat layers. Cover and refrigerate for at least 2 hours or overnight.

Cheesecakes and Other Goodies

Chocolate Chip Cheesecakes

Kathy's favorite flavor is vanilla, but her husband, David, prefers chocolate. This dessert is the perfect compromise: vanilla-flavored cheesecake with mini chocolate chips and just the right amount of chocolate ganache.

Tip

Do not let cheesecakes stand at room temperature for more than 2 hours. When you're entertaining, set out just those that will be eaten within 2 hours, and replenish with chilled cheesecakes as needed.

- Food processor
- Paper liners

Crusts

6	cream-filled chocolate sandwich cookies	6
1 tbsp	granulated sugar	15 mL
2 tbsp	unsalted butter, melted	30 mL

Filling

8 oz	cream cheese, softened	250 g
¼ cup	granulated sugar	60 mL
1 tbsp	all-purpose flour	15 mL
1	large egg, at room temperature	1
1	large egg yolk, at room temperature	1
1 tsp	vanilla extract	5 mL
¼ cup	mini semisweet chocolate chips	60 mL

Topping

Chocolate Ganache (page 116)

1. *Crusts:* In food processor, process cookies to fine, even crumbs. Add sugar and butter; pulse to blend.

2. Place a paper liner in each well. Spoon about 1½ tsp (7 mL) crumb mixture into the bottom of each liner. Use the pie forming tool to tap crust into liner.

3. *Filling:* In a medium bowl, using an electric mixer on medium speed, beat cream cheese for 1 minute or until fluffy. Beat in sugar and flour until smooth. Reduce mixer speed to low and beat in egg, egg yolk and vanilla just until smooth (do not overbeat). Stir in chocolate chips.

4. Spoon about 1½ tbsp (22 mL) filling over crust in each liner. Bake for 10 to 12 minutes or until filling is puffed at the edges and softly set at the center. Using a small offset spatula, carefully transfer cheesecakes to a wire rack to cool. Repeat with the remaining crumb mixture and filling.

5. Place cooled cheesecakes in an airtight container and refrigerate for at least 3 hours, until chilled and set, or for up to 5 days.

6. *Topping:* Drizzle about ¾ tsp (3 mL) Chocolate Ganache onto each cheesecake.

Red Velvet Cheesecakes

Makes 14
to 16 cheesecakes

Kathy's daughter Amanda loves cheesecakes and all things red, so it's no surprise that she declared these red velvet cheesecakes a favorite. Their mild chocolate flavor and deep red color make a winning combination.

Tip

If desired, omit the ganache and instead dollop cheesecakes with sweetened whipped cream. To prepare, in a deep bowl, using an electric mixer on medium speed, beat ½ cup (125 mL) heavy or whipping (35%) cream until frothy. Beat in 1 tbsp (15 mL) confectioners' (icing) sugar until stiff peaks form. For the most attractive presentation, use a pastry bag fitted with a large open star tip to pipe the whipped cream onto each cheesecake.

- Food processor
- Paper liners

Crusts

6	cream-filled chocolate sandwich cookies	6
1 tbsp	granulated sugar	15 mL
2 tbsp	unsalted butter, melted	30 mL

Filling

8 oz	cream cheese, softened	250 g
⅓ cup	granulated sugar	75 mL
1 tbsp	unsweetened cocoa powder	15 mL
1 tbsp	all-purpose flour	15 mL
2 tsp	red food coloring	10 mL
1	large egg, at room temperature	1
1	large egg yolk, at room temperature	1
½ tsp	vanilla extract	2 mL

Topping

White Chocolate Ganache (page 116)

1. *Crusts:* In food processor, process cookies to fine, even crumbs. And sugar and melted butter; pulse to blend.

2. Place a paper liner in each well. Spoon about 1½ tsp (7 mL) crumb mixture into the bottom of each liner. Use the pie forming tool to tap crust into liner.

3. *Filling:* In a medium bowl, using an electric mixer on medium speed, beat cream cheese for 1 minute or until fluffy. Beat in sugar, cocoa and flour until smooth. Beat in food coloring. Reduce mixer speed to low and beat in egg, egg yolk and vanilla just until smooth (do not overbeat).

4. Spoon about 1½ tbsp (22 mL) filling over crust in each liner. Bake for 10 to 12 minutes or until filling is puffed at the edges and softly set at the center. Using a small offset spatula, carefully transfer cheesecakes to a wire rack to cool. Repeat with the remaining crumb mixture and filling.

5. Place cooled cheesecakes in an airtight container and refrigerate for at least 3 hours, until chilled and set, or for up to 5 days.

6. *Topping:* Just before serving, drizzle with White Chocolate Ganache.

Piña Colada Cheesecakes

. . . .

That famous tropical drink combines coconut, pineapple and rum — an enticing flavor combination for a cheesecake.

. . . .

Tips

Use a food processor fitted with a metal blade to quickly make fine crumbs from the cookies. You'll need about 14 vanilla wafers to make ½ cup (125 mL) crumbs. If you don't have a food processor, place the wafers in a sealable plastic bag and use a rolling pin to crush them. Measure out ½ cup (125 mL) crumbs.

Cream of coconut is a sweetened canned product often used for cocktails. It should not be confused with coconut milk.

To toast coconut, spread it in a thin layer on a baking sheet. Bake at 300°F (150°C) for about 20 minutes, stirring every 5 minutes, until coconut is evenly browned.

- Paper liners

Crusts

½ cup	vanilla wafer crumbs (see tip, at left)	125 mL
¼ cup	sweetened flaked coconut	60 mL
1 tbsp	unsalted butter, melted	15 mL

Filling

8 oz	cream cheese, softened	250 g
¼ cup	granulated sugar	60 mL
1 tbsp	all-purpose flour	15 mL
1	large egg, at room temperature	1
1	large egg yolk, at room temperature	1
¼ cup	cream of coconut	60 mL
¼ tsp	rum extract	1 mL

Topping

1	can (8 oz/227 mL) crushed pineapple, with juice	1
2 tsp	cornstarch	10 mL

Garnish

Toasted sweetened flaked coconut (see tip, at left)

1. *Crusts:* In a small bowl, combine wafer crumbs and coconut. Stir in butter.

2. Place a paper liner in each well. Spoon about 1½ tsp (7 mL) crumb mixture into the bottom of each liner. Use the pie forming tool to tap crust into liner.

3. *Filling:* In a medium bowl, using an electric mixer on medium speed, beat cream cheese for 1 minute or until fluffy. Beat in sugar and flour until smooth. Reduce mixer speed to low and beat in egg and egg yolk until just combined. Beat in cream of coconut and rum extract just until incorporated (do not overbeat).

4. Spoon about 1½ tbsp (22 mL) filling over crust in each liner. Bake for 10 to 12 minutes or until filling is puffed at the edges and softly set at the center. Using a small offset spatula, carefully transfer cheesecakes to a wire rack to cool. Repeat with the remaining crumb mixture and filling. Let stand for 15 minutes.

5. *Topping:* Drain pineapple juice into a glass measuring cup. If necessary, add enough water to equal ½ cup (125 mL). In a small microwave-safe glass bowl, combine cornstarch and pineapple juice, stirring well. Microwave on High for 60 seconds, stirring halfway through, until thickened and bubbly. Stir in pineapple. Let cool for 15 minutes. Spoon topping over cheesecakes.

6. Place cooled cheesecakes in an airtight container and refrigerate for at least 3 hours, until chilled and set, or for up to 5 days.

7. *Garnish:* Just before serving, garnish with toasted coconut.

Strawberry Swirl Cheesecakes

**Makes 14
to 16 cheesecakes**

Decorating cheesecakes with strawberries is an elegant tradition that will never go out of style. In this recipe, fresh strawberries are also swirled through the cheesecake.

Tip

Use a food processor fitted with a metal blade to quickly make fine crumbs from the cookies. You'll need about 14 vanilla wafers to make ½ cup (125 mL) crumbs. If you don't have a food processor, place the wafers in a sealable plastic bag and use a rolling pin to crush them. Measure out ½ cup (125 mL) crumbs.

- Paper liners
- Blender

Crusts

½ cup	vanilla wafer crumbs (see tip, at left)	125 mL
1 tbsp	granulated sugar	15 mL
2 tbsp	unsalted butter, melted	30 mL

Filling

8 oz	cream cheese, softened	250 g
¼ cup	granulated sugar	60 mL
1 tbsp	all-purpose flour	15 mL
1	large egg, at room temperature	1
1	large egg yolk, at room temperature	1
1 tsp	vanilla extract	5 mL
½ cup	hulled strawberries, cut in half	125 mL
4 to 5	drops red food coloring	4 to 5

Topping

1 cup	hulled strawberries, chopped	250 mL
1 tbsp	confectioners' (icing) sugar	15 mL

1. *Crusts:* In a small bowl, combine wafer crumbs and sugar. Stir in butter.

2. Place a paper liner in each well. Spoon about 1½ tsp (7 mL) crumb mixture into the bottom of each liner. Use the pie forming tool to tap crust into liner.

3. *Filling:* In a medium bowl, using an electric mixer on medium speed, beat cream cheese for 1 minute or until fluffy. Beat in sugar and flour until smooth. Reduce mixer speed to low and beat in egg, egg yolk and vanilla just until smooth (do not overbeat).

4. In blender, combine strawberries and food coloring; purée until smooth. Measure out 3 tbsp (45 mL) purée, dollop over cheesecake batter and swirl just once, very gently. Do not mix in completely. Transfer the remaining purée to a bowl, cover and refrigerate until ready to use.

Variation

Substitute graham wafer crumbs for the vanilla wafer crumbs. Graham wafer crumbs can be purchased ready-made, but if you can't find them, you'll need about two 4¾- by 2¼-inch (11.5 by 5.5 cm) wafers to make ½ cup (125 mL).

5. Spoon about 1½ tbsp (22 mL) filling over crust in each liner. Bake for 11 to 13 minutes or until filling is puffed at the edges and softly set at the center. Using a small offset spatula, carefully transfer cheesecakes to a wire rack to cool. Repeat with the remaining crumb mixture and filling.

6. Place cooled cheesecakes in an airtight container and refrigerate for at least 3 hours, until chilled and set, or for up to 5 days.

7. *Topping:* Stir chopped strawberries and confectioners' sugar into the reserved strawberry purée. Just before serving, spoon about 1 tbsp (15 mL) topping onto each cheesecake.

Bananas Foster Cheesecakes

Makes 14 to 16 cheesecakes

For Roxanne and Kathy, trips to New Orleans wouldn't be complete without sampling bananas Foster. We created this recipe in tribute to those memorable culinary adventures.

Tip

Classic bananas Foster is sometimes ignited (a technique called flambé), and it makes a beautiful presentation. Once liquor is warmed, it can be ignited, but use caution. To safely flambé, pour the liquor into the pan and let it heat for just a few moments. Then, using a long match, such as one designed for outdoor grills or fireplaces, light the liquor. The flame may shoot up, so stand well away from it and make sure it is not near anything flammable. The flame is often blue, which can be a bit difficult to see. Once the flame dies down, stir well and serve or proceed as the recipe directs.

- Paper liners

Crusts

½ cup	graham wafer crumbs (see tip, opposite)	125 mL
1 tbsp	granulated sugar	15 mL
¼ tsp	ground cinnamon	1 mL
2 tbsp	unsalted butter, melted	30 mL

Filling

8 oz	cream cheese, softened	250 g
¼ cup	granulated sugar	60 mL
1 tbsp	all-purpose flour	15 mL
1	large egg, at room temperature	1
1	large egg yolk, at room temperature	1
1 tsp	vanilla extract	5 mL

Bananas Foster Sauce

2 tbsp	unsalted butter	30 mL
⅔ cup	packed brown sugar	150 mL
¼ tsp	ground cinnamon	1 mL
2	small bananas, cut into ½-inch (1 cm) thick slices	2
3 tbsp	dark rum	45 mL

1. *Crusts:* In a small bowl, combine graham wafer crumbs, sugar and cinnamon. Stir in butter.

2. Place a paper liner in each well. Spoon about 1½ tsp (7 mL) crumb mixture into the bottom of each liner. Use the pie forming tool to tap crust into liner.

3. *Filling:* In a medium bowl, using an electric mixer on medium speed, beat cream cheese for 1 minute or until fluffy. Beat in sugar and flour until smooth. Reduce mixer speed to low and beat in egg, egg yolk and vanilla just until smooth (do not overbeat).

4. Spoon about 1½ tbsp (22 mL) filling over crust in each liner. Bake for 10 to 12 minutes or until filling is puffed at the edges and softly set at the center. Using a small offset spatula, carefully transfer cheesecakes to a wire rack to cool. Repeat with the remaining crumb mixture and filling.

5. Place cooled cheesecakes in an airtight container and
   refrigerate for at least 3 hours, until chilled and set, or
   for up to 5 days.

6. *Bananas Foster Sauce:* In a small skillet, melt butter
   over medium heat. Stir in brown sugar and cinnamon;
   cook, stirring often, until bubbly and melted. Stir
   in bananas and cook, stirring occasionally, until just
   tender. Stir in rum and cook, stirring, for 1 minute.
   Spoon about 1½ tbsp (22 mL) warm sauce over each
   cheesecake. Serve immediately.

Greek Honey Nut Bites

• •

Makes 16 bites

These treats are much
easier to prepare than
baklava, but they're
just as tasty.

• •

Variation
For a honey lemon syrup,
replace the vanilla with
1 tbsp (15 mL) freshly
squeezed lemon juice.

1 cup	chopped walnuts (not toasted)	250 mL
1 tbsp	packed brown sugar	15 mL
½ tsp	ground cinnamon	2 mL
16	Phyllo Cups (page 44)	16
⅓ cup	granulated sugar	75 mL
¼ cup	water	60 mL
¼ cup	liquid honey	60 mL
1 tsp	vanilla extract	5 mL

1. In a small bowl, combine walnuts, brown sugar and
   cinnamon. Spoon about 1 tbsp (15 mL) into each
   phyllo cup.

2. In a small saucepan, combine granulated sugar, water
   and honey. Bring to a boil over medium-high heat.
   Reduce heat and simmer, stirring occasionally, for 8 to
   10 minutes or until slightly thickened. Stir in vanilla.
   Drizzle syrup evenly over nut mixture in phyllo cups.
   Serve immediately.

Dulce de Leche Cheesecakes

Makes 14 to 16 cheesecakes

Combine a rich, creamy cheesecake with dulce de leche — the sweet, velvety caramel from Latin America — and the result is an absolutely fantastic dessert.

Tip
Dulce de leche is readily available in cans or jars and can often be found shelved with the Latin American foods at well-stocked grocery stores.

• Paper liners

Crusts

½ cup	graham wafer crumbs (see tip, page 85)	125 mL
1 tbsp	granulated sugar	15 mL
2 tbsp	unsalted butter, melted	30 mL

Filling

8 oz	cream cheese, softened	250 g
¼ cup	granulated sugar	60 mL
1 tbsp	all-purpose flour	15 mL
¼ cup	dulce de leche	60 mL
1	large egg, at room temperature	1
1	large egg yolk, at room temperature	1
1 tsp	vanilla extract	5 mL

Topping

¼ cup	dulce de leche	60 mL

1. *Crusts:* In a small bowl, combine graham wafer crumbs and sugar. Stir in butter.

2. Place a paper liner in cupcake wells. Place about 1½ tsp (7 mL) crumb mixture into the bottom of each liner. Use the pie forming tool to tap crust into liner.

3. *Filling:* In a medium bowl, using an electric mixer on medium speed, beat cream cheese for 1 minute or until fluffy. Beat in sugar, flour and dulce de leche until smooth. Reduce mixer speed to low and beat in egg, egg yolk and vanilla just until smooth (do not overbeat).

4. Spoon about 1½ tbsp (22 mL) filling over crust in each liner. Bake for 10 to 12 minutes or until filling is puffed at the edges and softly set at the center. Using a small offset spatula, carefully transfer cheesecakes to a wire rack to cool. Repeat with the remaining crumb mixture and filling.

5. Place cooled cheesecakes in an airtight container and refrigerate for at least 3 hours, until chilled and set, or for up to 5 days.

6. *Topping:* Place dulce de leche in a small microwave-safe glass bowl. Microwave on High for 15 seconds or until warm. Stir well. Spoon about ¾ tsp (3 mL) dulce de leche over each cheesecake. Refrigerate for 1 hour or until topping is well chilled.

Triple-Nut Bites

Three kinds of nuts provide decadent, rich, crunchy flavor in every bite.

Tips

For optimum flavor and a crisp crust, serve Triple-Nut Bites the same day they are baked.

If desired, serve Triple-Nut Bites with a dollop of sweetened whipped cream (see tip, page 79).

You can substitute any nuts you prefer. You could also use just one kind of nut or combine two of your favorites.

Crusts

Cream Cheese Pastry (page 92)

Filling

¾ cup	packed brown sugar	175 mL
⅛ tsp	salt	0.5 mL
1	egg, lightly beaten	1
1 tbsp	unsalted butter	15 mL
1 tsp	vanilla extract	5 mL
⅓ cup	chopped pecans	75 mL
¼ cup	chopped macadamia nuts	60 mL
¼ cup	chopped almonds	60 mL

1. *Crusts:* Use the large circle of the crust cutting tool to cut 14 to 16 crusts, rerolling scraps as necessary. Place 8 crusts evenly on top of wells and gently press into wells with the pie forming tool. If desired, crimp the edges. Cover the remaining crusts with plastic wrap and set aside.

2. *Filling:* In a small saucepan, combine brown sugar, salt, egg, butter and vanilla. Cook over medium-low heat, stirring constantly, until blended and emulsified; do not boil.

3. In a small bowl, combine pecans, macadamia nuts and almonds. Sprinkle about $1\frac{1}{2}$ tsp (7 mL) nut mixture into bottom of each pastry-lined well. Spoon about 1 tbsp (15 mL) egg mixture over nuts in each well.

4. Bake for 10 to 12 minutes or until filling is set. Transfer bites to a wire rack to cool. Let appliance cool for 5 minutes. Repeat with the remaining crusts and filling.

Cherry Strudels

A warm and wonderful cherry filling nestled inside a crisp crust makes for a popular dessert!

Tips

The flavors of almonds and cherries complement each other; in fact, the small amount of almond extract intensifies the cherry flavor.

Toasting almonds intensifies their flavor. Spread chopped almonds in a single layer on a baking sheet. Bake at 350°F (180°C) for 5 to 7 minutes or until lightly browned. Let cool, then measure.

If using a store-bought refrigerated pie crust, let come to room temperature, then unroll according to package directions and proceed with the recipe. You can cut 14 Babycakes™ single crusts from one packaged pie crust (half a 14-oz/400 g package) by rerolling the scraps.

Filling

½ cup	granulated sugar	125 mL
1	can (14½ oz/435 mL) pitted tart red cherries, drained	1
3 tbsp	sweetened dried cranberries	45 mL
4 tsp	cornstarch	20 mL
1 tbsp	cold water	15 mL
¼ tsp	almond extract	1 mL
¼ cup	chopped almonds, toasted (see tip, at left)	60 mL

Crusts

Favorite Buttery Pie Crust (page 38) or store-bought refrigerated pie crust (see tip, at left)
Puff pastry (see tip, page 94)

Egg Wash

1	large egg, at room temperature	1
1 tbsp	water	15 mL

1. *Filling:* In a small saucepan, combine sugar, cherries and cranberries. Cook over medium-low heat, stirring often, for 3 to 4 minutes or until liquid is boiling and cranberries are tender.

2. In a small bowl, whisk together cornstarch and cold water until smooth. Stir into cherry mixture and cook, stirring constantly, for 2 to 3 minutes or until liquid is glossy and mixture is thickened. Remove from heat and stir in almond extract. Stir in almonds. Spoon mixture into a small bowl and let cool completely.

3. *Crusts:* Use the large circle of the crust cutting tool to cut 16 bottom crusts from the pie crust, rerolling scraps as necessary. Place 8 crusts evenly on top of wells and gently press into wells with the pie forming tool. Cover the remaining crusts with plastic wrap and set aside.

Variations

Substitute walnuts for the almonds.

Bake 16 Phyllo Cups (page 44), then spoon a heaping tablespoon (15 mL) of cherry filling into each cup just before serving.

4. On a lightly floured surface, roll out puff pastry to about $1/8$ inch (3 mm) thick, pressing any perforated seams together. Use the small circle of the crust cutting tool to cut 16 top crusts.

5. Spoon $1\frac{1}{2}$ tbsp (22 mL) cooled filling into each bottom crust; do not overfill. Place a top crust directly over the center of each filled shell. Cover the remaining top crusts with plastic wrap and set aside.

6. *Egg Wash:* In a small bowl, whisk together egg and water. Brush lightly over top crusts.

7. Bake for 10 to 12 minutes or until crusts are browned and crisp. Transfer strudels to a wire rack to cool. Let appliance cool for 5 minutes. Repeat with remaining crusts and filling.

Quick Berry Cobblers

Makes 8 servings

Kathy comes from a long line of cobbler bakers. This recipe, based on the old-fashioned, homey desserts, is quick to prepare, so it's a great option on a busy day.

Tips

Cut any large berries in half before cooking.

This cobbler tastes best made with warm, freshly baked scones.

2 tbsp	unsalted butter	30 mL
3 cups	fresh or thawed frozen berries (see tip, at left)	750 mL
1/3 to 1/2 cup	granulated sugar	75 to 125 mL
1/4 tsp	ground cinnamon	1 mL
1/2 tsp	cornstarch	2 mL
2 tbsp	cold water	30 mL
8	Classic Scones (page 131)	8
	Vanilla ice cream, whipped cream or frozen whipped topping, thawed (optional)	

1. In a medium saucepan, melt butter over medium-low heat. Stir in berries. Add sugar to taste and cinnamon. Cook, stirring often, until berries are tender and sugar has dissolved, about 5 minutes.

2. In a small bowl, whisk together cornstarch and cold water until smooth. Stir into berry mixture and cook, stirring often, for 3 to 5 minutes or until bubbly and thickened.

3. Cut each scone in half crosswise and place 2 halves in each dessert dish. Spoon about 1/4 cup (60 mL) berry mixture over the scones in each dish. Just before serving, dollop with ice cream, if desired.

Pies and Tarts

Cream Cheese Pastry

Cream cheese and butter make a richly flavored pie crust. This pastry is perfect for the bottom crust on treats such as Maple Pecan Tarts (page 103) and Parmesan and Bacon Tarts (page 212).

Tip

Wrap leftover dough tightly in plastic wrap and refrigerate; use within 3 days or freeze for up to 2 months. Let thaw overnight in the refrigerator, then roll out and use as desired.

• Food processor

4 oz	cold cream cheese, cut into 1-inch (2.5 cm) pieces	125 g
½ cup	cold unsalted butter, cut into 1-inch (2.5 cm) pieces	125 mL
1¼ cups	all-purpose flour	300 mL
¼ tsp	salt	1 mL

1. In food processor, process cream cheese and butter until combined, scraping down sides of bowl as necessary to ensure even mixing. Add flour and salt; pulse just until mixture begins to form a ball. Form dough into a disk, wrap in plastic wrap and refrigerate for at least 30 minutes, until chilled, or for up to 24 hours.

2. If firmly chilled, let dough stand at room temperature for 10 minutes. On a lightly floured surface, lightly dust top of dough with flour. Roll out gently, picking dough up after each roll, dusting underneath with flour as necessary and rotating it from 12 o'clock to 3 o'clock. (This keeps the dough from sticking.) Roll and rotate until dough is about ⅛ inch (3 mm) thick.

3. Use as directed in the recipe or, to bake single crusts blind (empty), see page 39. To bake single-crust mini pies, see page 41. To bake two-crust hand pies, see page 43.

Berry Peach Hand Pies

Summer's finest fruits combine to make juicy, sweet hand pies with a gorgeous jewel-toned filling. And, if you use frozen fruit, you can enjoy these all year long.

Tips

If using a store-bought refrigerated pie crust, let come to room temperature, then unroll according to package directions and proceed with the recipe. You can cut 14 Babycakes™ single crusts from one packaged pie crust (half a 14-oz/400 g package) by rerolling the scraps.

Partially thawed blueberries may still be cold and somewhat icy, but will no longer be solidly frozen.

Crusts

Favorite Buttery Pie Crust (page 38) or store-bought refrigerated pie crust (see tip, at left)
Puff pastry (see tip, page 94)

Filling

¾ cup	finely chopped peeled peaches or thawed frozen peaches	175 mL
3 tbsp	fresh or frozen blueberries, partially thawed and drained if frozen	45 mL
1 tsp	freshly squeezed lemon juice	5 mL
1 tbsp	packed brown sugar	15 mL
¼ tsp	ground cinnamon	1 mL
2 tbsp	peach preserves	30 mL
2 tsp	cornstarch	10 mL
1 tbsp	cold water	15 mL

1. *Crusts:* Use the large circle of the crust cutting tool to cut 8 bottom crusts from the pie crust. Place crusts evenly on top of wells and gently press into the wells with the pie forming tool.

2. On a lightly floured surface, roll out puff pastry to about ⅛ inch (3 mm) thick, pressing any perforated seams together. Use the small circle of the crust cutting tool to cut 8 top crusts. Cover with plastic wrap and set aside.

3. *Filling:* In a small saucepan, combine peaches and blueberries. Add lemon juice and toss to coat. Stir in brown sugar, cinnamon and preserves; bring to a simmer over low heat. Simmer, stirring often, for 5 to 6 minutes or until fruit is tender.

4. In a small bowl, whisk together cornstarch and cold water until smooth. Stir into fruit mixture and simmer, stirring constantly, for about 2 minutes or until thickened and bubbly. Remove from heat and let cool for 10 minutes.

5. Spoon 1½ tbsp (22 mL) filling into each bottom crust; do not overfill. Place a top crust directly over the center of each filled shell.

6. Bake for 10 to 12 minutes or until crusts are browned and crisp. Transfer pies to a wire rack to cool slightly. Serve warm.

Dutch Apple Hand Pies

∙ ∙

**Makes
8 hand pies**

The brown sugary,
buttery flavor of Dutch
apple pie is hidden
inside these two-crust
bundles. What a treat!

∙ ∙

Tips

Puff pastry is a flaky, rich
pastry that is readily
available in the freezer
section of grocery stores.
It is sold as sheets, shells
or blocks — choose any of
these and thaw according
to package directions. If
using sheets, you can cut
15 or 16 top crusts from one
sheet of puff pastry (half of
a 17.4 oz/490 g box) if you
reroll the scraps. If using
shells, plan on cutting 2 top
crusts from each shell; thaw
only the number you need
and keep the rest frozen for
another use. Because puff
pastry puffs so much, it is
not recommended for the
bottom crust of a two-crust
hand pie.

Crusts

| | Favorite Buttery Pie Crust (page 38) or store-bought refrigerated pie crust (see tip, page 93) | |
| | Puff pastry (see tip, at left) | |

Filling

1¾ cups	finely chopped peeled tart cooking apples (such as Granny Smith)	425 mL
2 tbsp	cold water, divided	30 mL
1 tsp	freshly squeezed lemon juice	5 mL
3 tbsp	granulated sugar	45 mL
½ tsp	ground cinnamon	2 mL
Pinch	salt	Pinch
1 tsp	cornstarch	5 mL
1 tbsp	all-purpose flour	15 mL
1 tbsp	packed brown sugar	15 mL
1 tbsp	cold unsalted butter, cut into small pieces	15 mL

1. *Crusts:* Use the large circle of the crust cutting tool to cut 8 bottom crusts from the pie crust. Place crusts evenly on top of wells and gently press into the wells with the pie forming tool.

2. On a lightly floured surface, roll out puff pastry to about ⅛ inch (3 mm) thick, pressing any perforated seams together. Use the small circle of the crust cutting tool to cut 8 top crusts. Cover with plastic wrap and set aside.

3. *Filling:* In a small saucepan, toss together apples, 1 tbsp (15 mL) of the cold water and lemon juice.

4. In a small bowl, whisk together granulated sugar, cinnamon and salt. Pour over apples and toss to coat evenly. Cook over low heat, stirring often, for 8 to 9 minutes or until apples are tender.

5. In another small bowl, whisk together cornstarch and the remaining cold water until smooth. Stir into apple mixture and cook, stirring constantly, for about 2 minutes or until thickened and bubbly. Remove from heat and let cool for 5 minutes.

6. Meanwhile, in another small bowl, whisk together flour and brown sugar. Using your fingertips or a pastry blender, cut in butter until mixture is coarse and crumbly.

7. Spoon about 1½ tbsp (22 mL) apple mixture into each bottom crust; do not overfill. Spoon 1 to 1½ tsp (5 to 7 mL) flour mixture over the apple mixture in each crust. Place a top crust directly over the center of each filled shell.

8. Bake for 10 to 12 minutes or until crusts are browned and crisp. Transfer pies to a wire rack to cool slightly. Serve warm.

Linzer Hand Pies

**Makes
8 hand pies**

The classic flavor combination of almonds and raspberry preserves was made famous in the Austrian linzertorte, and later in linzer cookies, and it shines in these elegant little pies.

Tip

Almond paste comes in cans or tubes and is available at most grocery stores. Tightly cover any leftovers and store in the refrigerator for up to 1 month or freeze for up to 3 months.

Crusts

Favorite Buttery Pie Crust (page 38) or store-bought refrigerated pie crust (see tip, page 98)
Puff pastry (see tip, page 94)

Filling

8 tsp	seedless raspberry preserves	40 mL
1 tbsp	granulated sugar	15 mL
¼ cup	almond paste	60 mL
1	large egg yolk, at room temperature	1
1 tsp	grated orange zest	5 mL
8 tsp	chopped toasted slivered almonds	40 mL

1. *Crusts:* Use the large circle of the crust cutting tool to cut 8 bottom crusts from the pie crust. Place crusts evenly on top of wells and gently press into the wells with the pie forming tool.

2. On a lightly floured surface, roll out puff pastry to about ⅛ inch (3 mm) thick, pressing any perforated seams together. Use the small circle of the crust cutting tool to cut 8 top crusts. Cover with plastic wrap and set aside.

3. *Filling:* Spoon 1 tsp (5 mL) raspberry preserves into each bottom crust.

4. In a medium bowl, using a fork, stir together sugar and almond paste. Stir in egg yolk and orange zest until well blended. Spoon about 2 tsp (10 mL) almond mixture over preserves in each well. Sprinkle each with 1 tsp (5 mL) chopped almonds. Place a top crust directly over the center of each filled shell.

5. Bake for 10 to 12 minutes or until crusts are browned and crisp. Transfer pies to a wire rack to cool slightly. Serve warm.

Lemon Drop Cupcakes (page 28)

Southern-Style Pecan Mini Pies (page 40)

Italian Cream Cake Bites (page 52)

Raspberry Lemonade Cupcakes (page 57)

Cranberry Orange Blondies (page 70)
and Traditional Brownie Bites (page 67)

Piña Colada Cheesecakes (page 80)

Triple-Nut Bites (page 87)

Berry Peach Hand Pies (page 93)

Cinnamon Pecan Hand Pies

**Makes
10 hand pies**

Here, pecans are hidden inside a crust that is surprisingly easy to prepare. Fans of nuts and cinnamon will make this treat again and again.

Tips

Toasting pecans intensifies their flavor. Spread chopped pecans in a single layer on a baking sheet. Bake at 350°F (180°C) for 5 to 7 minutes or until lightly browned. Let cool, then measure.

For easy cleaning, let the appliance cool between batches and wipe it clean with a paper towel to remove any residual sugar.

1	can (7.3 oz/207 g) refrigerated cinnamon roll dough (5 rolls)	1
¼ cup	chopped pecans, toasted (see tip, at left)	60 mL
	Nonstick baking spray	

1. Separate cinnamon rolls, reserving package of glaze. On a lightly floured surface, roll each round of dough, cinnamon side up, into a 3½-inch (8.5 cm) circle. Cut each circle in half.

2. Spoon 1¼ to 1½ tsp (6 to 7 mL) pecans into the middle of each half circle. Gather up all sides to enclose the nuts in a packet.

3. Spray wells with nonstick baking spray. Place a packet, seam side down, in each well. Bake for 3 minutes. Using a small offset spatula, carefully turn packets over. Bake for 2 to 3 minutes or until golden brown. Transfer pies to a wire rack to cool slightly. Let appliance cool for 5 minutes. Repeat with the remaining packets.

4. Drizzle warm pies with the reserved glaze.

Chocolate Silk Mini Pies

Bob Bateman,
Roxanne's husband,
likes to celebrate any
special occasion with
chocolate cream pie.
Roxanne prepares
these pies for him any
chance she gets.

Tips

If using a store-bought
refrigerated pie crust, let
come to room temperature,
then unroll according to
package directions and
proceed with the recipe.
You can cut 14 Babycakes™
single crusts from one
packaged pie crust (half a
14-oz/400 g package) by
rerolling the scraps.

Garnish with chocolate
shavings, if desired.

Crusts

	Favorite Buttery Pie Crust (page 38) or store-bought refrigerated pie crust (see tip, at left)	

Filling

1½ cups	mini marshmallows	375 mL
4 oz	unsweetened chocolate, chopped	125 g
⅓ cup	semisweet chocolate chips	75 mL
1 tsp	espresso powder	5 mL
1 cup	sweetened condensed milk	250 mL
2 tbsp	unsalted butter	30 mL
3 tbsp	heavy or whipping (35%) cream	45 mL

Topping

1 cup	heavy or whipping (35%) cream	250 mL
2 tbsp	confectioners' (icing) sugar	30 mL

1. *Crusts:* Follow the instructions on page 39 for baking single crusts blind.

2. *Filling:* In a medium saucepan, combine marshmallows, chocolate, chocolate chips, espresso powder, milk and butter. Cook over low heat, stirring often, for 10 to 12 minutes or until chocolate and marshmallows are melted and mixture is combined. Stir in cream.

3. Pour about 2 tbsp (30 mL) filling into each cooled crust. Place pies on a baking sheet and refrigerate for 2 hours, until firm, or for up to 4 hours.

4. *Topping:* In a chilled medium bowl, using an electric mixer on medium-high speed, beat cream until frothy. Beat in confectioners' sugar until stiff peaks form. Dollop onto pies just before serving.

Banana Cream Mini Pies

Makes 10 to 12 mini pies

When our days are rocky, we turn to comfort foods. Serve up a spoonful of creamy, delicious stress relief when you present these little pies, reminiscent of the banana cream pie you used to get at Grandma's house.

Tips

Wrap leftover dough tightly in plastic wrap and refrigerate; use within 3 days or freeze for up to 2 months. Let thaw overnight in the refrigerator, then roll out and use as directed. Or cut all of the dough into circles and stack the extra circles, separating them with waxed paper or parchment paper, then wrap the stack tightly in plastic wrap and freeze.

For an easier version, substitute 1 cup (250 mL) prepared vanilla or French vanilla pudding for the custard prepared in steps 2 and 3.

Garnish with chocolate curls, if desired.

Crusts

Favorite Buttery Pie Crust (page 38) or store-bought refrigerated pie crust (see tip, page 98)

Filling

¼ cup	granulated sugar	60 mL
4 tsp	cornstarch	20 mL
Pinch	salt	Pinch
1 cup	milk	250 mL
2	large egg yolks	2
½ tsp	vanilla extract	2 mL
½ tsp	unsalted butter	2 mL
1	banana, cut crosswise into ⅛- to ¼-inch (3 to 5 mm) slices	1

Topping

½ cup	heavy or whipping (35%) cream	125 mL
1 tbsp	confectioners' (icing) sugar	15 mL

1. *Crusts:* Follow the instructions on page 39 for baking single crusts blind.

2. *Filling:* In a small saucepan, whisk together sugar, cornstarch and salt. Gradually whisk in milk. Bring to a boil over medium heat, whisking constantly. Boil for 2 minutes, whisking constantly.

3. In a small bowl, whisk egg yolks. Gradually whisk in about ½ cup (125 mL) of the hot milk mixture until well blended. Pour into the remaining milk mixture and cook, whisking constantly, for 2 minutes. Remove from heat and stir in vanilla and butter.

4. Place 2 banana slices in each cooled crust. Spoon about 1½ tbsp (22 mL) filling on top. Place pies on a baking sheet and cover with plastic wrap, pressing plastic down lightly on the filling on each pie. Refrigerate for at least 1 hour, until firm, or for up to 4 hours.

5. *Topping:* In a chilled small bowl, using an electric mixer on medium-high speed, beat cream until frothy. Beat in confectioners' sugar until stiff peaks form. Pipe or dollop onto pies just before serving.

Key Lime Mini Pies

**Makes
12 mini pies**

Key lime pie is especially popular right now, and many restaurants and bakeries feature it. These bite-size versions are easy to prepare, but so good you'll make them often!

Tips

Key limes are smaller, more yellow in color and more flavorful than the commonly available Persian lime. But if you can't find Key limes, it's fine to use regular lime zest and juice.

For a more natural look, omit the food coloring or add just a small drop.

These pies can be stored in an airtight container in the refrigerator for up to 5 days.

• Paper liners

Crusts

1/3 cup	graham wafer crumbs (see tip, page 85)	75 mL
1 tbsp	granulated sugar	15 mL
2 tbsp	unsalted butter, melted	30 mL

Filling

2	large egg yolks	2
2/3 cup	sweetened condensed milk	150 mL
1 tsp	grated Key lime zest (see tip, at left)	5 mL
1/4 cup	freshly squeezed Key lime juice	60 mL
1 to 2	drops green food coloring (optional)	1 to 2

Topping

1/2 cup	heavy or whipping (35%) cream	125 mL
1 tbsp	confectioners' (icing) sugar	15 mL

1. *Crusts:* In a small bowl, combine graham wafer crumbs and sugar. Stir in butter.

2. Place a paper liner in each well. Spoon about 1 1/2 tsp (7 mL) crumb mixture into the bottom of each liner. Use the pie forming tool to tap crust into liner.

3. *Filling:* In a medium bowl, whisk together egg yolks and milk until blended. Stir in lime zest, lime juice and food coloring (if using).

4. Spoon about 1 1/2 tbsp (22 mL) filling over crust in each liner. Bake for 10 to 12 minutes or until softly set. Using a small offset spatula, carefully transfer pies to a wire rack to cool. Repeat with the remaining crumb mixture and filling.

5. Place pies on a baking sheet and refrigerate for 3 to 4 hours, until firm.

6. *Topping:* In a chilled small bowl, using an electric mixer on medium-high speed, beat cream until frothy. Beat in confectioners' sugar until stiff peaks form. Dollop or pipe onto pies just before serving.

Eggnog Pumpkin Mini Pies

Two favorite holiday flavors — pumpkin and eggnog — combine to make one spectacular dessert!

Tips

If using a store-bought refrigerated pie crust, let come to room temperature, then unroll according to package directions and proceed with the recipe. You can cut 14 Babycakes™ single crusts from one packaged pie crust (half a 14-oz/400 g package) by rerolling the scraps.

Substitute heavy or whipping (35%) cream for eggnog.

Crusts

	Favorite Buttery Pie Crust (page 38) or store-bought refrigerated pie crust (see tip, at left)	

Filling

3 tbsp	granulated sugar	45 mL
½ tsp	ground cinnamon	2 mL
¼ tsp	ground ginger	1 mL
⅛ tsp	ground cloves	0.5 mL
1	large egg, at room temperature	1
⅓ cup	canned pumpkin purée (not pie filling)	75 mL
⅓ cup	eggnog	75 mL

Topping

½ cup	heavy or whipping (35%) cream	125 mL
1 tbsp	confectioners' (icing) sugar	15 mL
1 tbsp	crystallized ginger, finely minced	15 mL

1. *Crusts:* Use the large circle of the crust cutting tool to cut 8 crusts from the pie crust. Place crusts evenly on top of wells and gently press into wells with the pie forming tool. If desired, crimp the edges.

2. *Filling:* In a medium bowl, whisk together sugar, cinnamon, ginger, cloves, egg, pumpkin and eggnog until blended.

3. Spoon 1½ to 2 tbsp (22 to 30 mL) filling into each crust. Bake for 8 to 10 minutes or until filling is set and a tester inserted in the center of a pie comes out clean. Transfer pies to a wire rack to cool.

4. *Topping:* In a chilled small bowl, using an electric mixer on medium-high speed, beat cream until frothy. Beat in confectioners' sugar and ginger until stiff peaks form. Dollop or pipe onto pies just before serving.

Dark Chocolate Caramel Tarts

One night, when friends were over for dinner, Kathy served these decadent tarts as part of a dessert trio. They were such a hit, everyone begged for the recipe. Here it is!

Tip

If desired, garnish the tarts with sweetened whipped cream (see step 4 on page 98 for instructions on making sweetened whipped cream).

Crusts

Favorite Buttery Pie Crust (page 38) or store-bought refrigerated pie crust (see tip, page 101)

Filling

¾ cup	packed brown sugar	175 mL
3 tbsp	unsalted butter	45 mL
⅓ cup	heavy or whipping (35%) cream	75 mL
2 tsp	vanilla extract	10 mL
1	3½ oz (105 g) dark (bittersweet) chocolate bar, broken into pieces	1

1. *Crusts:* Follow the instructions on page 39 for baking single crusts blind.

2. *Filling:* In a small saucepan, combine brown sugar and butter. Cook over medium heat, stirring often, for 2 to 3 minutes or until butter is melted. Stir in cream and bring to a boil. Boil, stirring constantly, for 30 seconds. Remove from heat and stir in vanilla. Stir in chocolate until melted and smooth. Let cool for 10 minutes.

3. Spoon about 1 tbsp (15 mL) chocolate mixture into each cooled crust. Let cool completely.

Maple Pecan Tarts

**Makes
8 to 10 tarts**

The goodness of pecan pie combines with the distinctive flavor of maple syrup to make a winning combination that is sure to become a favorite.

Tip

Toasting pecans intensifies their flavor. Spread chopped pecans in a single layer on a baking sheet. Bake at 350°F (180°C) for 5 to 7 minutes or until lightly browned. Let cool, then measure.

Variation

Substitute walnuts or cashews for the pecans.

Crusts

	Favorite Buttery Pie Crust (page 38) or store-bought refrigerated pie crust (see tip, page 101)	

Filling

¼ cup	packed brown sugar	60 mL
1 tbsp	all-purpose flour	15 mL
Pinch	ground cinnamon	Pinch
Pinch	salt	Pinch
1	large egg, at room temperature	1
2 tbsp	pure maple syrup	30 mL
1 tbsp	unsalted butter, melted	15 mL
½ cup	finely chopped pecans, toasted (see tip, at left)	125 mL

1. *Crusts:* Use the large circle of the crust cutting tool to cut 8 to 10 crusts from the pie crust. Place 8 crusts evenly on top of wells and gently press into wells with the pie forming tool. If desired, crimp the edges. Cover the remaining crusts with plastic wrap and set aside.

2. *Filling:* In a medium bowl, whisk together brown sugar and flour. Stir in cinnamon, salt, egg, maple syrup and butter. Stir in pecans.

3. Spoon 1½ to 2 tbsp (22 to 30 mL) filling into each crust. Bake for 10 to 12 minutes or until filling is set and crusts are golden brown. Transfer tarts to a wire rack to cool. Let appliance cool for 5 minutes. Repeat with the remaining crusts and filling.

Frostings and Glazes

Vanilla Buttercream Frosting

This is a very popular frosting and you will turn to it often — for good reason. It can be tinted any color and its flavor complements just about any cupcake!

Tips

Double the recipe if preparing a larger batch of cupcakes.

To tint frosting to the desired color, add a few drops of food coloring. Use colored paste or gel food coloring for the brightest or boldest colors.

Store leftover frosting in an airtight container in the refrigerator for up to 2 weeks. Let warm to room temperature before using.

¼ cup	unsalted butter, softened	60 mL
1¾ cups	confectioners' (icing) sugar	425 mL
2 to 3 tbsp	milk	30 to 45 mL
1 tsp	vanilla extract	5 mL

1. In a small bowl, using an electric mixer on medium-high speed, beat butter for 1 minute or until creamy. Gradually beat in sugar until blended. Beat in 2 tbsp (30 mL) milk and vanilla until light and fluffy.

2. If a thinner frosting is desired, beat in an additional 1 tbsp (15 mL) milk.

VEGAN VARIATION

Replace the butter with 2 tbsp (30 mL) vegan butter substitute and 2 tbsp (30 mL) vegan shortening, and replace the milk with 2 to 3 tbsp (30 to 45 mL) unsweetened almond milk.

Classic Chocolate Buttercream Frosting

Sometimes you just have to have chocolate — at least, this is true for Roxanne. And we think it is true for lots of others, too. How about you?

Tip

Do you like firm, rich frosting or thin, fluffy frosting? Both are wonderful — it's a matter of personal preference. If you plan to pipe the frosting, you may prefer to prepare slightly thinner frosting, as it will flow from the bag with less pressure.

Variation

For a mocha kick, substitute strong cold coffee for half of the cream.

½ cup	unsalted butter, softened	125 mL
1½ cups	confectioners' (icing) sugar	375 mL
¼ cup	unsweetened cocoa powder	60 mL
2½ to 3½ tbsp	heavy or whipping (35%) cream	37 to 52 mL
1 tsp	vanilla extract	5 mL

1. In a small bowl, using an electric mixer on medium-high speed, beat butter for 1 minute or until creamy. Gradually beat in sugar and cocoa until blended. Beat in 2½ tbsp (37 mL) cream and vanilla until light and fluffy.

2. If a thinner frosting is desired, beat in an additional 1 tbsp (15 mL) cream.

Shirley Temple Buttercream Frosting

Pretty and pink — isn't that the look Shirley Temple portrayed as a famous child actress? Capture that fun in this tasty frosting.

Tip

Although some people sift confectioners' (icing) sugar, we haven't found it necessary, especially since we prepare frosting with an electric mixer. If you do feel the need to sift the sugar, sift after measuring.

½ cup	unsalted butter, softened	125 mL
3 cups	confectioners' (icing) sugar	750 mL
2 tbsp	grenadine syrup	30 mL
1 to 2 tbsp	milk	15 to 30 mL
½ tsp	vanilla extract	2 mL

1. In a medium bowl, using an electric mixer on medium-high speed, beat butter for 1 minute or until creamy. Gradually beat in sugar until blended. Beat in grenadine syrup. Beat in 1 tbsp (15 mL) milk and vanilla until light and fluffy.

2. If a thinner frosting is desired, beat in an additional 1 tbsp (15 mL) milk.

Hazelnut Buttercream Frosting

**Makes
about 1½ cups
(375 mL)**

Chocolate hazelnut
spread adds depth of
flavor to this frosting.
It's perfect for Hazelnut
Cupcakes (page 64),
but is delicious good on
any chocolate or white
cupcakes.

Tip

Store leftover frosting in
an airtight container in
the refrigerator for up to
2 weeks. Let warm to room
temperature before using.

½ cup	chocolate hazelnut spread (such as Nutella)	125 mL
2 tbsp	unsalted butter, softened	30 mL
1¾ cups	confectioners' (icing) sugar	425 mL
4 to 5 tbsp	heavy or whipping (35%) cream	60 to 75 mL

1. In a small bowl, using an electric mixer on medium-high speed, beat hazelnut spread and butter for 1 minute or until creamy. Gradually beat in sugar until blended. Beat in 4 tbsp (60 mL) cream until light and fluffy.

2. If a thinner frosting is desired, beat in an additional 1 tbsp (15 mL) cream.

Orange Frosting

**Makes
about 1 cup
(250 mL)**

A hint of orange in this
creamy frosting makes
it a perfect partner for
Orange Marmalade
Cupcakes (page 223),
but it's wonderful atop
any yellow or vanilla
cupcakes.

Variation

Cherry Frosting: Substitute
2 to 3 tbsp (30 to 45 mL)
maraschino cherry juice for
the orange juice.

¼ cup	unsalted butter, softened	60 mL
1¾ cups	confectioners' (icing) sugar	425 mL
2 to 3 tbsp	freshly squeezed orange juice	30 to 45 mL
½ tsp	vanilla extract	2 mL

1. In a small bowl, using an electric mixer on medium-high speed, beat butter for 1 minute or until creamy. Gradually beat in sugar until blended. Beat in 2 tbsp (30 mL) orange juice and vanilla until light and fluffy.

2. If a thinner frosting is desired, beat in an additional 1 tbsp (15 mL) orange juice.

White Chocolate Frosting

1 oz	white chocolate, chopped	30 g
3 tbsp	heavy or whipping (35%) cream	45 mL
¼ cup	unsalted butter, softened	60 mL
1¾ cups	confectioners' (icing) sugar	425 mL
½ tsp	vanilla extract	2 mL

White chocolate is not actually chocolate, because it doesn't contain chocolate liquor, but it's still one of Kathy's favorite flavors.

Tip

For the creamiest texture, use a 1-oz (30 g) square of white chocolate (not vanilla baking chips) for this recipe. Do not substitute other kinds of chocolate in recipes designed for white chocolate.

1. In a small microwave-safe glass bowl, combine white chocolate and cream. Microwave on High for 30 to 40 seconds or until cream is hot. Stir well. Set aside and let white chocolate melt, stirring occasionally. Let cool for 10 minutes.

2. In a medium bowl, using an electric mixer on medium-high speed, beat butter for 1 minute or until creamy. Beat in melted white chocolate mixture. Gradually beat in sugar until blended. Beat in vanilla.

Variation

White Chocolate Peppermint Frosting: Substitute peppermint extract for the vanilla.

Lemon Frosting

¼ cup	unsalted butter, softened	60 mL
1¾ cups	confectioners' (icing) sugar	425 mL
2 to 3 tbsp	freshly squeezed lemon juice	30 to 45 mL
¼ tsp	vanilla extract	1 mL

Lemon is a popular flavor, and it is wonderful on lemon cupcakes, of course. But we like it so much we use it on yellow and white cupcakes, too.

Tip

If you want the frosting to be a brighter yellow, tint it with 1 or 2 drops of yellow food coloring.

1. In a small bowl, using an electric mixer on medium-high speed, beat butter for 1 minute or until creamy. Gradually beat in sugar until blended. Beat in 2 tbsp (30 mL) lemon juice and vanilla until light and fluffy.

2. If a thinner frosting is desired, beat in an additional 1 tbsp (15 mL) lemon juice.

Raspberry Lemonade Frosting

**Makes
about 1 cup
(250 mL)**

Tart and sweet flavors
make such a fabulous
combination —
especially when the
balance between the
two is perfect. You will
enjoy this frosting on
Raspberry Lemonade
Cupcakes (page 57),
but it is great on
any yellow or vanilla
cupcake.

Tip

Remember that any
frosting — especially one
made with butter — will
soften and melt easily. Keep
frosted cupcakes in a cool
spot until serving time.

⅓ cup	unsalted butter, softened	75 mL
1¾ cups	confectioners' (icing) sugar	425 mL
3 to 4 tbsp	frozen raspberry lemonade concentrate, thawed	45 to 60 mL
2 to 3	drops red food coloring	2 to 3 drops

1. In a small bowl, using an electric mixer on medium-high speed, beat butter for 1 minute or until creamy. Gradually beat in sugar until blended. Beat in 3 tbsp (45 mL) raspberry lemonade concentrate and food coloring until light and fluffy.

2. If a thinner frosting is desired, beat in an additional 1 tbsp (15 mL) raspberry lemonade concentrate.

Variation

Pink Lemonade Frosting: Substitute frozen pink lemonade concentrate for the raspberry lemonade concentrate.

Peppermint Frosting

Makes about ⅔ cup (150 mL)

Peppermint adds such a fresh flavor to frosting, it's no wonder it's so popular! This frosting is the crowning glory on any chocolate, white or yellow cupcake, and we love it on brownies.

Tips

If you prefer, you can replace the milk and peppermint extract with 2 to 3 tbsp (30 to 45 mL) crème de menthe.

Double the recipe if preparing a larger batch of cupcakes.

Add a few drops of green food coloring to the frosting to create a festive look.

¼ cup	unsalted butter, softened	60 mL
2 cups	confectioners' (icing) sugar	500 mL
2 to 3 tbsp	milk	30 to 45 mL
1 tsp	peppermint extract	5 mL

1. In a small bowl, using an electric mixer on medium-high speed, beat butter for 1 minute or until creamy. Gradually beat in sugar until blended. Beat in 2 tbsp (30 mL) milk and peppermint extract until light and fluffy.

2. If a thinner frosting is desired, beat in an additional 1 tbsp (15 mL) milk.

Creamy Coconut Frosting

Makes about 1½ cups (375 mL)

This frosting pairs perfectly with Creamy Coconut Cupcakes (page 58). Roxanne also likes to pipe it onto chocolate cupcakes, then sprinkle them with toasted coconut and almonds and pretend she is enjoying a popular chocolate bar.

½ cup	unsalted butter, softened	125 mL
2½ cups	confectioners' (icing) sugar	625 mL
2 to 3 tbsp	cream of coconut	30 to 45 mL
½ tsp	vanilla extract	2 mL

1. In a medium bowl, using an electric mixer on medium-high speed, beat butter for 1 minute or until creamy. Gradually beat in sugar until blended. Beat in 2 tbsp (30 mL) cream of coconut and vanilla until light and fluffy.

2. If a thinner frosting is desired, beat in an additional 1 tbsp (15 mL) cream of coconut.

> **Tip**
> Store leftover frosting in an airtight container in the refrigerator for up to 2 weeks. Let warm to room temperature before using.

Maple Frosting

Makes about ¾ cup (175 mL)

So many cupcake flavors pair well with maple — chocolate, gingerbread, white and yellow, to name a few.

Variation

Stir in ¼ cup (60 mL) toasted chopped pecans once the confectioners' sugar is well blended.

⅓ cup	packed brown sugar	75 mL
¼ cup	unsalted butter	60 mL
3 tbsp	milk	45 mL
½ tsp	vanilla extract	2 mL
1 tsp	maple flavoring	5 mL
1 cup	confectioners' (icing) sugar	250 mL

1. In a small saucepan, combine brown sugar and butter. Bring to a boil over medium-high heat, stirring constantly. Boil for 2 minutes. Stir in milk, vanilla and maple flavoring. Return to a boil, then remove from heat. Let cool slightly, for 3 to 5 minutes.

2. Transfer milk mixture to a medium bowl and, using an electric mixer on medium-high speed, beat in confectioners' sugar for 30 seconds or until thickened.

Southern Praline Frosting

**Makes about
1 cup (250 mL)**

This recipe is perfect for Southern Caramel Chocolate Chip Cakes (page 62) and Praline Cupcakes (page 63). You might enjoy the praline flavor of this frosting on a favorite chocolate cupcake, too.

Tips

Toasting pecans intensifies their flavor. Spread chopped pecans in a single layer on a baking sheet. Bake at 350°F (180°C) for 5 to 7 minutes or until lightly browned. Let cool, then measure.

If desired, garnish frosted cupcakes with toasted pecan halves or chopped pecans.

1/3 cup	packed brown sugar	75 mL
1/4 cup	unsalted butter	60 mL
3 tbsp	milk	45 mL
1/2 tsp	vanilla extract	2 mL
1 cup	confectioners' (icing) sugar	250 mL
1/4 cup	chopped pecans, toasted (see tip, at left)	60 mL

1. In a small saucepan, combine brown sugar and butter. Bring to a boil over medium-high heat, stirring constantly. Boil for 2 minutes. Stir in milk and vanilla. Return to a boil, then remove from heat. Let cool slightly, for 3 to 5 minutes.

2. Transfer milk mixture to a medium bowl and, using an electric mixer on medium-high speed, beat in confectioners' sugar for 30 seconds or until thickened. Stir in pecans.

Apple Cider Frosting

**Makes
about 1 3/4 cups
(425 mL)**

We have served Apple Cider Cupcakes (page 55), filled with apple butter and frosted with this luscious frosting, several times at public events. They are always a hit!

3 cups	confectioners' (icing) sugar	750 mL
1/2 cup	unsalted butter, softened	125 mL
2 tbsp	unsweetened apple cider	30 mL
1 tbsp	apple butter	15 mL

1. In a medium bowl, using an electric mixer on medium-high speed, beat sugar and butter until blended. Beat in apple cider and apple butter until smooth.

Cola Frosting

Makes about 1¼ cups (300 mL)

This is a natural topping choice for Cola Cupcakes (page 65), but also makes a good partner for Old-Fashioned White Cupcakes (page 34).

Tip

If a thicker consistency is desired, whisk in up to ¼ cup (60 m) more confectioners' sugar, 1 tbsp (15 mL) at a time.

Variation

Root Beer Frosting: Substitute root beer for the cola.

1½ tbsp	unsweetened cocoa powder	22 mL
¼ cup	unsalted butter	60 mL
3 tbsp	cola	45 mL
2 cups	confectioners' (icing) sugar	500 mL
1 tsp	vanilla extract	5 mL

1. In a small saucepan, combine cocoa, butter and cola. Bring to a boil over medium heat, stirring, until butter is melted. Remove from heat and whisk in confectioners' sugar and vanilla until blended and smooth.

VEGAN VARIATION

For a vegan frosting, replace the butter with 2 tbsp (30 mL) vegan butter substitute and 2 tbsp (30 mL) vegan shortening.

Cream Cheese Frosting

Makes about 1¾ cups (425 mL)

This creamy, classic frosting is just perfect for all kinds of cupcakes.

4 oz	cream cheese, softened	125 g
¼ cup	unsalted butter, softened	60 mL
2 cups	confectioners' (icing) sugar	500 mL
½ tsp	vanilla extract	2 mL

1. In a medium bowl, using an electric mixer on medium-high speed, beat cream cheese and butter for 1 minute or until light and creamy. Gradually beat in sugar until blended. Beat in vanilla.

Tips

Store leftover frosting in an airtight container in the refrigerator for up to 10 days.

If desired, double the recipe and use an entire 8-oz (250 g) package of cream cheese.

Caramel Cream Cheese Frosting

Makes about 2 cups (500 mL)

4 oz	cream cheese, softened	125 g
¼ cup	unsalted butter, softened	60 mL
½ cup	caramel sauce	125 mL
2 cups	confectioners' (icing) sugar	500 mL

Kathy's philosophy is that any frosting recipe that calls for cream cheese is a winner!

Tip

If baking a small batch of cupcakes or brownies, such as Turtle Brownies (page 74), prepare just half of the frosting recipe.

1. In a medium bowl, using an electric mixer on medium-high speed, beat cream cheese and butter for 1 minute or until creamy. Beat in caramel sauce until well blended. Gradually beat in sugar until blended.

Tips

If a thicker consistency is desired, whisk in up to ¼ cup (60 m) more confectioners' sugar, 1 tbsp (15 mL) at a time.

Store leftover frosting in an airtight container in the refrigerator for up to 5 days. Let warm to room temperature before using.

Peanut Butter Cream Cheese Frosting

Makes about 1¾ cups (425 mL)

3 oz	cream cheese, softened	90 g
¼ cup	unsalted butter, softened	60 mL
3 tbsp	creamy peanut butter	45 mL
2 cups	confectioners' (icing) sugar	500 mL
1 tsp	vanilla extract	5 mL

When it comes to peanut butter and cream cheese, more is always better. We can think of so many ways to use this creamy, rich frosting. Try it on Peanut Butter Brownies (page 72) or All-American Chocolate Cupcakes (page 32).

1. In a medium bowl, using an electric mixer on medium-high speed, beat cream cheese, butter and peanut butter for 1 minute or until creamy. Gradually beat in sugar until blended. Beat in vanilla.

Tip

Store cupcakes frosted with cream cheese frosting in the refrigerator until serving them. Frostings made with cream cheese should not be at room temperature for longer than 2 hours.

Chocolate Ganache

A drizzle of chocolate ganache turns an ordinary treat into a showstopping indulgence. Drizzle this rich ganache over a cheesecake, a brownie or a vanilla-frosted cupcake.

¼ cup	semisweet chocolate chips	60 mL
2 tbsp	heavy or whipping (35%) cream	30 mL
¼ tsp	vanilla extract	1 mL

1. Place chocolate chips and cream in a small microwave-safe glass bowl. Microwave on High for 30 seconds or until cream comes to a boil. Stir until chocolate is melted and mixture is smooth. Stir in vanilla. Let cool for 5 minutes.

> **Tip**
> For a truly sophisticated presentation, drizzle both this ganache and White Chocolate Ganache (below) over the cupcakes in a decorative fashion.

White Chocolate Ganache

Rich and decadent white chocolate is the perfect accent for mini cheesecakes. Or try this ganache as a flavor and color highlight on a chocolate-frosted cupcake or brownie.

3 tbsp	heavy or whipping (35%) cream	45 mL
2 oz	white chocolate, chopped	60 g
½ tsp	vanilla extract	2 mL

1. Place cream in a small microwave-safe glass bowl. Microwave on High for 30 to 45 seconds or until it just comes to a boil. Stir in white chocolate. Let stand, stirring occasionally, until white chocolate is melted. Stir in vanilla. Let cool for 10 minutes or until slightly thickened.

> **Tip**
> Be sure to use good-quality white chocolate for the ganache. It will melt into a smoother texture and it will taste richer. Do not substitute white or vanilla baking chips.

Vanilla Glaze

· ·

You will find so many
excuses to make this
easy but delectable
glaze, perfect for
scones, muffins and
even biscuits.

1/3 cup	confectioners' (icing) sugar	75 mL
1 to	milk	5 to
1 1/2 tsp		7 mL
Dash	vanilla extract	Dash

1. In a small bowl, whisk together sugar, milk and vanilla until smooth.

> **Tip**
> For easy drizzling, fill a sealable food storage bag with glaze, then snip off the corner.

Chocolate Glaze

· ·

We love to make
cream-filled cupcakes
and top them with
this wonderful, old-
fashioned glaze. But
it's fabulous on any
chocolate, vanilla or
yellow cupcake, with
or without filling.

2 tbsp	unsweetened cocoa powder	30 mL
1/4 cup	unsalted butter	60 mL
3 tbsp	milk	45 mL
2 cups	confectioners' (icing) sugar	500 mL
1/2 tsp	vanilla extract	2 mL

1. In a medium microwave-safe glass bowl, combine cocoa, butter and milk. Microwave on High for 45 to 60 seconds or until butter is melted and milk is boiling. Stir until smooth.

2. Using an electric mixer on medium-high speed, beat in sugar and vanilla until glossy and thick.

Orange Glaze

Makes about ¼ cup (60 mL)

This light citrus glaze adds the perfect finishing touch to biscuits, scones, muffins or cupcakes.

½ cup	confectioners' (icing) sugar	125 mL
½ tsp	grated orange zest	2 mL
1 tbsp	freshly squeezed orange juice	15 mL

1. In a small bowl, whisk together sugar, orange juice and orange zest until smooth.

Lemon Glaze

Makes about ¼ cup (60 mL)

We love the sweet and tart flavor of lemon glaze over cupcakes, scones and muffins. You'll find yourself coming back to this recipe again and again.

½ cup	confectioners' (icing) sugar	125 mL
1 tbsp	freshly squeezed lemon juice	15 mL

1. In a small bowl, whisk together sugar and lemon juice until smooth.

Chocolate Drizzle

- -

Makes about ¼ cup (60 mL)

A little chocolate drizzle transforms cupcakes into an elegant, show-stopping dessert.

¼ cup	semisweet chocolate chips	60 mL
2 tbsp	unsalted butter	30 mL

1. Place chocolate chips and butter in a small microwave-safe glass bowl. Microwave on High for 30 seconds. Stir. Microwave on High in 15-second intervals, stirring after each, until melted and smooth.

Tip
For easy drizzling, fill a sealable food storage bag with chocolate drizzle, then snip off the corner.

Vanilla Cream Filling

- -

Makes about ¾ cup (175 mL)

Add a surprise flavor boost to your cupcakes with this creamy, easy-to-prepare filling.

Tip
To fill a cupcake, fit a pastry bag with a medium writing tip, such as a Wilton #3, and spoon the filling into the bag. Insert the tip of the bag into the top of the cooled cupcake and gently squeeze the bag. The filling will flow into the cupcake, swelling it slightly. Do not overfill.

¼ cup	granulated sugar	60 mL
⅓ cup	shortening	75 mL
¼ cup	confectioners' (icing) sugar	60 mL
3 tbsp	milk	45 mL
Pinch	salt	Pinch
¼ tsp	vanilla extract	1 mL

1. In a medium bowl, using an electric mixer on medium-high speed, beat granulated sugar and shortening for 1 minute or until creamy. Beat in confectioners' sugar and milk until well blended. Beat in salt and vanilla. Continue beating for 5 to 7 minutes or until very fluffy.

Part 3

Mealtime Favorites

Muffins and Breads

Granola Muffins

● ●

**Makes
13 to 15 muffins**

Incorporate your favorite granola into these hearty muffins. Kathy uses a granola with raisins and nuts, but Roxanne prefers a maple-flavored granola. Serve these bundles freshly baked with a crowning dollop of honey butter (see tip, below), apple butter or marmalade.

● ●

Tips

To make honey butter, in a small bowl, combine 2 tbsp (30 mL) confectioners' (icing) sugar, ¼ tsp (1 mL) ground cinnamon, ¼ cup (60 mL) softened butter and 3 tbsp (45 mL) liquid honey until blended and smooth.

Granola stays fresher longer if stored in an airtight container in the freezer.

● Paper liners (optional)

1 cup	granola	250 mL
⅔ cup	all-purpose flour	150 mL
¼ cup	packed brown sugar	60 mL
1 tsp	ground cinnamon	5 mL
½ tsp	baking powder	2 mL
½ tsp	baking soda	2 mL
Pinch	salt	Pinch
1	large egg, at room temperature	1
½ cup	buttermilk	125 mL
2 tbsp	vegetable oil	30 mL
1 tsp	vanilla extract	5 mL

1. In a large bowl, combine granola, flour, brown sugar, cinnamon, baking powder, baking soda and salt. Set aside.

2. In a small bowl, whisk together egg, buttermilk, oil and vanilla. Stir into flour mixture until just blended.

3. If desired, place paper liners in wells. Fill each well with about 1½ tbsp (22 mL) batter. Bake for 5 to 7 minutes or until a tester inserted in the center of a muffin comes out clean. Transfer muffins to a wire rack to cool slightly. Repeat with the remaining batter.

Orange Nut Muffins

**Makes
16 to 18 muffins**

Begin your morning
with a freshly baked,
honey-sweetened
orange muffin — the
perfect way to start
your day.

Tip

If you prefer, you can use
Orange Glaze (page 118)
instead of Honey Orange
Glaze.

• Paper liners (optional)

Muffins

1½ cups	all-purpose flour	375 mL
1 tsp	baking powder	5 mL
½ tsp	baking soda	2 mL
¼ tsp	ground ginger	1 mL
¼ tsp	salt	1 mL
½ cup	liquid honey	125 mL
¼ cup	unsalted butter, softened	60 mL
1	large egg, at room temperature	1
¼ cup	frozen orange juice concentrate, thawed	60 mL
1 tsp	grated orange zest	5 mL
⅓ cup	chopped pecans, toasted (see tip, page 125)	75 mL

Honey Orange Glaze

2 tsp	cornstarch	10 mL
3 tbsp	freshly squeezed orange juice	45 mL
1 tbsp	liquid honey	15 mL

1. *Muffins:* In a large bowl, whisk together flour, baking powder, baking soda, ginger and salt. Set aside.

2. In a medium bowl, using an electric mixer on medium-high speed, beat honey and butter until light and fluffy. Beat in egg, orange juice concentrate and orange zest. Stir into flour mixture until just blended. Stir in pecans.

3. If desired, place paper liners in wells. Fill each well with about 1½ tbsp (22 mL) batter. Bake for 5 to 7 minutes or until a tester inserted in the center of a muffin comes out clean. Transfer muffins to a wire rack to cool. Repeat with the remaining batter.

4. *Glaze:* In a small microwave-safe glass bowl, combine cornstarch, orange juice and honey. Microwave on High for 45 to 60 seconds or until boiling, stirring halfway through. Stir until blended and smooth. Let cool for 5 minutes, then brush over muffins.

Grandma's Old-Fashioned Corn Muffins

You don't have to visit Grandma's house to indulge in old-fashioned corn muffins. This recipe transforms a few pantry ingredients into fantastic cornbread — without using a mix.

Tips

No buttermilk on hand? Stir 2 tsp (10 mL) lemon juice or white vinegar into ¾ cup (175 mL) milk. Let stand for 5 to 10 minutes or until thickened. Proceed with the recipe.

Should cornbread contain sugar? That controversy has been going on for years, and the answer probably depends on where you live and on your family traditions. If you like sweetened cornbread, add 1 to 2 tbsp (15 to 30 mL) granulated sugar to the dry ingredients.

1 cup	yellow cornmeal	250 mL
¼ cup	all-purpose flour	60 mL
1½ tsp	baking powder	7 mL
½ tsp	baking soda	2 mL
¼ tsp	salt	1 mL
1	large egg, at room temperature	1
¾ cup	buttermilk	175 mL
2 tbsp	vegetable oil	30 mL
2 tbsp	unsalted butter, melted	30 mL

1. In a large bowl, whisk together cornmeal, flour, baking powder, baking soda and salt. Set aside.

2. In a small bowl, whisk together egg, buttermilk and oil. Stir into cornmeal mixture just until blended.

3. Brush wells with melted butter. Fill each well with about 1½ tbsp (22 mL) batter. Bake for 6 to 8 minutes or until a tester inserted in the center of a muffin comes out clean. Transfer muffins to a wire rack to cool slightly. Repeat with the remaining batter. Serve warm.

Cinnamon-Filled Sour Cream Coffee Cakes

Makes 17 to 19 cakes

Pair steaming hot coffee with this breakfast or mid-morning snack and your day is off to a great start.

Tip

Toasting pecans intensifies their flavor. Spread chopped pecans in a single layer on a baking sheet. Bake at 350°F (180°C) for 5 to 7 minutes or until lightly browned. Let cool, then measure.

- Paper liners (optional)

Coffee Cakes

1 cup	all-purpose flour	250 mL
1/2 tsp	baking soda	2 mL
Pinch	salt	Pinch
1/2 cup	granulated sugar	125 mL
1/2 cup	unsalted butter, softened	125 mL
1	large egg, at room temperature	1
1/2 cup	sour cream	125 mL
1 tsp	vanilla extract	5 mL

Cinnamon Crumb Filling

1/3 cup	chopped pecans, toasted (see tip, at left)	75 mL
3 tbsp	packed brown sugar	45 mL
1 tbsp	granulated sugar	15 mL
1/2 tsp	ground cinnamon	2 mL

1. *Coffee Cakes:* In a small bowl, whisk together flour, baking soda and salt. Set aside.

2. In a medium bowl, using an electric mixer on medium speed, beat granulated sugar and butter for 1 to 2 minutes or until fluffy. Beat in egg. Reduce mixer speed to low and beat in flour mixture until just blended. Stir in sour cream and vanilla.

3. *Filling:* In another small bowl, combine pecans, brown sugar, granulated sugar and cinnamon.

4. If desired, place paper liners in wells. Fill each well with about 1 tbsp (15 mL) batter. Sprinkle each with about 1 1/2 tsp (7 mL) filling, then top with 1 1/2 tsp (7 mL) batter. Bake for 6 to 8 minutes or until a tester inserted in the center of a coffee cake comes out clean. Transfer coffee cakes to a wire rack to cool. Repeat with the remaining batter.

Beer Cheese Bread Bites

· ·

These tender bites, infused with the malt flavor of beer and the tang of sharp Cheddar cheese, make a tasty sidekick to almost any soup or stew. On St. Patrick's Day, Roxanne's family serves Beer Cheese Bread with corned beef and cabbage.

· ·

Tips

You can use any type of beer you like. We think the dry, crisp flavor of lager is perfect for these bread bites, but if you prefer a fuller flavor, feel free to use an ale.

Depending on the entrée you plan to serve these with, you may choose to omit the Cheddar.

1½ cups	all-purpose flour	375 mL
1½ tbsp	granulated sugar	22 mL
1½ tsp	baking powder	7 mL
¾ tsp	salt	3 mL
¾ cup	beer, at room temperature	175 mL
¾ cup	shredded sharp (old) Cheddar cheese	175 mL
1 tbsp	unsalted butter, melted	15 mL

1. In a medium bowl, whisk together flour, sugar, baking powder and salt. Stir in beer until just moistened. Fold in cheese.

2. Fill each well with about 1½ tbsp (22 mL) batter. Brush lightly with butter. Bake for 9 to 10 minutes or until golden brown. Transfer bread bites to a wire rack to cool slightly. Repeat with the remaining batter. Serve warm.

Garlic Cheese Crescent Rolls

These rolls are so easy to make, and they are the perfect accompaniment to a soup, salad or a plate of spaghetti and meatballs.

Tip

If desired, you can add 1 to 2 tbsp (15 to 30 mL) minced fresh parsley to the cheese mixture. Or substitute 1 tbsp (15 mL) minced fresh basil for the Italian seasoning.

1	can (8 oz/227 g) refrigerated crescent roll dough	1
1 tbsp	unsalted butter, softened	15 mL
1/4 cup	freshly grated Parmesan cheese	60 mL
1/2 tsp	dried Italian seasoning	2 mL
1/4 tsp	garlic powder	1 mL
	Nonstick baking spray	

1. On a lightly floured surface, carefully unroll crescent roll dough in one piece. Press seams together to make an 11- by 8-inch (28 by 20 cm) rectangle. Spread butter lightly over the dough. Set aside.

2. In a small bowl, whisk together cheese, Italian seasoning and garlic powder. Sprinkle evenly over dough. Starting from a long end, roll up dough like a jelly roll. Pinch seam to seal. Slice roll into 14 spirals, each about 3/4 inch (2 cm) thick.

3. Spray wells with nonstick baking spray. Place 1 spiral in each well and bake for 3 to 4 minutes or until bottoms are golden brown. Using a small offset spatula, carefully turn rolls over and bake for 3 minutes or until golden brown. Transfer rolls to a wire rack to cool slightly. Repeat with the remaining spirals. Serve warm.

Mom's Buttermilk Biscuits

Roxanne's mother, Colleen, taught Roxanne the art of biscuit-baking when Roxanne was quite young. Colleen is famous for her biscuits and gravy, which she served almost every weekend. It was an aha moment for Roxanne when she realized that biscuits complement so many meals — they aren't just for breakfast anymore.

Tip

No buttermilk on hand? Stir 1 tsp (5 mL) lemon juice or white vinegar into 1/3 cup (75 mL) milk. Let stand for 5 to 10 minutes or until thickened. Proceed with the recipe.

1 cup	all-purpose flour	250 mL
1 tsp	baking powder	5 mL
1/2 tsp	salt	2 mL
1/4 tsp	baking soda	1 mL
3 tbsp	shortening	45 mL
1/3 cup	buttermilk	75 mL
1 tbsp	unsalted butter, melted	15 mL

1. In a medium bowl, whisk together flour, baking powder, salt and baking soda. Using your fingertips or a pastry blender, blend in shortening until mixture is coarse and crumbly. Using a fork, stir in buttermilk just until dough comes together.

2. Turn dough out onto a floured surface and gently knead 3 or 4 times. Divide dough into 8 even pieces and shape each piece into a disk about 1 1/2 inches (4 cm) thick.

3. Place a biscuit in each well. Brush biscuits with half the butter. Bake for 5 minutes. Using a small offset spatula, carefully turn biscuits over. Brush with the remaining butter. Bake for 5 to 6 minutes or until golden brown on top. Transfer hot biscuits to a serving plate.

Spicy Texas Cheese Biscuits

We enjoyed testing
recipes with our
colleague Julie
Bondank. Julie is
known far and wide
as a fabulous cook.
She is also known
for her love of spicy,
pepper-laden dishes.
This recipe gets her
thumbs-up.

Tip

No buttermilk on hand? Stir
1½ tsp (7 mL) lemon juice
or white vinegar into ½ cup
(125 mL) milk. Let stand
for 5 to 10 minutes or until
thickened. Proceed with
the recipe.

1 cup	all-purpose flour	250 mL
2 tsp	granulated sugar	10 mL
¼ tsp	salt	1 mL
¼ cup	cold unsalted butter, cut into small pieces	60 mL
⅓ cup	shredded Cheddar cheese	75 mL
2 tbsp	chopped drained pickled jalapeño	30 mL
½ cup	buttermilk	125 mL

1. In a medium bowl, whisk together flour, sugar and salt. Using your fingertips or a pastry blender, blend in butter until mixture is coarse and crumbly. Add cheese and jalapeño; toss lightly. Using a fork, stir in buttermilk just until dough comes together.

2. Turn dough out onto a floured surface and gently knead 3 or 4 times. Divide dough into 11 even pieces and shape each piece into a disk about 1½ inches (4 cm) thick.

3. Place a biscuit in each well. Bake for 5 minutes. Using a small offset spatula, carefully turn biscuits over. Bake for 5 to 6 minutes or until golden brown on top. Transfer hot biscuits to a serving plate. Repeat with the remaining biscuits.

Ham-Flecked Biscuits

**Makes
11 to 13 biscuits**

A long-time Southern belle wannabe, Roxanne grew up enjoying the flavors of the old South. Country ham tops her list, and if she ever spies it on a menu, you can be sure she will order the dish. So it came as no surprise that she wanted to include this recipe. Southerners rejoice!

Tips

Dry-cured, salty country ham has a distinctive flavor, but if it isn't available in your area, substitute thick-cut peppered bacon, cooked until very crisp, then crumbled.

No buttermilk on hand? Stir 1 tbsp (15 mL) lemon juice or white vinegar into 1 cup (250 mL) milk. Let stand for 5 to 10 minutes or until thickened. Proceed with the recipe.

1½ cups	biscuit mix (such as Bisquick)	375 mL
½ cup	finely diced cooked country ham	125 mL
1 cup	buttermilk	250 mL

1. In a medium bowl, combine biscuit mix, ham and buttermilk, stirring with a fork just until dough comes together.

2. Fill each well with about 1½ tbsp (22 mL) dough. Bake for 8 to 9 minutes or until golden brown. Transfer hot biscuits to a serving plate. Repeat with the remaining dough.

Classic Scones

Kathy and Roxanne both enjoy afternoon tea, and their favorite part of the menu might just be the scones with clotted cream.

Variation
Gently stir ⅓ cup (75 mL) dried currants into the dough at the end of step 2.

- 1½-inch (4 cm) round cookie cutter

1 cup	all-purpose flour	250 mL
1 tbsp	granulated sugar	15 mL
1½ tsp	baking powder	7 mL
3 tbsp	cold unsalted butter, cut into small pieces	45 mL
1	large egg, at room temperature	1
⅓ cup	heavy or whipping (35%) cream	75 mL

1. In a large bowl, whisk together flour, sugar and baking powder. Using your fingertips or a pastry blender, blend in butter until mixture is coarse and crumbly.

2. In a small bowl, whisk together egg and cream. Add to flour mixture and, using a fork, stir just until moistened (do not overmix).

3. Turn dough out onto a floured surface and gently knead 4 or 5 times. Pat into a ¾-inch (2 cm) thick circle. Using the cookie cutter, cut out 8 to 10 scones, rerolling scraps as necessary.

4. Place a scone in each well. Bake for 5 minutes. Using a small offset spatula, carefully turn scones over. Bake for 4 to 5 minutes or until golden brown on top. Transfer hot scones to a serving plate. Repeat with the remaining scones, if necessary. Serve immediately.

Cherry Scones

There's no need
to enroll in pastry
school to learn how
to prepare bakeshop
goodies. These scones
will rival any pastry
shop's creations and
are mixed together
in minutes.

Tips

If your dried cherries are
quite large, chop them
before adding them to the
dough.

Toasting almonds intensifies
their flavor. Spread sliced
almonds in a single layer
on a baking sheet. Bake
at 350°F (180°C) for 5 to
7 minutes or until lightly
browned. Let cool, then
measure.

For scones with a darker
golden brown color, brush
them with egg wash before
baking. In a small bowl,
combine 1 egg and 1 tbsp
(15 mL) water. Use a pastry
brush to lightly brush each
scone with egg wash.

• 1½-inch (4 cm) round cookie cutter

1 cup + 2 tbsp	all-purpose flour	280 mL
¼ cup	granulated sugar	60 mL
1 tsp	baking powder	5 mL
¼ tsp	salt	1 mL
¼ cup	cold unsalted butter, cut into small pieces	60 mL
1	large egg yolk, at room temperature	1
⅓ cup	sour cream	75 mL
¼ tsp	almond extract	1 mL
½ cup	dried cherries	125 mL
	Vanilla Glaze (page 117)	
2 tbsp	sliced almonds, toasted (see tip, at left)	30 mL

1. In a medium bowl, whisk together flour, sugar, baking powder and salt. Using your fingertips or a pastry cutter, blend in butter until mixture is coarse and crumbly.

2. In a small bowl, whisk together egg yolk, sour cream and almond extract. Add to flour mixture and, using a fork, stir just until moistened (do not overmix). Gently stir in cherries.

3. Turn dough out onto a floured surface and gently knead 4 or 5 times. Pat into a ¾-inch (2 cm) thick circle. Using the cookie cutter, cut out 9 to 11 scones, rerolling scraps as necessary.

4. Place a scone in each well. Bake for 5 minutes. Using a small offset spatula, carefully turn scones over. Bake for 5 to 6 minutes or until golden brown on top. Transfer hot scones to a serving plate. Repeat with the remaining scones.

5. Drizzle Vanilla Glaze over scones. Sprinkle with almonds. Serve immediately.

Lemon Scones with Fruit Bits

We had such fun testing recipes for this book in the state-of-the-art kitchen at Kansas State University Olathe. For most of our testing, we worked with Julie Bondank and Mandy Totoro, whose assistance was invaluable. The day we tested this recipe, the four of us swooned over the results. We hate to admit it, but all the scones were gone by lunchtime!

Tip
Dried fruit bits are a convenient way to add a variety of fruit flavors to these scones. They are readily available at most grocery stores, with the other dried fruits. If you prefer, you can finely chop a variety of your favorite dried fruits, such as raisins, apples, apricots, peaches, plums and/or tart cherries.

Variation
Substitute dried blueberries for the fruit bits.

1 cup	all-purpose flour	250 mL
1 tsp	baking powder	5 mL
1/4 tsp	baking soda	1 mL
Pinch	salt	Pinch
1/4 cup	cold unsalted butter, cut into small pieces	60 mL
2 tbsp	granulated sugar	30 mL
1	large egg, at room temperature	1
1/4 cup	sour cream	60 mL
1/4 cup	heavy or whipping (35%) cream	60 mL
1 tsp	grated lemon zest	5 mL
1/2 cup	dried fruit bits	125 mL
	Lemon Glaze (page 118)	

1. In a medium bowl, whisk together flour, baking powder, baking soda and salt. Using your fingertips or a pastry cutter, blend in butter until mixture is coarse and crumbly.

2. In a small bowl, whisk together sugar, egg, sour cream and whipping cream. Stir in lemon zest. Add to flour mixture, along with fruit bits, and, using a fork, stir just until moistened (do not overmix).

3. Drop about 1 1/2 tbsp (22 mL) dough into each well. Bake for 3 minutes. Using a small offset spatula, carefully turn scones over. Bake for 3 to 4 minutes or until golden brown on top. Transfer hot scones to a serving plate. Repeat with the remaining dough.

4. Drizzle scones with Lemon Glaze. Serve immediately.

Breakfast and Brunch Bites

Cheesy Scrambled Egg and Bacon Cups

Weekend breakfasts are always an occasion at Roxanne's house, and she often makes these breakfast cups as a fun alternative to the traditional bacon-and-egg breakfast.

Tips

This recipe works best with fresh bread that can be rolled very thin.

If you prefer, you can use 3 tbsp (45 mL) finely chopped back bacon (Canadian bacon) in place of the regular bacon.

8	slices sandwich bread	8
2 tsp	unsalted butter, softened	10 mL
3	large eggs	3
2	slices bacon, cooked crisp and crumbled	2
	Salt and freshly ground black pepper	
8 tsp	shredded Cheddar cheese	40 mL

1. Using a rolling pin, roll each slice of bread until it is very thin. Use the large circle of the crust cutting tool to cut a circle from each slice (discard scraps or reserve for another use). Spread one side of each circle with butter.

2. Place 1 bread circle, buttered side down, on top of each well and gently press into well with the pie forming tool, making a cup. Bake for 5 to 6 minutes or until lightly toasted.

3. In a small bowl, whisk together eggs and bacon. Season with salt and pepper. Spoon about $1\frac{1}{2}$ tbsp (22 mL) egg mixture into each bread cup.

4. Bake for 6 to 8 minutes or until egg mixture is set. Transfer breakfast cups to a serving plate and immediately sprinkle with cheese. Let stand for 2 to 3 minutes. Serve warm.

Classic Quiches Lorraine

**Makes
8 quiches**

We traveled to France one spring about 10 years ago. One day, we stopped at a bakery in a small rural town and bought individual quiches to take with us. We then found a place to sit outside, on some rocks that overlooked the vast vineyards. We so enjoyed the sights, weather, friendship and scrumptious quiches Lorraine. Here is a tribute to that unforgettable day.

Tip

If using a store-bought refrigerated pie crust, let come to room temperature, then unroll according to package directions and proceed with the recipe. You can cut 14 Babycakes™ single crusts from one packaged pie crust (half a 14-oz/400 g package) by rerolling the scraps.

Crusts

Favorite Buttery Pie Crust (page 38) or store-bought refrigerated pie crust (see tip, at left)

Filling

2	slices bacon, cooked crisp and crumbled	2
½ cup	shredded Gruyère or Swiss cheese	125 mL
Pinch	ground nutmeg	Pinch
1	large egg	1
⅓ cup	milk	75 mL
	Salt and freshly ground black pepper	

1. *Crusts:* Use the large circle of the crust cutting tool to cut 8 crusts. Place crusts evenly on top of wells and gently press into the wells with the pie forming tool. If desired, crimp the top edge.

2. *Filling:* Spoon bacon into crusts, dividing evenly. Sprinkle cheese on top.

3. In a small bowl, whisk together nutmeg, egg and milk. Season with salt and pepper. Spoon about 1 tbsp (15 mL) egg mixture into each crust.

4. Bake for 10 to 12 minutes or until a tester inserted in the center of a quiche comes out clean and crusts are golden brown. Transfer quiches to a wire rack to cool slightly.

Springtime Onion and Gruyère Quiches

Green onions add subtle flavor to these delightful quiches. And the Gruyère transports us to the cafés of France. Serve them for breakfast or brunch — or pair them with a glass of white wine and enjoy them for lunch.

Variation

Leek and Gruyère Quiches: Substitute ¼ cup (60 mL) finely chopped leek (white and green parts only) for the green onions.

Crusts

	Favorite Buttery Pie Crust (page 38) or store-bought refrigerated pie crust (see tip, page 136)	

Filling

1 tbsp	unsalted butter	15 mL
¼ cup	sliced green onions, white portion only	60 mL
½ cup	shredded Gruyère cheese	125 mL
Pinch	garlic powder	Pinch
1	large egg	1
⅓ cup	half-and-half (10%) cream	75 mL
	Salt and freshly ground black pepper	

1. *Crusts:* Use the large circle of the crust cutting tool to cut 8 crusts. Place crusts evenly on top of wells and gently press into the wells with the pie forming tool. If desired, crimp the top edge.

2. *Filling:* In a small skillet, melt butter over medium-low heat. Add green onions and cook, stirring, for 2 to 3 minutes or until just tender.

3. Spoon about 1½ tsp (7 mL) green onions into each crust. Sprinkle cheese on top.

4. In a small bowl, whisk together garlic powder, egg and cream. Season with salt and pepper. Spoon about 1 tbsp (15 mL) egg mixture into each crust.

5. Bake for 10 to 12 minutes or until a tester inserted in the center of a quiche comes out clean and crusts are golden brown. Transfer quiches to a wire rack to cool slightly.

Mushroom Garlic Quiches

Makes
8 quiches

Garlic enhances the flavor of mushrooms in this quiche. For an even richer flavor, substitute more exotic mushrooms, such as enoki or shiitake.

Tip

If you don't have shallots on hand, you can substitute 2 tbsp (30 mL) finely chopped onion.

Crusts

Favorite Buttery Pie Crust (page 38) or store-bought refrigerated pie crust (see tip, page 136)

Filling

1 tbsp	unsalted butter	15 mL
2 tbsp	minced shallot	30 mL
2	cloves garlic, minced	2
⅔ cup	chopped mushrooms	150 mL
	Salt and freshly ground black pepper	
2 tbsp	minced fresh parsley	30 mL
⅓ cup	shredded Gruyère or Swiss cheese	75 mL
1 tbsp	freshly grated Parmesan cheese	15 mL
1	large egg	1
¼ cup	half-and-half (10%) cream	60 mL

1. *Crusts:* Use the large circle of the crust cutting tool to cut 8 crusts. Place crusts evenly on top of wells and gently press into the wells with the pie forming tool. If desired, crimp the top edge.

2. *Filling:* In a medium skillet, melt butter over medium heat. Add shallots and cook, stirring, for 2 to 3 minutes or until softened. Add garlic and mushrooms; cook, stirring often, for 5 to 8 minutes or until moisture evaporates from mushrooms and mushrooms are tender. Remove from heat. Season to taste with salt and pepper. Stir in parsley.

3. Spoon mushroom mixture into crusts, dividing evenly. Sprinkle Gruyère and Parmesan on top.

4. In a small bowl, whisk together egg and cream. Spoon egg mixture into crusts, dividing evenly.

5. Bake for 10 to 12 minutes or until a tester inserted in the center of a quiche comes out clean and crusts are golden brown. Transfer quiches to a wire rack to cool slightly.

Ham, Mushroom and Spinach Quiches

Makes 8 quiches

Quiches are one of those special foods that you can enjoy for either a simple family meal or a holiday feast.

Tips

Wrap leftover pie crust dough tightly in plastic wrap and refrigerate; use within 3 days or freeze for up to 2 months. Let thaw overnight in the refrigerator, then roll out and use as desired.

Substitute milk for the half-and-half (10%) cream, if desired.

Crusts

Favorite Buttery Pie Crust (page 38) or store-bought refrigerated pie crust (see tip, page 136)

Filling

⅓ cup	frozen chopped spinach	75 mL
1 tbsp	unsalted butter	15 mL
⅓ cup	finely chopped mushrooms	75 mL
⅓ cup	finely chopped cooked ham	75 mL
⅓ cup	shredded Cheddar cheese	75 mL
1	large egg	1
⅓ cup	half-and-half (10%) cream	75 mL
1 tsp	Dijon mustard	5 mL
	Salt and freshly ground black pepper	

1. *Crusts:* Use the large circle of the crust cutting tool to cut 8 crusts. Place large crusts evenly on top of wells and gently press into the wells with the pie forming tool. If desired, crimp the top edge.

2. *Filling:* Place spinach in a tea strainer or small colander and rinse with hot water until thawed. Drain well, then squeeze until dry.

3. In a small skillet, melt butter over medium-high heat. Add mushrooms and cook, stirring often, for 5 to 8 minutes or until moisture evaporates from mushrooms and mushrooms are tender. Stir in spinach and ham; cook, stirring often, for 1 minute or until heated through.

4. Spoon ham mixture into crusts, dividing evenly. Sprinkle cheese on top.

5. In a medium bowl, whisk together egg, cream and mustard. Season with salt and pepper. Spoon egg mixture into crusts, dividing evenly.

6. Bake for 10 to 12 minutes or until a tester inserted in the center of a quiche comes out clean and crusts are golden brown. Transfer quiches to a wire rack to cool slightly.

Country Ham and Potato Quiches

- -

Dry-cured, salty
country ham has a
distinctive flavor and
makes a wonderful
addition to this quiche.
If country ham isn't
available in your area,
thick-cut peppered
bacon, cooked until
crisp, tastes wonderful
in its place.

Tips

You can replace the
Cheddar with your favorite
cheese — Swiss and
provolone work particularly
well — or try a blend of
cheeses.

Substitute snipped fresh
chives for the green onion,
if desired.

Crusts

	Favorite Buttery Pie Crust (page 38) or store-bought refrigerated pie crust (see tip, page 136)	

Filling

½ cup	finely chopped country ham	125 mL
½ cup	frozen Southern-style or diced hash brown potatoes, thawed	125 mL
½ cup	shredded Cheddar cheese	125 mL
1 tsp	finely minced green onion	5 mL
1	large egg	1
¼ cup	milk	60 mL
	Salt and freshly ground black pepper	

1. *Crusts:* Use the large circle of the crust cutting tool to cut 8 crusts. Place crusts evenly on top of wells and gently press into the wells with the pie forming tool. If desired, crimp the top edge.

2. *Filling:* In a small skillet, over medium-high heat, cook ham for 4 to 5 minutes or until well browned and edges are crisp.

3. Spoon ham into crusts, dividing evenly. Sprinkle potatoes and cheese on top.

4. In a small bowl, whisk together green onion, egg and milk. Season with salt and pepper. Spoon about 1 tbsp (15 mL) egg mixture into each crust.

5. Bake for 10 to 12 minutes or until a tester inserted in the center of a quiche comes out clean and crusts are golden brown. Transfer quiches to a wire rack to cool slightly.

Sausage Phyllo Quiches

We love recipes, like this one, that come together easily but look like they took hours to prepare. These quiches are great for breakfast, but also make delectable appetizers.

Variation

Add 2 tbsp (30 mL) diced drained roasted red bell peppers with the cheese.

8	sheets frozen phyllo dough (see tip, page 45), thawed	8
4 oz	sausage (bulk or casings removed)	125 g
3 tbsp	finely chopped green onion	45 mL
2 tbsp	finely chopped celery	30 mL
½ cup	shredded mozzarella cheese	125 mL
½ tsp	poultry seasoning	2 mL
1	egg, beaten	1
3 tbsp	half-and-half (10%) cream	45 mL
	Salt and freshly ground black pepper	
	Chopped fresh chives or parsley	

1. Form phyllo dough into cups as directed on page 45.

2. In a small skillet, over medium-high heat, cook sausage, green onion and celery, breaking sausage up with the back of a spoon, for 8 to 10 minutes or until sausage is no longer pink and celery is tender. Drain off fat.

3. Transfer sausage mixture to a medium bowl. Stir in cheese, poultry seasoning, egg and cream until well combined. Season with salt and pepper. Spoon 1 heaping tbsp (15 mL) sausage mixture into each phyllo cup.

4. Bake for 10 to 12 minutes or until cups are crisp and a tester inserted in the center of a quiche comes out clean. Carefully transfer quiches to a wire rack to cool slightly. Serve garnished with chives.

Mexican Breakfast Bites

● ●

Makes 8 tortilla cups

Roxanne's family loves Mexican food, and this recipe is a great way to add Mexican flair to breakfast.

● ● ● ● ● ● ● ● ● ● ● ● ● ● ● ● ● ● ● ●

Variation
Add 2 tbsp (30 mL) chopped pickled jalapeño peppers with the cheese.

4 oz	sausage (bulk or casings removed)	125 g
1	large egg, beaten	1
1	green onion, chopped	1
½ cup	shredded Cheddar cheese	125 mL
1 tbsp	minced fresh cilantro	15 mL
2	8- or 10-inch (20 or 25 cm) flour tortillas	2
4 tsp	salsa	20 mL
4 tsp	sour cream	20 mL
	Fresh cilantro leaves	

1. In a small skillet, over medium-high heat, cook sausage, breaking it up with the back of a spoon, for 8 to 10 minutes or until no longer pink. Drain off fat.

2. Transfer sausage to a medium bowl. Stir in egg, green onion, cheese and minced cilantro until well combined.

3. Working with 1 tortilla at a time, wrap tortilla in a paper towel and microwave on High for about 20 seconds or until just warm. Using the large circle of the crust cutting tool, cut 4 circles from the warm tortilla (discard scraps or reserve for another use).

4. Place 1 tortilla circle on top of each well and very gently press into well with the pie forming tool, making a cup.

5. Spoon about 2 tbsp (30 mL) of the sausage mixture into each tortilla cup. Bake for 9 to 10 minutes or until tortilla cups are crisp and a tester inserted in the center of the filling comes out clean. Carefully transfer tortilla cups to a wire rack to cool slightly. Dollop with salsa and sour cream, and sprinkle with cilantro leaves. Serve warm.

Hash Brown Casserole

Spoil your overnight guests with these breakfast bites, served alongside eggs and fresh fruit.

Tips

If you can't find Cheddar-Jack cheese, substitute Cheddar, Colby-Jack or Monterey Jack.

If desired, top each baked breakfast bite with ½ tsp (2 mL) salsa.

These casserole morsels are bite-size, so be sure to serve at least a few per person. If you don't need quite so many, feel free to cut the recipe in half.

8	slices bacon, cooked crisp and crumbled	8
2	green onions, chopped	2
½ cup	finely chopped red bell pepper	125 mL
1½ cups	frozen country-style hash browns, thawed	375 mL
1½ cups	shredded Cheddar-Jack cheese	375 mL
½ cup	biscuit mix (such as Bisquick)	125 mL
¼ tsp	salt	1 mL
⅛ tsp	coarsely ground black pepper	0.5 mL
2	large eggs	2
1 cup	milk	250 mL
¼ cup	sour cream	60 mL
	Nonstick baking spray	

1. In a large bowl, combine bacon, green onions, red pepper, hash browns, cheese, biscuit mix, salt, pepper, eggs, milk and sour cream; stir well.

2. Spray wells with nonstick baking spray. Fill each well with 1½ tbsp (22 mL) hash brown mixture. Bake for 7 to 9 minutes or until set and lightly browned. Transfer breakfast bites to a serving plate. Repeat with the remaining hash brown mixture.

Orange Breakfast Rolls

**Makes
14 rolls**

These are so easy to
make, yet they taste so
very good! Bake them
for a quick weekday
breakfast, a leisurely
weekend breakfast,
a holiday brunch, an
afternoon snack or a
late-night sweet treat.

Tips

Grate only the colored
portion of the orange peel,
avoiding the bitter white
pith underneath.

For easier cleanup, spray the
wells with nonstick baking
spray between batches.
Once you're finished using
the appliance, use a wet
paper towel to carefully wipe
out the wells before the unit
has cooled completely and
the sugars have set.

Rolls

1	can (8 oz/227 g) refrigerated crescent roll dough	1
1/4 cup	granulated sugar	60 mL
2 tsp	grated orange zest	10 mL
2 oz	cream cheese, softened	60 g
	Nonstick baking spray	

Glaze

1/4 cup	confectioners' (icing) sugar	60 mL
1/4 tsp	vanilla extract	1 mL
2 to 4 tsp	freshly squeezed orange juice	10 to 20 mL

1. *Rolls:* On a lightly floured surface, carefully unroll crescent roll dough in one piece. Press seams together to make an 11- by 8-inch (28 by 20 cm) rectangle. Set aside.

2. In a small bowl, using an electric mixer on medium speed, beat sugar, orange zest and cream cheese until smooth. Spread evenly over dough, leaving a 1/8-inch (3 mm) border. Starting from a long end, roll up dough like a jelly roll. Pinch seam to seal. Slice roll into 14 spirals, each about 3/4 inch (2 cm) thick.

3. Spray wells with nonstick baking spray. Place 1 spiral in each well and bake for 3 to 4 minutes or until bottoms are golden brown. Using a small offset spatula, carefully turn rolls over and bake for 3 minutes or until golden brown. Transfer rolls to a wire rack to cool slightly. Repeat with the remaining spirals.

4. *Glaze:* In a small bowl, whisk together confectioner's sugar, vanilla and 2 tsp (10 mL) orange juice. If a thinner glaze is desired, whisk in more orange juice, 1 tsp (5 mL) at a time, until the desired consistency is reached. Drizzle glaze over warm rolls.

Chocolate Silk Mini Pies (page 98)

Lemon Scones with Fruit Bits (page 133)

Cheesy Scrambled Egg
and Bacon Cups (page 135)

Swiss Chicken Hand Pies (page 147)

Root Beer Float Cupcakes (page 164)

Raspberry Coffee Cake Bites (page 169)

Mississippi Mud Pies (page 174)

Inside-Out Rocky Road Cupcakes (page 184)

Avocado Dip Cups (page 195)

Bayou Cakes with Rémoulade (page 202)

King Cupcakes (page 221)

Candy Cane Cupcakes (page 229)

Lunch and Dinner Pies

Parmesan Herb Crust

Makes enough pastry for 8 two-crust hand pies or 16 single-crust mini pies

This is a perfect crust for any savory pie, meat pie or quiche. Parmesan cheese and a subtle yet distinctive hint of basil add just the right amount of flavor.

Tips

Substitute dried Italian seasoning, oregano, tarragon, thyme or another dried herb for the basil. You might want to complement the flavor of the filling — for example, tarragon or thyme for a chicken pie or Italian seasoning for the Italian Grinder Hand Pies (page 177).

Wrap leftover dough tightly in plastic wrap and refrigerate; use within 3 days or freeze for up to 2 months. Let thaw overnight in the refrigerator, then roll out and use as desired.

• Pastry blender or blending fork

1½ cups	all-purpose flour	375 mL
¼ cup	freshly grated Parmesan cheese	60 mL
½ tsp	garlic salt	2 mL
½ tsp	dried basil	2 mL
½ cup	shortening	125 mL
5 to 6 tbsp	ice water	75 to 90 mL

1. In a large bowl, whisk together flour, Parmesan, garlic salt and basil. Using a pastry blender or blending fork, cut in shortening until mixture is crumbly.

2. Sprinkle 5 tbsp (75 mL) ice water evenly over flour mixture and let stand for 30 seconds. Blend with a fork until dough holds together and cleans the sides of the bowl, adding more ice water, if needed. Form dough into a disk, wrap in plastic wrap and refrigerate for at least 30 minutes, until chilled, or for up to 24 hours.

3. On a lightly floured surface, lightly dust top of dough with flour. Roll out gently, picking dough up after each roll, dusting underneath with flour as necessary and rotating it from 12 o'clock to 3 o'clock. (This keeps the dough from sticking.) Roll and rotate until dough is about ⅛ inch (3 mm) thick.

4. Use as directed in the recipe or, to bake single crusts blind (empty), see page 39. To bake single-crust mini pies, see page 41. To bake two-crust hand pies, see page 43.

Swiss Chicken Hand Pies

Makes 12 to 14 hand pies

We love this recipe! It's easy, yet it doesn't taste ordinary.

Tip

Puff pastry is a flaky, rich pastry that is readily available in the freezer section of grocery stores. It is sold as sheets, shells or blocks — choose any of these and thaw according to package directions. If using sheets, you can cut 15 or 16 top crusts from one sheet of puff pastry (half of a 17.4 oz/490 g box) if you reroll the scraps. If using shells, plan on cutting 2 top crusts from each shell; thaw only the number you need and keep the rest frozen for another use. Because puff pastry puffs so much, it is not recommended for the bottom crust of a two-crust hand pie.

Crusts

Favorite Buttery Pie Crust (page 38) or store-bought refrigerated pie crust (see tip, page 148)
Puff pastry (see tip, at left)

Filling

2 tbsp	unsalted butter	30 mL
1/3 cup	finely chopped onion	75 mL
1 cup	very finely chopped cooked chicken	250 mL
2 tbsp	chopped drained roasted red bell peppers	30 mL
1/2 cup	light Alfredo sauce	125 mL
	Salt and freshly ground black pepper	
1/2 cup	shredded Swiss cheese	125 mL

1. *Crusts:* Use the large circle of the crust cutting tool to cut 12 to 14 bottom crusts from the pie crust, rerolling scraps as necessary. Place 8 large crusts evenly on top of wells and gently press into wells with the pie forming tool. Cover the remaining crusts with plastic wrap and set aside.

2. On a lightly floured surface, roll out puff pastry to about 1/8 inch (3 mm) thick, pressing any perforated seams together. Use the small circle of the crust cutting tool to cut 12 to 14 top crusts. Cover with plastic wrap and set aside.

3. *Filling:* In a medium skillet, melt butter over medium-high heat. Add onion and cook, stirring often, for 2 to 3 minutes or until tender. Stir in chicken, roasted peppers and Alfredo sauce. Season to taste with salt and pepper. Remove from heat and stir in Swiss cheese.

4. Spoon about 1 1/2 tbsp (22 mL) filling into each bottom crust; do not overfill. Place a top crust directly over the center of each filled shell.

5. Bake for 10 to 12 minutes or until crusts are browned and crisp. Transfer pies to a wire rack to cool slightly. Let appliance cool for 5 minutes. Repeat with the remaining crusts and filling. Serve warm.

Mushroom Goat Cheese Empanadas

The lively flavors of jalapeño and oregano combine with warm, comforting goat cheese and cumin to make these appetizers a favorite for all.

Tip

If using a store-bought refrigerated pie crust, let come to room temperature, then unroll according to package directions and proceed with the recipe. You can cut 14 Babycakes™ single crusts from one packaged pie crust (half a 14-oz/400 g package) by rerolling the scraps.

Crusts

Favorite Buttery Pie Crust (page 38) or store-bought refrigerated pie crust (see tip, at left)
Puff pastry (see tip, at right)

Filling

2 tbsp	unsalted butter	30 mL
2	cloves garlic, minced	2
1/3 cup	finely chopped onion	75 mL
1/3 cup	finely chopped red bell pepper	75 mL
1/2	jalapeño pepper, seeded and minced	1/2
1/3 cup	sliced mushrooms	75 mL
1 tsp	dried oregano	5 mL
1/2 tsp	ground cumin	2 mL
	Salt and freshly ground black pepper	
1/2 cup	shredded Monterey Jack cheese	125 mL
3 oz	goat cheese	90 g

1. *Crusts:* Use the large circle of the crust cutting tool to cut 8 bottom crusts from the pie crust. Place crusts evenly on top of wells and gently press into wells with the pie forming tool.

2. On a lightly floured surface, roll out puff pastry to about 1/8 inch (3 mm) thick, pressing any perforated seams together. Use the small circle of the crust cutting tool to cut 8 top crusts. Cover with plastic wrap and set aside.

Tip

Puff pastry is a flaky, rich pastry that is readily available in the freezer section of grocery stores. It is sold as sheets, shells or blocks — choose any of these and thaw according to package directions. If using sheets, you can cut 15 or 16 top crusts from one sheet of puff pastry (half of a 17.4 oz/490 g box) if you reroll the scraps. If using shells, plan on cutting 2 top crusts from each shell; thaw only the number you need and keep the rest frozen for another use. Because puff pastry puffs so much, it is not recommended for the bottom crust of a two-crust hand pie.

3. *Filling:* In a medium skillet, melt butter over medium-high heat. Add garlic and onion; cook, stirring often, for 2 to 3 minutes or until tender. Add red pepper and jalapeño; cook, stirring often, for 3 minutes. Stir in mushrooms and cook, stirring often, for 3 to 4 minutes or until mushrooms and peppers are tender. Stir in oregano, cumin and salt and pepper to taste. Reduce heat to low and stir in Monterey Jack and goat cheese. Cook, stirring often, until cheese is melted. Remove from heat.

4. Spoon about $1\frac{1}{2}$ tbsp (22 mL) filling into each bottom crust; do not overfill. Place a top crust directly over the center of each filled shell.

5. Bake for 10 to 12 minutes or until crusts are browned and crisp. Transfer empanadas to a wire rack to cool slightly. Serve warm.

Herbed Turkey Pot Pies

**Makes
8 hand pies**

A little extra cooked turkey will never be viewed as mere leftovers again! These are so good — with either turkey or chicken — that you will be tempted to serve them often.

Tip

You can substitute Favorite Buttery Pie Crust (page 38) for the Parmesan Herb Crust. If desired, puff pastry may be used for the top crusts.

Variation

Substitute cooked chicken for the cooked turkey.

Crusts

	Parmesan Herb Crust (page 146) or store-bought refrigerated pie crust (see tip, page 148)	

Filling

2 tbsp	unsalted butter	30 mL
1/3 cup	frozen mixed vegetables, partially thawed	75 mL
2/3 cup	finely chopped cooked turkey	150 mL
1/4 tsp	poultry seasoning	1 mL
	Salt and freshly ground black pepper	
1 tbsp	all-purpose flour	15 mL
1/2 cup	chicken broth	125 mL
1 tbsp	minced fresh parsley	15 mL

1. *Crusts:* Use the large circle of the crust cutting tool to cut 8 bottom crusts from the pie crust, and use the small circle of the crust cutting tool to cut 8 top crusts, rerolling scraps as necessary. Place large crusts evenly on top of wells and gently press into wells with the pie forming tool. Cover the top crusts with plastic wrap and set aside.

2. *Filling:* In a small skillet, melt butter over medium heat. Add mixed vegetables and cook, stirring often, for 4 to 5 minutes or until tender. Stir in turkey and poultry seasoning. Season to taste with salt and pepper. Cook, stirring constantly, until turkey is heated through. Stir in flour until smooth. Cook, stirring constantly, for 1 minute. Stir in broth and cook, stirring constantly, until bubbling. Stir in parsley.

3. Spoon about 1 1/2 tbsp (22 mL) filling into each bottom crust. Place a top crust directly over the center of each filled shell.

4. Bake for 10 to 12 minutes or until crusts are browned and crisp. Transfer pies to a wire rack to cool slightly. Serve warm.

Pizza Pot Pies

Pot pie becomes new
and exciting when
stuffed with popular
pizza fillings.

Variations

Hamburger Pizza Pot Pies:
Substitute ground beef for
the Italian sausage. Season
to taste with salt and
pepper after stirring in the
pizza sauce.

Adjust the filling to suit
your preferences, using
any combination of cooked
meat and vegetables
totaling about 1 cup
(250 mL). For example, try
pepperoni slices, chopped
Canadian bacon, diced
cooked ham, sliced pitted
olives, chopped tomatoes,
minced fresh basil or
caramelized onions. Stir in
1/2 cup (125 mL) pizza sauce
before spooning filling into
crusts.

Crusts

	Favorite Buttery Pie Crust (page 38) or store-bought refrigerated pie crust (see tip, page 148) Puff pastry (see tip, page 149)	

Filling

4 oz	Italian sausage (bulk or casings removed)	125 g
1/4 cup	chopped red bell pepper	60 mL
1/4 cup	chopped mushrooms	60 mL
1/2 cup	pizza sauce	125 mL
1/2 cup	shredded Italian cheese blend or pizza cheese blend	125 mL

1. *Crusts:* Use the large circle of the crust cutting tool to cut 8 bottom crusts from the pie crust. Place crusts evenly on top of wells and gently press into wells with the pie forming tool.

2. On a lightly floured surface, roll out puff pastry to about 1/8 inch (3 mm) thick, pressing any perforated seams together. Use the small circle of the crust cutting tool to cut 8 top crusts. Cover with plastic wrap and set aside.

3. *Filling:* In a small skillet, over medium-high heat, cook sausage, breaking it up with the back of a spoon, for 8 to 10 minutes or until no longer pink. Drain off fat. Add red pepper and mushrooms; cook, stirring often, for 3 to 5 minutes or until tender. Stir in pizza sauce.

4. Spoon about 1 1/2 tbsp (22 mL) sausage mixture into each bottom crust; do not overfill. Top each with about 1 tbsp (15 mL) Italian blend cheese. Place a top crust directly over the center of each filled shell.

5. Bake for 10 to 12 minutes or until crusts are browned and crisp. Transfer pies to a wire rack to cool slightly. Serve warm.

Green Chile Sausage Hand Pies

Easy, yet with a captivating flavor, these little pies are perfect for lunch or supper, and also make delightful appetizers! You'll want to serve them often.

Tip

For the very best two-crust pies, use Favorite Buttery Pie Crust for the bottom crust and puff pastry for the top crust. The puff pastry bakes up light, crisp and golden brown. But because puff pastry puffs so much, it is not recommended for the bottom crust.

Crusts

	Favorite Buttery Pie Crust (page 38) or store-bought refrigerated pie crust (see tip, page 148)	
	Puff pastry (see tip, page 149)	

Filling

8 oz	sausage (bulk or casings removed)	250 g
1	can (4½ oz/127 mL) green chiles, drained and chopped	1
1 cup	shredded sharp (old) Cheddar cheese	250 mL
¼ cup	ranch salad dressing	60 mL

1. *Crusts:* Use the large circle of the crust cutting tool to cut 16 bottom crusts from the pie crust, rerolling scraps as necessary. Place 8 large crusts evenly on top of wells and gently press into wells with the pie forming tool. Cover the remaining crusts with plastic wrap and set aside.

2. On a lightly floured surface, roll out puff pastry to about ⅛ inch (3 mm) thick, pressing any perforated seams together. Use the small circle of the crust cutting tool to cut 16 top crusts. Cover with plastic wrap and set aside.

3. *Filling:* In a medium skillet, over medium-high heat, cook sausage, breaking it up with the back of a spoon, for 8 to 10 minutes or until no longer pink. Drain off fat and transfer sausage to a medium bowl. Stir in green chiles, cheese and ranch dressing.

4. Spoon 1 to 1½ tbsp (15 to 22 mL) filling into each bottom crust; do not overfill. Place a top crust directly over the center of each filled shell.

5. Bake for 12 to 14 minutes or until crusts are browned and crisp. Transfer pies to a wire rack to cool slightly. Let appliance cool for 5 minutes. Repeat with the remaining crusts and filling. Serve warm.

Country Ham and Egg Hand Pies

Makes 8 hand pies

Roxanne's dad, Kenny Wyss, retired from the grocery industry. His specialty was merchandising meat products for a large grocery chain. One of his favorite delights is country ham. Roxanne has fond memories of sharing country ham and eggs with her father at their family cottage on the Lake of the Ozarks, and she credits her love of great food to her dad's influence.

Tips

Dry-cured, salty country ham has a distinctive flavor, but if it isn't available in your area, substitute chopped thick-cut peppered bacon and omit the butter. In step 2, cook bacon over medium-high heat until very crisp. Using a slotted spoon, transfer bacon to a plate lined with paper towels. Drain all but 1 tbsp (15 mL) fat from pan. Add mushrooms to the pan and continue with step 3 as directed. Return the bacon to the pan with the cheese.

Add a pinch of dry mustard to the filling, if desired.

Crusts

Favorite Buttery Pie Crust (page 38) or store-bought refrigerated pie crust (see tip, page 148)
Puff pastry (see tip, page 149)

Filling

2 tbsp	unsalted butter	30 mL
1/3 cup	chopped country ham	75 mL
1/4 cup	chopped mushrooms	60 mL
1 tbsp	all-purpose flour	15 mL
	Salt and freshly ground black pepper	
1/2 cup	milk	125 mL
3 tbsp	freshly grated Parmesan cheese	45 mL
1	hard-cooked egg, chopped	1

1. *Crusts:* Use the large circle of the crust cutting tool to cut 8 bottom crusts from the pie crust. Place crusts evenly on top of wells and gently press into wells with the pie forming tool.

2. On a lightly floured surface, roll out puff pastry to about 1/8 inch (3 mm) thick, pressing any perforated seams together. Use the small circle of the crust cutting tool to cut 8 top crusts. Cover with plastic wrap and set aside.

3. *Filling:* In a small saucepan, melt butter over medium heat. Add ham and cook, stirring, for 4 to 5 minutes or until browned and crisp. Add mushrooms and cook, stirring often, for 1 to 2 minutes or until tender. Stir in flour until smooth. Cook, stirring constantly, for 1 minute. Season to taste with salt and pepper. Gradually stir in milk; cook, stirring constantly, for 1 to 2 minutes or until thickened and bubbly. Stir in cheese.

4. Spoon egg into bottom crusts, dividing evenly. Top each with about 1 tbsp (15 mL) ham mixture. Place a top crust directly over the center of each filled shell.

5. Bake for 10 to 12 minutes or until crusts are browned and crisp. Transfer pies to a wire rack to cool slightly. Serve warm.

Beef Pie Bites

**Makes
8 hand pies**

Cornish pasties are a time-honored favorite for many families. This version adapts the classic treat into bite-size pies, perfect for a luncheon, a supper or as appetizers. In the traditional version, the crust is filled with uncooked meat and vegetables, but we find that precooked beef and vegetables, or even leftover ingredients, make a delightful, quick alternative.

Variation

Omit the potatoes and use 1¼ cups (300 mL) meat, or substitute chopped cooked mushrooms, carrots or other vegetables for the potato.

Crusts

Favorite Buttery Pie Crust (page 38), Parmesan Herb Crust (page 146) or store-bought refrigerated pie crust (see tip, page 148)

Filling

2 tbsp	unsalted butter	30 mL
¾ cup	chopped cooked beef steak or roast	175 mL
½ cup	chopped cooked peeled potato	125 mL
½ tsp	instant beef bouillon powder	2 mL
⅛ tsp	dried thyme	0.5 mL
½ tsp	Worcestershire sauce	2 mL
	Salt and freshly ground black pepper	

Egg Wash

1	large egg	1
1 tbsp	water	15 mL

1. *Crusts:* Use the large circle of the crust cutting tool to cut 8 bottom crusts from the pie crust, and use the small circle of the crust cutting tool to cut 8 top crusts, rerolling scraps as necessary. Place large crusts evenly on top of wells and gently press into wells with the pie forming tool. Cover the top crusts with plastic wrap and set aside.

2. *Filling:* In a small skillet, melt butter over medium-high heat. Add beef and potato; cook, stirring often, for about 1 minute or until heated through. Stir in bouillon, thyme and Worcestershire sauce. Season to taste with salt and pepper. Cook, stirring, for 1 minute to blend the flavors.

3. Spoon about 2 tbsp (30 mL) filling into each bottom crust, mounding slightly. Place a top crust directly over the center of each filled shell.

4. *Egg Wash:* In a small bowl, whisk together egg and water. Brush lightly over top crusts.

5. Bake for 12 to 15 minutes or until crusts are golden brown. Transfer pies to a wire rack to cool slightly. Serve hot.

Beef and Broccoli Bites

**Makes
12 to 14 packets**

Beef and broccoli pair well together. The tangy vegetable cream cheese and the crisp phyllo crust will convert even the staunchest of broccoli-challenged folks.

Tips

Different brands of phyllo come in different-size sheets. We used sheets that are 14 by 9 inches (35 by 23 cm), which is about half of a 16-oz (454 g) package. Some sheets are larger (17 by 12 inches/43 by 30 cm or 18 by 14 inches/ 45 by 35 cm), so use 3 to 4 and cut them in half crosswise before proceeding with step 2.

If desired, substitute plain cream cheese for the garden vegetable–flavored cream cheese.

8 oz	lean ground beef	250 g
½ cup	chopped onion	125 mL
1 cup	finely chopped broccoli florets	250 mL
	Salt and freshly ground black pepper	
¼ cup	sour cream	60 mL
¼ cup	garden vegetable–flavored cream cheese	60 mL
6 to 7	sheets frozen phyllo dough, thawed	6 to 7
	Nonstick baking spray	

1. In a medium skillet, over medium-high heat, cook beef and onion, breaking beef up with the back of a spoon, for 8 to 10 minutes or until beef is no longer pink and onion is tender. Drain off fat. Add broccoli and cook, stirring often, for 3 to 4 minutes or until tender. Season to taste with salt and pepper. Stir in sour cream and cream cheese; reduce heat to low and cook, stirring constantly, until cream cheese is melted.

2. Place 1 sheet of phyllo on a cutting board. (Immediately cover the remaining sheets with plastic wrap and then a lightly dampened towel, keeping them covered to prevent them from drying out.) Cut phyllo sheet in half crosswise.

3. Fold 1 half-sheet in half crosswise. Mound 1 to 1½ tbsp (15 to 22 mL) beef mixture in the center. Fold in longer sides, then shorter sides, enclosing the filling and making a packet that will fit in a well. Repeat with the remaining phyllo and filling.

4. Spray wells with nonstick baking spray. Place a packet in each well, pushing it down lightly. Spray tops of packets with baking spray. Bake for 5 to 6 minutes. Using a small offset spatula, carefully turn packets over. Bake for 5 to 6 minutes or until golden brown on top. Carefully transfer packets to a wire rack to cool slightly. Repeat with the remaining packets. Serve warm.

Caramelized Onion Mini Pies

**Makes
8 mini pies**

Roxanne would love to move to Paris. On days when the gravitational pull toward France is hard to resist, she prepares these caramelized onion pies, makes a crisp salad with French vinaigrette, pours a glass of French wine and dreams about past trips to the city on the Seine.

Tip

To create a truly French experience, add 2 tbsp (30 mL) shredded Gruyère cheese to the egg mixture.

Crusts

	Favorite Buttery Pie Crust (page 38) or store-bought refrigerated pie crust (see tip, page 148)	

Filling

¼ cup	caramelized onions (see box, below), chopped	60 mL
1	large egg	1
2 tbsp	half-and-half (10%) cream	30 mL
¼ cup	sour cream	60 mL
	Salt and freshly ground black pepper	

1. *Crusts:* Use the large circle of the crust cutting tool to cut 8 crusts from the pie crust. Place crusts evenly on top of wells and gently press into wells with the pie forming tool. If desired, crimp the edges.

2. *Filling:* Spoon about $1\frac{1}{2}$ tsp (7 mL) caramelized onions into each crust.

3. In a small bowl, whisk together egg and cream. Stir in sour cream until smooth. Season with salt and pepper.

4. Spoon about 1 tbsp (15 mL) egg mixture over onions in each crust. Bake for 7 to 9 minutes or until crusts are golden brown. Transfer pies to a wire rack to cool slightly. Serve warm.

Caramelized Onions

The easiest way to caramelize onions is to prepare them in a slow cooker. Thinly slice 5 to 6 sweet onions and place in a 4- to 6-quart slow cooker. Drizzle with 2 tbsp (30 mL) olive oil and 2 tbsp (30 mL) melted butter. Cover and cook on High for 6 to 8 hours or until onions are caramelized. Season to taste with salt and freshly ground black pepper. Let cool, then spoon onions into small airtight containers and freeze for up to 5 months. Let thaw overnight in the refrigerator before use.

If desired, to make just enough caramelized onions for this recipe, thinly slice 1 sweet onion. In a skillet, heat 2 tbsp (30 mL) butter or olive oil over medium-high heat. Sauté onion for 5 to 6 minutes or until tender. Reduce heat to low and cook, stirring often, for 15 to 20 minutes or until onions are golden brown and very tender. Season to taste with salt and pepper.

Part 4

Babycakes™ for Everybody

Gluten-Free and Vegan Treats

Grandma's Chocolate Mayonnaise Cupcakes

Makes 16 to 18 cupcakes

Chocolate mayonnaise cake is an old-time favorite, and it never loses its appeal. When Kathy first started working in a test kitchen after college, chocolate mayonnaise cake was enjoying a surge in popularity. Now the trend has returned, and we think these mini versions make it better than ever.

Tip

Ground flax seeds are quite perishable. Store in an airtight container in the refrigerator for up to 3 months or in the freezer for up to 6 months.

- Paper liners (optional)

2 tbsp	ground flax seeds (flaxseed meal)	30 mL
6 tbsp	hot water	90 mL
1 cup	gluten-free chocolate cake mix	250 mL
1/2 cup	mayonnaise	125 mL
1/2 cup	water	125 mL
1/2 cup	gluten-free miniature semisweet chocolate chips	125 mL
2 tbsp	gluten-free confectioners' (icing) sugar	30 mL

1. In a large bowl, combine flax seeds and hot water. Let stand for 10 minutes.

2. Add cake mix, mayonnaise and water to the flaxseed mixture and, using an electric mixer on low speed, beat for 30 seconds or until moistened. Beat on medium speed for 2 minutes. Stir in chocolate chips.

3. If desired, place paper liners in wells. Fill each well with about $1\frac{1}{2}$ tbsp (22 mL) batter. Bake for 7 to 9 minutes or until a tester inserted in the center of a cupcake comes out clean. Transfer cupcakes to a wire rack to cool. Repeat with the remaining batter.

4. Just before serving, sprinkle with confectioners' (icing) sugar.

VEGAN VARIATION

Substitute vegan mayonnaise spread for the mayonnaise, use vegan miniature chocolate chips and check the label to make sure the cake mix is vegan.

Chocolate Ale Cupcakes

**Makes
34 to 36 cupcakes**

These cupcakes may be gluten-free, but they are so rich and moist, they'll be the hit of any party.

Tips

Frost these with chocolate frosting or, for even more decadent treats, frost with caramel frosting, then drizzle with caramel topping and sprinkle with coarse sea salt.

Always read labels to be sure all products are gluten-free and were not processed in a plant that also produces products that contain gluten.

Variation

For a dairy-free version, use vegan hard margarine in place of the butter and dairy-free sour cream substitute in place of the sour cream.

• Paper liners (optional)

½ cup	gluten-free ale or beer	125 mL
⅓ cup	unsalted butter, cut into small pieces	75 mL
1 cup	packed brown sugar	250 mL
⅓ cup	unsweetened cocoa powder	75 mL
1 cup	almond flour	250 mL
¼ cup	gluten-free all-purpose baking mix (see tips, page 165)	60 mL
1¼ tsp	baking soda	6 mL
2	large eggs, at room temperature	2
⅓ cup	sour cream	75 mL
1½ tsp	vanilla extract	7 mL

1. In a large saucepan, combine ale and butter. Heat over medium heat, stirring frequently, until butter is melted. Remove from heat and stir in brown sugar and cocoa. Set aside.

2. In a small bowl, whisk together almond flour, baking mix and baking soda. Set aside.

3. In a large bowl, using an electric mixer on medium-high speed, beat eggs, sour cream and vanilla until combined. Beat in beer mixture until smooth. Reduce mixer speed to low and beat in dry ingredients until smooth.

4. If desired, place paper liners in wells. Fill each well with about 1½ tbsp (22 mL) batter. Bake for 7 to 9 minutes or until a tester inserted in the center of a cupcake comes out clean. Transfer cupcakes to a wire rack to cool. Repeat with the remaining batter.

Cherry Pecan Cupcakes

GLUTEN-FREE

Makes 15 to 17 cupcakes

For years we traveled to Wichita, Kansas, to tape a television show, and we loved to stop at a local drive-in for lunch. The restaurant served wonderful ice cream. Roxanne's favorite — cherry pecan — is the inspiration for these cupcakes.

Tips

Frost with Cherry Frosting (variation, page 108), made with gluten-free confectioners' (icing) sugar, then garnish with toasted chopped pecans.

Toasting pecans intensifies their flavor. Spread chopped pecans in a single layer on a baking sheet. Bake at 350°F (180°C) for 5 to 7 minutes or until lightly browned. Let cool, then measure.

- Paper liners (optional)

1/4 cup	chopped dried cherries	60 mL
1/3 cup	boiling water	75 mL
1 cup	gluten-free yellow cake mix	250 mL
1	large egg, at room temperature	1
1	large egg yolk, at room temperature	1
1/4 cup	unsalted butter, softened	60 mL
1 tsp	vanilla extract	5 mL
1/2 tsp	almond extract	2 mL
3 to 5	drops red food coloring (optional)	3 to 5
1/4 cup	chopped pecans, toasted (see tip, at left)	60 mL

1. In a large bowl, combine cherries and boiling water. Let stand for 5 minutes, stirring occasionally. Using an electric mixer on low speed, beat in cake mix, egg, egg yolk, butter, vanilla, almond extract and food coloring (if using) for 30 seconds or until moistened. Beat on medium speed for 2 minutes. Stir in pecans.
2. If desired, place paper liners in wells. Fill each well with about 1 1/2 tbsp (22 mL) batter. Bake for 6 to 8 minutes or until a tester inserted in the center of a cupcake comes out clean. Transfer cupcakes to a wire rack to cool. Repeat with the remaining batter.

Lemon Ricotta Cupcakes

Lemon gives baked goods a light, refreshing flavor, and the addition of ricotta creates moist, rich cupcakes. These are perfect any time of year.

Tips

Lemon curd is a thick mixture of cooked lemon juice, sugar, butter and eggs. It is readily available in jars and can often be found with the jams and jellies at the grocery store. Commercially prepared lemon curd may be kept tightly covered and refrigerated for up 6 months. Homemade lemon curd is highly perishable; while the exact storage time will vary with the recipe used, in general it should be used within 1 to 2 weeks.

For a more intense vanilla flavor, substitute 1 tsp (5 mL) vanilla bean paste for the vanilla extract.

• Paper liners (optional)

1/4 cup	unsalted butter, cut into pieces	60 mL
1/2 cup	gluten-free all-purpose baking mix (see tips, page 165)	125 mL
1/2 cup	almond flour	125 mL
3/4 tsp	gluten-free baking powder	3 mL
1/2 cup	granulated sugar	125 mL
2	large eggs, at room temperature	2
1/2 cup	ricotta cheese	125 mL
1 tbsp	lemon curd (see tip, at left)	15 mL
	Grated zest of 1 lemon	
1 tbsp	freshly squeezed lemon juice	15 mL
1 tsp	vanilla extract	5 mL

1. In a small microwave-safe glass bowl, microwave butter on High for 45 to 60 seconds or until melted. Set aside to cool.

2. In a small bowl, whisk together baking mix, almond flour and baking powder. Set aside.

3. In a large bowl, using an electric mixer on medium-high speed, beat sugar and eggs for 2 to 3 minutes or until pale yellow. Beat in melted butter, ricotta, lemon curd, lemon zest, lemon juice and vanilla. Reduce mixer speed to low and beat in dry ingredients until well combined.

4. If desired, place paper liners in wells. Fill each well with about 1 1/2 tbsp (22 mL) batter. Bake for 8 to 10 minutes or until a tester inserted in the center of a cupcake comes out clean. Transfer cupcakes to a wire rack to cool. Repeat with the remaining batter.

Margarita Cupcakes

VEGAN

Who says we outgrow fun treats? This cupcake, inspired by the famous cocktail, will add fun to any party.

Tip

Frost with the vegan variation of Vanilla Buttercream Frosting (page 105). Garnish with a lime zest curl or lime wedge, then sprinkle lightly with margarita salt.

• Paper liners (optional)

1 1/3 cups	all-purpose flour	325 mL
1/2 tsp	baking powder	2 mL
1/2 tsp	salt	2 mL
1/4 tsp	baking soda	1 mL
3/4 cup	granulated sugar	175 mL
1 cup	unsweetened plain almond milk	250 mL
1/4 cup	vegetable oil	60 mL
1 tsp	grated lime zest	5 mL
1/4 cup	freshly squeezed lime juice	60 mL
1 tbsp	tequila	15 mL

1. In a large bowl, whisk together flour, baking powder, salt and baking soda. Set aside.

2. In a medium bowl, whisk together sugar, almond milk, oil, lime zest, lime juice and tequila until well combined. Stir into flour mixture until well combined.

3. If desired, place paper liners in wells. Fill each well with about 1 1/2 tbsp (22 mL) batter. Bake for 6 to 8 minutes or until a tester inserted in the center of a cupcake comes out clean. Transfer cupcakes to a wire rack to cool. Repeat with the remaining batter.

Root Beer Float Cupcakes

Roxanne's dad, Kenneth Wyss, adores root beer floats. Roxanne has wonderful childhood memories of sharing root beer floats with him at the local root beer stand, Mugs Up. Although she can't always take him out for root beer these days, she can always bake up one of his favorite flavors.

Tip

To make each cupcake look like a root beer float, mound fluffy puffs of Vanilla Buttercream Frosting (page 105), made with gluten-free confectioners' (icing) sugar, on top. Cut a bendy straw in half (discarding the bottom half) and insert it into the cupcake.

• Paper liners (optional)

1 cup	gluten-free chocolate cake mix	250 mL
2	large eggs, at room temperature	2
1/2 cup	root beer, at room temperature	125 mL
1/2 cup	butter, softened	125 mL

1. In a medium bowl, using an electric mixer on low speed, beat cake mix, eggs, root beer and butter for 30 seconds or until moistened. Beat on medium speed for 2 minutes.

2. If desired, place paper liners in wells. Fill each well with about 1 1/2 tbsp (22 mL) batter. Bake for 6 to 8 minutes or until a tester inserted in the center of a cupcake comes out clean. Transfer cupcakes to a wire rack to cool. Repeat with the remaining batter.

Gluten-Free Pie Pastry

GLUTEN-FREE

Makes enough pastry for 8 two-crust hand pies or 16 single-crust mini pies

Don't let a gluten-free diet prevent you from enjoying wonderful pies. This gluten-free pie crust recipe makes it possible.

Tips

Gluten-free all purpose baking mix is a blend of several kinds of gluten-free flours and starches. The exact blend used varies from brand to brand, so you might prefer the baking qualities and flavor of one over another. Popular brands include King Arthur and Bob's Red Mill, but stores and websites that specialize in gluten-free baking ingredients offer a large array of brands and package sizes.

To make your own gluten-free all-purpose baking mix, whisk together 3 parts white rice flour (not sweet), 3 parts brown rice flour, 2 parts potato starch and 1 part tapioca starch. Store in an airtight container in the refrigerator for up to 4 months or in the freezer for up to 1 year.

- Pastry blender or blending fork

1¼ cups	gluten-free all-purpose baking mix (see tips, at left)	300 mL
1½ tbsp	granulated sugar	22 mL
½ tsp	guar gum (see tip, page 169)	2 mL
⅛ tsp	salt	0.5 mL
2 tbsp	shortening	30 mL
6 tbsp	cold unsalted butter, cut into small pieces	90 mL
¼ cup	ice water	60 mL

1. In a large bowl, whisk together baking mix, sugar, guar gum and salt. Using a pastry blender or blending fork, cut in shortening until mixture resembles coarse crumbs. Cut in butter until mixture resembles fine crumbs. Sprinkle with ice water and blend with a fork until dough holds together. Form dough into a disk, wrap in plastic wrap and refrigerate for at least 30 minutes, until chilled, or for up to 24 hours.

2. Place a sheet of plastic wrap on a work surface. Place dough on top and cover with another sheet of plastic wrap. Roll out gently between sheets of plastic wrap, picking dough up after each roll and rotating it from 12 o'clock to 3 o'clock. (This keeps the dough from sticking.) Roll and rotate until dough is about ⅛ inch (3 mm) thick.

3. Use as directed in the recipe or, to bake single crusts blind (empty), see page 39. To bake single-crust mini pies, see page 41. To bake two-crust hand pies, see page 43.

VEGAN VARIATION

Use vegan shortening in place of the shortening and vegan hard margarine in place of the butter.

Bourbon Pecan Fig Hand Pies

These are such rich and elegant pies — perfect for any holiday or dinner party — yet they're so easy!

Tips

If you don't need to follow a gluten-free diet, you can use your favorite pastry for the bottom crusts (see recipes on pages 38, 92 and 146) and puff pastry for the top crusts.

Toasting pecans intensifies their flavor. Spread chopped pecans in a single layer on a baking sheet. Bake at 350°F (180°C) for 5 to 7 minutes or until lightly browned. Let cool, then measure.

Crusts

| | Gluten-Free Pie Pastry (page 165) | |
| 1 tbsp | unsweetened plain almond milk | 15 mL |

Filling

½ cup	fig spread or preserves	125 mL
2 tbsp	bourbon	30 mL
¼ cup	chopped pecans, toasted (see tip, at left)	60 mL

1. *Crusts:* Use the large circle of the crust cutting tool to cut 8 bottom crusts from the pie crust, and use the small circle of the crust cutting tool to cut 8 top crusts, rerolling scraps as necessary. Place large crusts evenly on top of wells and gently press into wells with the pie forming tool. Cover the top crusts with plastic wrap and set aside.

2. *Filling:* In a small saucepan, combine fig spread and bourbon. Bring to a boil over medium heat, stirring frequently. Remove from heat and stir in pecans.

3. Spoon about 1½ tbsp (22 mL) filling into each bottom crust. Place a top crust directly over the center of each filled shell. Brush top crusts lightly with almond milk.

4. Bake for 15 to 17 minutes or until top crusts are golden brown and crisp. Transfer pies to a wire rack to cool slightly. Serve warm.

VEGAN VARIATION

Use the Vegan Variation when making the pastry.

Salted Caramel Apple Mini Pies

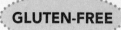

Sweet and salty flavors make a captivating combination. These mini pies are so good that this recipe may become your all-time apple pie favorite.

Tip

One cup (250 mL) of apple pie filling is about half of a 21-oz (597 mL) can. Leftover filling can be stored in an airtight container in the refrigerator for up to 1 week.

Crusts

Gluten-Free Pie Pastry (page 165)

Filling

1 cup	gluten-free canned apple pie filling	250 mL
1 tsp	coarse sea salt	5 mL
3 tbsp	gluten-free caramel sauce	45 mL

Topping

2 tbsp	packed brown sugar	30 mL
2 tbsp	certified gluten-free large-flake (old-fashioned) rolled oats	30 mL
1 tbsp	gluten-free all-purpose baking mix (see tips, page 165)	15 mL
1½ tsp	unsalted butter	7 mL

1. *Crusts:* Use the large circle of the crust cutting tool to cut 12 to 14 crusts from the pie crust. Place 8 crusts evenly on top of wells and gently press into wells with the pie forming tool. If desired, crimp the edges. Cover the remaining crusts with plastic wrap and set aside.

2. *Filling:* Pour apple pie filling into a shallow dish and chop the apple slices. In a small bowl, combine pie filling, salt and caramel sauce.

3. *Topping:* In another small bowl, combine brown sugar, oats and baking mix. Using your fingertips or a pastry blender, cut in butter until mixture resembles coarse crumbs.

4. Spoon 1½ tbsp (22 mL) filling into each crust. Sprinkle 1 to 1½ tsp (5 to 7 mL) topping over the filling in each crust.

5. Bake for 11 to 12 minutes or until crusts are golden brown. Transfer pies to a wire rack to cool. Let appliance cool for 5 minutes. Repeat with the remaining crusts, filling and topping.

VEGAN VARIATION

Use the Vegan Variation when making the pastry. Use vegan caramel sauce in the filling and vegan hard margarine in the topping.

Caramel Applesauce Muffins

**Makes
19 to 21 muffins**

Some flavor combos
are universally popular.
We capture one of
those natural fits —
caramel and apples —
in these muffins.

Tips

Vegan caramel sauce is sold
in health food and specialty
food stores. Read the label
carefully to select one that is
free of all animal products.

If desired, you can drizzle
additional vegan caramel
sauce over each muffin just
before serving.

• Paper liners (optional)

1 cup	all-purpose flour	250 mL
2/3 cup	packed brown sugar	150 mL
1 1/2 tsp	baking powder	7 mL
1/2 tsp	ground cinnamon	2 mL
1/4 tsp	salt	1 mL
1/2 cup	unsweetened applesauce	125 mL
1/3 cup	unsweetened plain almond milk	75 mL
2 tbsp	vegan caramel sauce	30 mL

1. In a large bowl, whisk together flour, brown sugar, baking powder, cinnamon and salt. Set aside.

2. In a small bowl, whisk together applesauce, almond milk and caramel sauce. Stir into flour mixture just until blended.

3. If desired, place paper liners in wells. Fill each well with about 1 1/2 tbsp (22 mL) batter. Bake for 6 to 8 minutes or until a tester inserted in the center of a muffin comes out clean. Transfer muffins to a wire rack to cool slightly. Repeat with the remaining batter. Serve warm.

Raspberry Coffee Cake Bites

Makes 15 to 17 cake bites

These pretty, fresh-tasting coffee cakes are the perfect treats to bake in the summer, when raspberries are plentiful. Serve them warm, and get ready to serve seconds — they are that good!

Tip

Guar gum is sold in health food and specialty food stores. The legume-based powder is added to foods as a binder, stabilizer and thickener. It is often used in gluten-free baking.

- Pastry blender or blending fork
- Paper liners

Filling

1/3 cup	raspberries	75 mL
2 tsp	granulated sugar	10 mL

Cake

2 tbsp	ground flax seeds (flaxseed meal)	30 mL
6 tbsp	hot water	90 mL
1 cup + 2 tbsp	gluten-free all-purpose baking mix (see tips, page 165)	280 mL
3/4 cup	granulated sugar	175 mL
1 tsp	guar gum (see tip, at left)	5 mL
1/2 tsp	salt	2 mL
1/2 cup	unsalted butter	125 mL

1. *Filling:* In a small bowl, combine raspberries and sugar. Let stand while preparing cake.

2. *Cake:* In a small bowl, combine flax seeds and hot water. Let stand for 10 minutes.

3. In a large bowl, whisk together baking mix, sugar, guar gum and salt. Using a pastry blender or blending fork, cut in butter until mixture resembles coarse crumbs. Using a fork, gently stir in flaxseed mixture.

4. Place paper liners in wells. Fill each well with about 1 1/2 tsp (7 mL) cake mixture. Top with 1 tsp (5 mL) filling, then another 1 1/2 tsp (7 mL) cake mixture.

5. Bake for 15 to 16 minutes or until set and golden brown. Transfer cake bites to a wire rack to cool slightly. Repeat with the remaining cake mixture and filling. Serve warm.

VEGAN VARIATION

Use vegan hard margarine in place of the butter. Choose firm sticks of vegan margarine rather than whipped tubs.

Treats
for Tots

Shirley Temple Cupcakes

The pink drink named for the famous child star is a favorite for all, and these delightful pink cupcakes capture its flavor and fun. Make your children feel like stars and prepare these special cupcakes together.

Tips

If you prefer, you can substitute your favorite vanilla or white frosting.

Garnish each frosted cupcake with pink sanding sugar or a maraschino cherry.

- Paper liners (optional)

2 cups	yellow cake mix	500 mL
2	large eggs, at room temperature	2
1/4 cup	vegetable oil	60 mL
1/4 cup	lemon-lime soda	60 mL
2 tbsp	grenadine syrup	30 mL
2 to 4	drops red food coloring	2 to 4
	Shirley Temple Buttercream Frosting (page 107)	

1. In a large bowl, using an electric mixer on low speed, beat cake mix, eggs, oil, soda, grenadine and food coloring for 30 seconds or until moistened. Beat on medium speed for 2 minutes.

2. If desired, place paper liners in wells. Fill each well with about 1 1/2 tbsp (22 mL) batter. Bake for 6 to 8 minutes or until a tester inserted in the center of a cupcake comes out clean. Transfer cupcakes to a wire rack to cool. Repeat with the remaining batter.

3. Frost with Shirley Temple Buttercream Frosting.

Sugar and Spice Cupcakes

Sugar and spice and everything nice — that's how you and your children will describe these cupcakes.

Tips

Frost with Caramel Cream Cheese Frosting (page 115) or Vanilla Buttercream Frosting (page 105).

Apple pie spice is a blend of ground cinnamon, nutmeg and allspice. If you don't have any on hand, use $1/2$ tsp (2 mL) ground cinnamon, $1/4$ tsp (1 mL) ground nutmeg and $1/4$ tsp (1 mL) ground allspice.

Yogurt often comes in 6-oz (175 g) containers, which hold $2/3$ cup (150 mL). But if you have a larger container, simply measure out what you need.

• Paper liners (optional)

2 cups	white cake mix	500 mL
1 tsp	apple pie spice	5 mL
1	large egg, at room temperature	1
$2/3$ cup	vanilla-flavored yogurt	150 mL
$1/3$ cup	milk	75 mL
2 tbsp	unsalted butter, melted	30 mL
$1/2$ tsp	vanilla extract	2 mL

1. In a medium bowl, using an electric mixer on low speed, beat cake mix, apple pie spice, egg, yogurt, milk, butter and vanilla for 30 seconds or until moistened. Beat for 2 minutes on medium speed.

2. If desired, place paper liners in wells. Fill each well with about $1\frac{1}{2}$ tbsp (22 mL) batter. Bake for 6 to 8 minutes or until a tester inserted in the center of a cupcake comes out clean. Transfer cupcakes to a wire rack to cool. Repeat with the remaining batter.

Frosted Banana Snack Cakes

**Makes
16 to 18 cupcakes**

It seems like we are always looking for ways to use bananas that are on the verge of being overripe. These delicious snack cakes offer a refreshing alternative to banana bread.

Variations

Omit the frosting and sprinkle the cooled snack cakes with confectioners' (icing) sugar.

Add ½ cup (125 mL) toasted chopped nuts, such as walnuts or pecans, to the batter with the mashed banana.

• Paper liners (optional)

1 cup	all-purpose flour	250 mL
½ tsp	baking soda	2 mL
Pinch	salt	Pinch
¼ cup	unsalted butter, softened	60 mL
¾ cup	granulated sugar	175 mL
1	large egg, at room temperature	1
½ cup	sour cream	125 mL
1 tsp	vanilla extract	5 mL
½ cup	mashed ripe banana (about 1 large)	125 mL
	Cream Cheese Frosting (page 114)	

1. In a small bowl, whisk together flour, baking soda and salt. Set aside.

2. In a medium bowl, using an electric mixer on medium-high speed, beat butter for 1 to 2 minutes or until fluffy. Beat in sugar, egg, sour cream and vanilla until well combined. Reduce mixer speed to low and beat in flour mixture until smooth. Stir in banana.

3. If desired, place paper liners in wells. Fill each well with about 1½ tbsp (22 mL) batter. Bake for 6 to 8 minutes or until a tester inserted in the center of a snack cake comes out clean. Transfer snack cakes to a wire rack to cool. Repeat with the remaining batter.

4. Frost with Cream Cheese Frosting.

Mississippi Mud Pies

Makes
8 mini pies

We were both born in Missouri, and the Mississippi River runs along the eastern side of the state. Mississippi mud cakes and pies are popular along either side of the river, because chocolate reminds people of the dark mud along the riverbanks.

Tips

Use a food processor to quickly crush cookies into fine crumbs. You'll need 4 to 5 cream-filled chocolate sandwich cookies (such as Oreos) to make ⅓ cup (75 mL) crumbs.

Garnish with chopped roasted peanuts or chopped toasted almonds, if desired.

Crusts

Favorite Buttery Pie Crust (page 38) or store-bought refrigerated pie crust (see tip, page 178)

Filling

¾ cup	chocolate ice cream, softened	175 mL
8 tsp	chocolate syrup	40 mL
⅓ cup	cream-filled chocolate sandwich cookie crumbs (see tip, at left)	75 mL

Topping

½ cup	hot fudge sauce	125 mL
	Whipped topping	

1. *Crusts:* Follow the instructions on page 39 for baking single crusts blind.

2. *Filling:* Spoon 1½ tbsp (22 mL) ice cream into each cooled crust. Drizzle each with 1 tsp (5 mL) chocolate syrup, then sprinkle with 2 tsp (10 mL) cookie crumbs, mounding crumbs slightly.

3. Place pies in an airtight container that is 2 to 3 inches (5 to 7.5 cm) deep. Freeze for at least 2 hours or overnight.

4. *Topping:* When ready to serve, let stand at room temperature for 5 minutes. Drizzle with hot fudge sauce and garnish with a dollop of whipped topping.

Variation

Make your own signature ice cream mini pies by substituting other flavors of ice cream and syrup. For example, for a summer strawberry party, substitute strawberry or vanilla ice cream and drizzle with strawberry syrup. Then, just before serving, top with fresh strawberries and additional strawberry syrup. For a minty version, substitute mint chocolate chip ice cream and drizzle with chocolate syrup. For an adult twist, drizzle with a dessert liqueur such as crème de menthe or crème de cacao.

Chocolate Chip Muffins

· ·

**Makes
12 to 13 muffins**

What child doesn't like
chocolate chip muffins?
And do we ever grow
out of that stage?
Kathy and Roxanne
never have — and with
muffins this good, they
serve them often.

· · · · · · · · · · · · · · · · · · ·

Variation

*Banana Chocolate Chip
Muffins:* Substitute ½ cup
(125 mL) mashed ripe
banana (about 1 large) for
the milk.

- Paper liners (optional)

1 cup	all-purpose flour	250 mL
⅓ cup	granulated sugar	75 mL
1 tsp	baking powder	5 mL
¼ tsp	salt	1 mL
1	large egg, at room temperature	1
⅓ cup	milk	75 mL
¼ cup	unsalted butter, melted and cooled	60 mL
1 tsp	vanilla extract	5 mL
⅔ cup	miniature semisweet chocolate chips	150 mL

1. In a large bowl, whisk together flour, sugar, baking powder and salt. Set aside.

2. In a small bowl, whisk egg until lightly beaten. Whisk in milk, butter and vanilla. Stir into flour mixture just until blended. Stir in chocolate chips.

3. If desired, place paper liners in wells. Fill each well with about 1½ tbsp (22 mL) batter. Bake for 6 to 8 minutes or until a tester inserted in the center of a muffin comes out clean. Transfer muffins to a wire rack to cool. Repeat with the remaining batter.

Ham and Cheese Muffins

Makes 15 to 17 muffins

In many cooking classes, one of the first foods students learn to make is muffins, because they are easy to prepare but teach measuring and baking skills. This recipe is especially easy, as it starts with a baking mix. Why not teach your child to bake these muffins? The treats will be devoured, and the cooking skills will last a lifetime.

Tip

These muffins are best served freshly baked and still slightly warm.

- Paper liners

1½ cups	baking mix (such as Bisquick)	375 mL
1 tsp	granulated sugar	5 mL
¾ cup	shredded Cheddar cheese	175 mL
½ cup	chopped cooked ham	125 mL
1	large egg, at room temperature	1
½ cup	milk	125 mL
2 tbsp	vegetable oil	30 mL

1. In a large bowl, whisk together baking mix and sugar. Stir in cheese and ham. Set aside.

2. In a small bowl, whisk together egg, milk and oil. Stir into baking mix mixture until just combined.

3. Place paper liners in wells. Fill each well with about 1½ tbsp (22 mL) batter. Bake for 5 to 7 minutes or until a tester inserted in the center of a muffin comes out clean. Transfer muffins to a wire rack to cool slightly. Repeat with the remaining batter. Serve warm.

Italian Grinder Hand Pies

Makes
8 hand pies

Lunch or supper could not be more fun to prepare! These little pies are going to be a favorite.

Tips

There are many brands of frozen cooked meatballs available. Choose the meat blend and flavor that suits your preference. This recipe was tested with appetizer-size meatballs (about 1¼ inches/3 cm in diameter), and the pieces filled the crusts about two-thirds full. If you choose larger home-style or entrée meatballs, decrease the number of meatballs and cut them into eighths, so that you don't overfill the crusts.

If you wish, you can use your favorite homemade meatballs. Form them into 1¼ inch (3 cm) balls, cook them, quarter them and proceed as directed.

Crusts

	Favorite Buttery Pie Crust (page 38) or store-bought refrigerated pie crust (see tip, page 178) Puff pastry (see tip, page 147)

Filling

8	frozen cooked Italian meatballs, thawed and quartered (see tips, at left)	8
8 tsp	shredded mozzarella cheese or Italian cheese blend	40 mL
¼ cup	marinara sauce	60 mL

1. *Crusts:* Use the large circle of the crust cutting tool to cut 8 bottom crusts from the pie crust. Place crusts evenly on top of wells and gently press into wells with the pie forming tool.

2. On a lightly floured surface, roll out puff pastry to about ⅛ inch (3 mm) thick, pressing any perforated seams together. Use the small circle of the crust cutting tool to cut 8 top crusts. Cover with plastic wrap and set aside.

3. *Filling:* Place 4 meatball quarters in each bottom crust. Top each with about 1 tsp (5 mL) cheese and drizzle with about 1½ tsp (7 mL) marinara sauce. Place a top crust directly over the center of each filled shell.

4. Bake for 10 to 12 minutes or until crusts are browned and crisp. Transfer pies to a wire rack to cool slightly. Serve warm.

Sloppy Joe Calzones

These calzones capture the tangy, cheesy flavors of sloppy Joes, but make for much less messy eating!

Tip

If using a store-bought refrigerated pie crust, let come to room temperature, then unroll according to package directions and proceed with the recipe. You can cut 14 Babycakes™ single crusts from one packaged pie crust (half a 14-oz/400 g package) by rerolling the scraps.)

Variation

Substitute ⅓ cup (75 mL) shredded Cheddar cheese for the American cheese slices. Spoon about 2 tsp (10 mL) cheese on top of the beef mixture in each crust.

Crusts

Favorite Buttery Pie Crust (page 38) or store-bought refrigerated pie crust (see tip, at left)
Puff pastry (see tip, page 147)

Filling

8 oz	lean ground beef	250 g
½ cup	canned sloppy Joe sauce	125 mL
2	slices American cheese, quartered	2
8	slices dill pickle, quartered (optional)	8

1. *Crusts:* Use the large circle of the crust cutting tool to cut 8 bottom crusts from the pie crust. Place crusts evenly on top of wells and gently press into wells with the pie forming tool.

2. On a lightly floured surface, roll out puff pastry to about ⅛ inch (3 mm) thick, pressing any perforated seams together. Use the small circle of the crust cutting tool to cut 8 top crusts. Cover with plastic wrap and set aside.

3. *Filling:* In a medium skillet, over medium-high heat, cook beef, breaking it up with the back of a spoon, for 8 to 10 minutes or until no longer pink. Drain off fat. Stir in sloppy Joe sauce.

4. Spoon about 2 tbsp (30 mL) meat mixture into each crust. Top with a piece of cheese. If desired, top with 4 pickle quarters. Place a top crust directly over the center of each filled shell.

5. Bake for 10 to 12 minutes or until crusts are browned and crisp. Transfer pies to a wire rack to cool slightly. Serve warm.

Cheeseburger Mini Pies

All three of our
daughters — Grace,
Laura and Amanda —
are cheeseburger
lovers, and we realized
long ago that serving
up cheeseburger pie
was the perfect way
to entice them to the
dinner table.

Tip

Some people like pickles on
their cheeseburger; others
prefer to omit the mustard.
Feel free to adjust the
flavors in these pies to suit
your preferences.

8	slices white bread	8
2 tsp	unsalted butter, softened	10 mL
5 oz	lean ground beef	150 g
	Salt and freshly ground black pepper	
2 tbsp	ketchup	30 mL
1 tbsp	prepared mustard	15 mL
8 tsp	shredded Cheddar cheese	40 mL

1. Using a rolling pin, roll each slice of bread until it is very thin. Use the large circle of the crust cutting tool to cut a circle from each slice (discard scraps or reserve for another use). Spread one side of each circle with butter.

2. Place 1 bread circle, buttered side down, on top of each well and gently press into well with the pie forming tool, making a cup.

3. In a small skillet, over medium-high heat, cook beef, breaking it up with the back of a spoon, for 8 to 10 minutes or until no longer pink. Drain off fat. Season to taste with salt and pepper. Stir in ketchup and mustard.

4. Spoon about 2 tbsp (30 mL) beef mixture into each bread cup. Sprinkle each with 1 tsp (5 mL) cheese.

5. Bake for 6 to 8 minutes or until toast cups are browned and crisp. Transfer pies to a wire rack to cool slightly. Serve warm.

Taco Teasers

● ●

**Makes
16 tortilla cups**

These Mexican treats
are a go-to after-
school snack, but they
also make fantastic
appetizers.

. . . .

Tip
Dollop taco teasers with
sour cream or guacamole,
if desired.

4	8- to 10-inch (20 to 25 cm) flour tortillas	4
8 oz	lean ground beef	250 g
1/2 cup	diced onion	125 mL
2/3 cup	shredded Mexican cheese blend or Cheddar cheese	150 mL
1/4 cup	salsa or picante sauce	60 mL
1 cup	shredded iceberg lettuce	250 mL
1	tomato, seeded and diced	1

1. Working with 1 tortilla at a time, wrap tortilla in a paper towel and microwave on High for 20 seconds or just until warm. Using the large circle of the crust cutting tool, cut 4 circles from the warm tortilla (discard scraps or reserve for another use).

2. Place 1 tortilla circle on top of each well and very gently press into well with the pie forming tool, making a cup.

3. In a medium skillet, over medium-high heat, cook beef and onion, breaking beef up with the back of a spoon, for 8 to 10 minutes or until no beef is longer pink. Drain off fat. Stir in cheese and salsa.

4. Spoon about $1\frac{1}{2}$ tbsp (22 mL) beef mixture into each tortilla cup. Bake for 7 to 9 minutes or until cheese is melted and tortilla cups are golden and crisp. Transfer tortilla cups to a wire rack to cool slightly. Let appliance cool for 5 minutes. Repeat with the remaining tortilla circles and beef mixture.

5. Sprinkle warm taco teasers with lettuce and tomato just before serving.

Small Servings

Boston Cream Cupcakes

**Makes
10 to 12 cupcakes**

The inspiration for these cupcakes is Boston cream pie, which is not a pie at all but rather two layers of sponge cake sandwiching a thick custard filling and topped with a chocolate glaze.

Tip

For optimum flavor and texture, these cupcakes should be served the day they are made.

Variation

Substitute chocolate pudding for the vanilla pudding.

• Paper liners (optional)

1 cup	yellow cake mix	250 mL
1	large egg, at room temperature	1
1/3 cup	water	75 mL
2 tbsp	vegetable oil	30 mL
2	vanilla pudding cups (each 4 oz/113 g)	2
1 oz	unsweetened chocolate, chopped	30 g
1 tbsp	unsalted butter	15 mL
1/2 cup	confectioners' (icing) sugar	125 mL
1/2 tsp	vanilla extract	2 mL
1 to 2 tbsp	hot water	15 to 30 mL

1. In a medium bowl, using an electric mixer on low speed, beat cake mix, egg, water and oil for 30 seconds or until moistened. Beat on medium speed for 2 minutes.

2. If desired, place paper liners in wells. Fill each well with about 1 1/2 tbsp (22 mL) batter. Bake for 6 to 8 minutes or until a tester inserted in the center of a cupcake comes out clean. Transfer cupcakes to a wire rack to cool. Repeat with the remaining batter.

3. If cupcakes are in liners, remove liners. Cut each cupcake in half crosswise. Spoon 2 to 3 tsp (10 to 15 mL) pudding onto each bottom half. Cover with top half. Refrigerate for at least 30 minutes, until chilled, or for up to 3 hours.

4. Place chocolate and butter in a small microwave-safe glass bowl. Microwave on High for 30 seconds. Stir. Microwave in 30-second intervals, stirring after each, until chocolate is melted. Whisk in confectioners' sugar and vanilla. Whisk in enough water to make a thick glaze.

5. Spoon about 2 tsp (10 mL) glaze over each cupcake. Refrigerate until ready to serve.

Tiramisu Cupcakes

**Makes
8 cupcakes**

The distinctive flavor of tiramisu shines through in these easy cupcakes — the perfect elegant dessert for your next dinner party.

Variation

Add ½ tsp (2 mL) brandy extract with the sugar when whipping the cream.

- Paper liners (optional)

¾ cup	white cake mix	175 mL
1	large egg, at room temperature	1
2 tbsp	buttermilk	30 mL
2 tbsp	vegetable oil	30 mL
¼ cup	toffee bits	60 mL
2½ tsp	confectioners' (icing) sugar, divided	12 mL
½ tsp	instant coffee granules	2 mL
1 tbsp	boiling water	15 mL
⅓ cup	heavy or whipping (35%) cream	75 mL
	Unsweetened cocoa powder	

1. In a small bowl, using an electric mixer on low speed, beat cake mix, egg, buttermilk and oil for 30 seconds or until moistened. Beat on medium speed for 2 minutes. Stir in toffee bits.

2. If desired, place paper liners in wells. Fill each well with about 1½ tbsp (22 mL) batter. Bake for 6 to 8 minutes or until a tester inserted in the center of a cupcake comes out clean. Transfer cupcakes to a wire rack to cool.

3. In another small bowl, combine 1½ tsp (7 mL) of the confectioners' sugar, instant coffee and boiling water, stirring until sugar is dissolved. Prick the top of each cupcake several times with a fork. Slowly and gradually brush coffee mixture over each cupcake, letting it seep inside.

4. In another small bowl, using an electric mixer on medium-high speed, beat cream until frothy. Beat in the remaining confectioners' sugar until stiff peaks form.

5. Frost cupcakes with whipped cream. Garnish each cupcake with a very light dusting of cocoa. Serve immediately.

Inside-Out Rocky Road Cupcakes

These quick and easy cupcakes, garnished with mini chocolate chips, marshmallows and peanuts, are as gourmet as any bake shop cupcakes.

Tip

For easy garnishing, combine chocolate chips, quartered marshmallows and peanuts in a small bowl. Gently dip the top of each frosted cupcake into the mixture, covering it completely.

- Paper liners (optional)

¾ cup	devil's food cake mix	175 mL
2 tsp	unsweetened cocoa powder	10 mL
1	large egg, at room temperature	1
2 tbsp	vegetable oil	30 mL
2 tbsp	water	30 mL
½	recipe Classic Chocolate Buttercream Frosting (page 106)	½
3 tbsp	miniature semisweet chocolate chips	45 mL
12	miniature marshmallows, quartered	12
3 tbsp	chopped dry-roasted peanuts	45 mL

1. In a large bowl, using an electric mixer on low speed, beat cake mix, cocoa, egg, oil and water for 30 seconds or until moistened. Beat on medium speed for 2 minutes.

2. If desired, place paper liners in wells. Fill each well with about 1½ tbsp (22 mL) batter. Bake for 6 to 8 minutes or until a tester inserted in the center of a cupcake comes out clean. Transfer cupcakes to a wire rack to cool.

3. Frost cupcakes with Classic Chocolate Buttercream Frosting. Garnish with chocolate chips, marshmallows and peanuts.

Lemon Muffins

If you crave old-fashioned lemon muffins, just sweet enough to be perfect with either breakfast or lunch, this is the recipe for you.

• Paper liners (optional)

⅔ cup	all-purpose flour	150 mL
¼ cup	granulated sugar	60 mL
½ tsp	baking powder	2 mL
¼ tsp	baking soda	1 mL
Pinch	salt	Pinch
1	large egg, at room temperature	1
2 tbsp	milk	30 mL
2 tbsp	unsalted butter, melted	30 mL
1 tsp	grated lemon zest	5 mL
1 tbsp	freshly squeezed lemon juice	15 mL
½	recipe Lemon Glaze (page 118)	½

1. In a medium bowl, whisk together flour, sugar, baking powder, baking soda and salt. Set aside.

2. In a small bowl, whisk egg until lightly beaten. Stir in milk, butter, lemon zest and lemon juice. Stir into flour mixture until just blended.

3. If desired, place paper liners in wells. Fill each well with about 1½ tbsp (22 mL) batter. Bake for 5 to 7 minutes or until a tester inserted in the center of a muffin comes out clean. Transfer muffins to a wire rack to cool slightly.

4. Drizzle each muffin with Lemon Glaze.

Monkey Bread Bites

Makes
8 bread bites

When Roxanne's nephew, Jarrod, and her niece, Libby, were tiny tots, they enjoyed sleepovers at Roxanne's house. Roxanne always made a version of monkey bread. Jarrod and Libby are now grown-ups with their own children, but they still remember monkey bread sleepovers. This recipe is for them, so they can begin their own food traditions with their little ones, creating lifelong memories.

Tip

Before preparing monkey bread bites, bake the remaining 4 biscuits in the Babycakes™ Cupcake Maker. Place one whole biscuit in each well, forming it a bit to fit. Bake for 6 to 8 minutes or until golden brown. Once cool, wrap and store biscuits to serve with lunch or dinner.

• Paper liners

1	can (10 oz/284 g) refrigerated buttermilk biscuit dough (10 small biscuits)	1
1 cup	packed brown sugar	250 mL
1 tsp	ground cinnamon	5 mL
3 tbsp	freshly squeezed orange juice	45 mL
	Nonstick baking spray	
¼ cup	unsalted butter, melted	60 mL

1. Cut 6 of the biscuits into quarters, reserving the remaining biscuits for another use (see tip, at left).

2. In a small saucepan, combine brown sugar, cinnamon and orange juice. Bring to a boil over medium-high heat, stirring often. Reduce heat and simmer, stirring often, for 5 minutes.

3. Place paper liners in wells. Spray liners with nonstick baking spray. Using the fork tool, dip a biscuit quarter in melted butter, then in the brown sugar mixture. Place in a paper liner. Repeat, placing 3 biscuit pieces in each liner. Reserve any remaining brown sugar mixture. Spray the inside lid of the cupcake maker with nonstick baking spray.

4. Bake for 7 to 8 minutes or until bread bites are golden brown. Using a small offset spatula, carefully transfer bread bites to a wire rack to cool slightly. Remove paper liners and transfer warm bread bites to a deep serving platter. Drizzle any remaining brown sugar mixture over top. Serve immediately.

Glazed Raisin Biscuits

In just minutes you can serve hot cinnamon raisin biscuits to your family — and they taste so much better than the ones you might have been tempted to pick up on the way to work or school.

Tip

Raisins must be stored in an airtight container so they don't dry out. One suggestion is to purchase raisins in individual-size boxes, packaged for lunch boxes and snacks. One 1½-oz (45 g) box holds just about what is needed for this recipe.

Variation

Substitute currants or sweetened dried cranberries for the raisins.

1 cup	all-purpose flour	250 mL
1 tsp	granulated sugar	5 mL
¾ tsp	baking powder	3 mL
½ tsp	ground cinnamon	2 mL
Pinch	salt	Pinch
2 tbsp	cold unsalted butter, cut into small pieces	30 mL
¼ cup	milk	60 mL
¼ cup	raisins	60 mL
	Nonstick baking spray	
	Vanilla Glaze (page 117)	

1. In a small bowl, whisk together flour, sugar, baking powder, cinnamon and salt. Using your fingertips or a pastry blender, blend in butter until mixture is coarse and crumbly. Using a fork, stir in milk just until moistened. Stir in raisins.

2. Spray wells with nonstick baking spray. Spoon about 1½ tbsp (22 mL) dough into each well. Bake for 5 minutes. Using a small offset spatula, carefully turn biscuits over. Bake for 3 minutes or until biscuits are browned. Transfer biscuits to a wire rack to cool slightly.

3. Drizzle each biscuit with Vanilla Glaze. Serve warm.

Vegetable Cheese Cups

Years ago, when we worked in a test kitchen, we developed a vegetable strudel recipe. To this day, we talk about the flavor of the fresh vegetables, melted cheese and crisp crust. This quick, versatile recipe was inspired by that old favorite. Serve these as part of a brunch, as a quick supper or lunch, as appetizers or as a side dish.

Tips

For the vegetables, select your favorites from what you have on hand or can pick up pre-chopped at the grocery store. Broccoli, cauliflower, zucchini, mushrooms, red pepper and onion are all great options. If possible, select a combination of several vegetables.

For the cheese, try shredded Cheddar, Swiss and/or Monterey Jack, or a shredded cheese blend. For optimum flavor, use a combination of cheeses. You might even add 1 tbsp (15 mL) crumbled blue cheese to the mix.

Crusts

8	slices white bread	8
2 tsp	butter, softened	10 mL

Filling

1 tbsp	unsalted butter	15 mL
1	clove garlic, minced	1
1 cup	finely chopped vegetables (see tip, at left)	250 mL
1/3 cup	shredded cheese (see tip, at left)	75 mL
2 tbsp	sour cream	30 mL
	Salt and freshly ground black pepper	

1. *Crusts:* Using a rolling pin, roll each slice of bread until it is very thin. Use the large circle of the crust cutting tool to cut a circle from each slice (discard scraps or reserve for another use). Spread one side of each circle with butter.

2. Place 1 bread circle, buttered side down, on top of each well and gently press into well with the pie forming tool, making a cup.

3. *Filling:* In a small skillet, melt butter over medium-high heat. Add garlic and vegetables; cook, stirring often, for 3 to 4 minutes or until vegetables are tender. Remove from heat and stir in cheese and sour cream. Season to taste with salt and pepper. Spoon about 1 1/2 tbsp (22 mL) vegetable mixture into each bread cup.

4. Bake for 6 to 8 minutes or until cups are crisp and brown. Carefully transfer toast cups to a wire rack to cool slightly. Serve warm.

Variation

Substitute Phyllo Cups for the toast cups. Form 8 sheets of frozen phyllo dough into cups as directed on page 45. Fill, then bake as directed above.

Individual Baked Brie

A wheel of warm
Brie enclosed in a
decorative pastry shell
is a classic appetizer,
and is the inspiration
for these little packets.
They're so very quick
to make, but so
elegant. Pour the wine!

Tips

Different brands of phyllo
come in different-size
sheets. We used sheets that
are 14 by 9 inches (35 by
23 cm), which is about half
of a 16-oz (454 g) package.
Some sheets are larger
(17 by 12 inches/43 by
30 cm or 18 by 14 inches/
45 by 35 cm), so use 2 and
cut them in half crosswise
before proceeding with
step 2.

Although commonly
available in wheels, Brie is
also sold in narrow 6-inch
(15 cm) logs — the perfect
shape for this recipe. Just
slice a log crosswise into
½-inch (1 cm) thick rounds
and use 1 slice in each
phyllo packet.

Party of two? This recipe can
easily be halved.

4	sheets frozen phyllo dough, thawed	4
3 oz	Brie cheese, cut into 8 pieces	90 g
8 tsp	apricot preserves	40 mL
	Nonstick baking spray	

1. Place 1 sheet of phyllo on a cutting board. (Immediately cover the remaining sheets with plastic wrap and then a lightly dampened towel, keeping them covered to prevent them from drying out.) Cut phyllo sheet in half crosswise.

2. Fold 1 half-sheet in half crosswise. Place 1 piece of Brie in the center. Dollop 1 tsp (5 mL) preserves on top. Fold in longer sides, then shorter sides, enclosing the filling and making a packet that will fit in a well. Repeat with the remaining phyllo, Brie and preserves.

3. Spray wells with nonstick baking spray. Place a packet in each well, pushing it down lightly. Spray tops of packets with baking spray. Bake for 5 to 6 minutes or until golden brown on the bottom. Using a small offset spatula, carefully turn packets over. Bake for 5 to 6 minutes or until golden brown. Carefully transfer packets to a wire rack to cool slightly. Serve warm.

Variations

Substitute other flavors of preserves or jam. Cherry and fig complement Brie well.

Use cream cheese in place of the Brie.

Toasted Cheese Pinwheels

These rolls make a wonderful snack or accompaniment to tomato soup. They may be bite-size, but they're packed with flavor. Trust us when we say you'll want to eat more than one.

Variation

Use spreadable garlic- and herb-flavored cheese in place of the pimento cheese spread.

1	can (4 oz/113 g) refrigerated crescent roll dough	1
3 tbsp	pimento cheese spread	45 mL
	Nonstick baking spray	

1. On a lightly floured surface, carefully unroll crescent roll dough. Place one rectangle of dough next to the other, with the long sides touching, making a 6-inch (15 cm) square. Press seams together. Spread cheese spread over the dough, leaving a 1/8-inch (3 mm) border.

2. Starting at one end, roll up dough like a jelly roll. Pinch seam to seal. Slice roll into 8 spirals, each about 3/4 inch (2 cm) thick.

3. Spray wells with nonstick baking spray. Place 1 spiral in each well and bake for 3 to 4 minutes or until bottoms are golden brown. Using a small offset spatula, carefully turn rolls over and bake for 3 minutes or until golden brown. Transfer rolls to a wire rack to cool slightly. Repeat with the remaining spirals. Serve warm.

Ham and Cheese Empanadas

Makes 8 empanadas

Warm ham and cheese empanadas are the ideal accompaniment to soup or salad for a light supper or lunch. Or serve them as appetizers when family and friends gather at your home.

Tip

Add 2 tbsp (30 mL) sliced stuffed green olives to the filling, if desired.

Crusts

	Favorite Buttery Pie Crust (page 38) or store-bought refrigerated pie crust (see tip, page 178) Puff pastry (see tip, page 147)	

Filling

½ cup	shredded Monterey Jack cheese	125 mL
½ cup	diced cooked ham	125 mL
2 tsp	minced fresh cilantro or flat-leaf (Italian) parsley	10 mL
⅛ tsp	garlic powder	0.5 mL
2 tbsp	sour cream	30 mL

1. *Crusts:* Use the large circle of the crust cutting tool to cut 8 bottom crusts from the pie crust. Place crusts evenly on top of wells and gently press into wells with the pie forming tool.

2. On a lightly floured surface, roll out puff pastry to about ⅛ inch (3 mm) thick, pressing any perforated seams together. Use the small circle of the crust cutting tool to cut 8 top crusts. Cover with plastic wrap and set aside.

3. *Filling:* In a medium bowl, combine cheese, ham, cilantro, garlic powder and sour cream.

4. Spoon about 2 tbsp (30 mL) filling into each bottom crust; do not overfill. Place a top crust directly over the center of each filled shell.

5. Bake for 10 to 12 minutes or until crusts are browned and crisp. Transfer empanadas to a wire rack to cool slightly. Serve warm.

Part 5

Entertaining Made Easy

Appetizers and Finger Food

Toast Cups

These easy, old-fashioned cups are the perfect base for a variety of wonderful appetizers. Fill the cups with a favorite dip or spread, or a prepared deli salad.

Tip

For hot appetizers, it also works well to fill the cups before baking, as we've done with the Inside-Out Pimento Cheese Fondues (page 198).

| 8 | slices white bread | 8 |
| 2 tsp | unsalted butter, softened, or spreadable margarine | 10 mL |

1. Using a rolling pin, roll each slice of bread until it is very thin. Use the large circle of the crust cutting tool to cut a circle from each slice (discard scraps or reserve for another use). Spread one side of each circle with butter.

2. Place 1 bread circle, buttered side down, on top of each well and gently press into well with the pie forming tool, making a cup.

3. Bake for 6 to 8 minutes or until toast cups are crisp and golden brown. Transfer cups to a wire rack to cool slightly.

Variation

Use any variety of soft, fresh bread, such as whole wheat or sourdough.

Tortilla Cups

Add some salsa and let the party begin. But don't stop at salsa — these cups are perfect for serving all kinds of dips.

Tip

Warming the tortillas one at a time in the microwave just as you are ready to cut and shape them ensures that they stay pliable.

| 2 | 10-inch (25 cm) flour tortillas | 2 |

1. Working with 1 tortilla one at a time, wrap tortilla in a paper towel and microwave on High for about 20 seconds or just until warm. Using the large circle of the crust cutting tool, cut 7 circles from the warm tortilla (discard scraps or save for another use).

2. Place 1 tortilla circle on top of each well and very gently press into well with the pie forming tool, making a cup.

3. Bake for 5 to 6 minutes or until tortilla cups are crisp. Transfer cups to a wire rack to cool. Repeat with the remaining tortilla.

Wonton Cups

Makes
8 cups

The Babycakes™ Cupcake Maker works magic on simple wonton wrappers, transforming them into crisp, golden brown shells. Once baked, fill them with any of your favorite dips, spreads or filling favorites such as chicken or ham salad.

| 8 | wonton wrappers (about 3½ inches/ 8.5 cm square) | 8 |

1. Place 1 wonton wrapper on top of each well and gently press down into well with the pie forming tool, making a cup.

2. Bake for 6 to 8 minutes or until crisp. Transfer cups to a wire rack to cool.

Tip
If desired, use the large circle of the crust cutting tool to cut a circle from each wonton wrapper (discard scraps). Proceed with step 1, placing 1 wonton circle on top of each well.

Avocado Dip Cups

Makes
16 tortilla cups

Tip
To make enough for a party or a larger family, bake up several batches of tortilla cups and place them on a baking sheet. Keep them warm in a 250°F (120°C) oven until ready to serve, for up to 20 minutes. Or let them cool and store in an airtight container at room temperature for up to 4 hours. Just before serving, reheat in a 250°F (120°C) oven for about 10 minutes.

2	large avocados, finely chopped	2
1	clove garlic, minced	1
⅓ cup	rinsed drained canned black beans	75 mL
¼ cup	chopped grape tomatoes	60 mL
3 tbsp	chopped red onion	45 mL
2 tbsp	chopped fresh cilantro	30 mL
2 tbsp	freshly squeezed lime juice	30 mL
1 tbsp	olive oil	15 mL
16	Tortilla Cups (page 194)	16

1. In a large bowl, gently combine avocados, garlic, beans, tomatoes, red onion, cilantro, lime juice and oil.

2. Spoon about 2 tbsp (30 mL) avocado dip into each tortilla cup. Serve immediately.

Tip
For a fun and fast presentation, cluster tortilla cups around a bowl of avocado dip rather than spooning the filling into the cups. We've found that the dip stretches farther when served this way, so you might want to bake a double batch of tortilla cups.

French Onion Dip Cups

Makes 16 toast cups

Many of us grew up dipping chips into a container of French onion dip. One bite of these appetizers and you'll never return to those white containers again!

Tip

This dip also makes an excellent spread for panini and other sandwiches.

1 tbsp	olive oil	15 mL
2	large onions, halved and thinly sliced	2
	Salt and freshly ground black pepper	
1½ tbsp	red wine vinegar	22 mL
4 oz	cream cheese, softened	125 g
½ cup	sour cream	125 mL
16	Toast Cups (page 194)	16

1. In a large skillet, heat oil over medium-high heat. Add onions, reduce heat to medium and cook, stirring occasionally, for about 15 minutes or until soft and golden. Cover, reduce heat to low and cook, stirring occasionally, for 20 to 30 minutes or until caramelized. Season to taste with salt and pepper. Stir in vinegar and cook, uncovered, until liquid has evaporated. Remove from heat and let cool slightly. Coarsely chop onions.

2. In a medium bowl, using an electric mixer on medium speed, beat cream cheese until smooth. Beat in sour cream. Fold onions into cream cheese mixture. Season to taste with salt and pepper, if desired.

3. Spoon about 2 tbsp (30 mL) onion dip into each toast cup. Serve immediately.

BLT Dip Cups

Makes 8 tortilla cups

Invite your friends over for a spur-of-the-moment gathering, turn on the game or pull out the cards, and whip up this quick and satisfying appetizer.

Tip

Try using thick-cut peppered bacon or any other favorite variety of bacon.

4	slices bacon, cooked crisp and crumbled	4
1	small plum (Roma) tomato, seeded and finely chopped	1
1 tbsp	finely chopped green onion	15 mL
Pinch	freshly ground black pepper	Pinch
⅓ cup	mayonnaise	75 mL
½ cup	shredded romaine or iceberg lettuce	125 mL
8	Tortilla Cups (page 194)	8

1. In a medium bowl, combine bacon, tomato, green onion, pepper and mayonnaise.

2. Spoon about 1 tbsp (15 mL) bacon dip into each tortilla cup. Garnish with lettuce.

Con Queso Cups

Makes
28 tortilla cups

Instead of serving hot queso dip with a basket of tortilla chips, offer these fun cups filled with spicy, cheesy goodness. Kathy's daughter Laura is a huge fan of these wonderful appetizers.

Tips

If you like heat, increase the jalapeño to 2 tbsp (30 mL) or garnish each cup with a pickled jalapeño slice.

Other garnishes work well with this recipe, too. Try minced green onion, salsa, guacamole or sliced pitted olives. For an attractive presentation, use a variety of garnishes.

4	10-inch (25 cm) flour tortillas	4
1 cup	shredded Colby-Jack cheese	250 mL
2 oz	cream cheese, softened	60 g
1 tbsp	chopped drained pickled jalapeño pepper	15 mL
1 1/2 tsp	ground cumin	7 mL
	Salt and freshly ground black pepper	
1/2 cup	diced seeded tomatoes	125 mL
2 tbsp	minced fresh cilantro	30 mL

1. Working with 1 tortilla at a time, wrap tortilla in a paper towel and microwave on High for about 20 seconds or until warm. Using the large circle of the crust cutting tool, cut 7 circles from the warm tortilla (discard scraps and reserve for another use).

2. Place 1 tortilla circle on top of each well and very gently press into well with the pie forming tool, making a cup.

3. In a medium bowl, combine Colby-Jack, cream cheese, jalapeño and cumin. Season to taste with salt and pepper. Spoon about 1 1/2 tsp (7 mL) cheese mixture into each tortilla cup.

4. Bake for 9 to 10 minutes or until tortillas are browned and crisp and cheese mixture is hot and melted. Transfer cups to a wire rack to cool slightly. Repeat with the remaining tortillas and cheese mixture. Garnish with tomatoes and cilantro. Serve warm.

Inside-Out Pimento Cheese Fondues

In traditional fondue, you dip bread cubes into melted cheese. We've turned that classic inside out, putting our tasty version of Southern pimento cheese fondue inside bread cups, perfect for serving as hot appetizers!

Tip

Do you have another favorite hot cheese dip, fondue recipe or flavored cream cheese? Follow steps 1 and 2 to make the cups, fill the cups with your cheese dip and bake as directed.

Variation

Add 4 slices bacon, cooked crisp and crumbled, with the pimentos.

Crusts

8	slices white bread	8
2 tsp	unsalted butter, softened, or spreadable margarine	10 mL

Filling

1 cup	shredded sharp (old) Cheddar cheese	250 mL
2 oz	cream cheese, softened	60 g
1/4 cup	heavy or whipping (35%) cream	60 mL
1	jar (2 oz/60 g) pimentos, well drained	1
1 tbsp	thinly sliced green onions	15 mL

1. *Crusts:* Using a rolling pin, roll each slice of bread until it is very thin. Use the large circle of the crust cutting tool to cut a circle from each slice (discard scraps or reserve for another use). Spread one side of each circle with butter.

2. Place 1 bread circle, buttered side down, on top of each well and gently press into well with the pie forming tool, making a cup.

3. *Filling:* In a large microwave-safe glass bowl, combine Cheddar, cream cheese and cream. Microwave on High in 60-second intervals, stirring after each, until cheeses are melted and mixture is smooth. Stir in pimentos and green onions.

4. Spoon about $1\frac{1}{2}$ tbsp (22 mL) filling into each bread cup. Bake for 6 to 8 minutes or until cups are browned and crisp and filling is hot. Transfer toast cups to a wire rack to cool slightly. Serve warm.

Goat Cheese, Pesto and Sun-Dried Tomato Cups

The bold, scrumptious flavors will make these appetizers the hit of any party.

Tip

For make-ahead convenience, prepare the filling up to 2 days ahead and store in an airtight container in the refrigerator. Let warm to room temperature, then fill the cups and bake as directed.

Variation

Substitute Phyllo Cups for the toast cups. Form 8 sheets of frozen phyllo dough into cups as directed on page 45. Fill, then bake as directed at right. Repeat with 6 to 8 more phyllo sheets.

Crusts

14 to 16	slices white bread	14 to 16
4 tsp	unsalted butter, softened, or spreadable margarine	20 mL

Filling

¼ cup	chopped drained oil-packed sun-dried tomatoes	60 mL
½ tsp	garlic salt	2 mL
½ tsp	dried basil	2 mL
¼ cup	mayonnaise	60 mL
2 oz	goat cheese, crumbled	60 g
2 oz	cream cheese, softened	60 g
⅓ cup	freshly grated Parmesan cheese	75 mL
8 tsp	basil pesto	40 mL
	Additional freshly grated Parmesan cheese	
3 tbsp	finely chopped grape tomatoes (optional)	45 mL
	Thinly sliced fresh basil (optional)	

1. *Crusts:* Using a rolling pin, roll each slice of bread until it is very thin. Use the large circle of the crust cutting tool to cut a circle from each slice (discard scraps or reserve for another use). Spread one side of each circle with butter.

2. Place 1 bread circle, buttered side down, on top of each well and gently press into well with the pie forming tool, making a cup.

3. *Filling:* In a small bowl, combine sun-dried tomatoes, garlic salt, dried basil, mayonnaise, goat cheese and cream cheese.

4. Spoon about 1 tbsp (15 mL) goat cheese mixture into each bread cup. Sprinkle each with about 1 tsp (5 mL) Parmesan. Bake for 6 to 8 minutes or until cups are browned and crisp and filling is hot. Transfer cups to a wire rack to cool slightly. Repeat with the remaining bread circles and filling.

5. Dollop about ½ tsp (2 mL) pesto on top of each cup. Garnish with additional Parmesan and, if desired, with tomatoes and fresh basil.

Potato Latkes

Makes 16 latkes

These bite-size potato pancakes are perfect when a crowd is gathering at your house. Although they're not deep-fried, they still bake up crispy and brown. Serve with sour cream and applesauce.

Tip

If desired, you can season the potato mixture with a pinch of garlic powder.

2	russet potatoes (about 1 lb/500 g), peeled	2
	Ice water	
¼ cup	shredded onion	60 mL
3 tbsp	all-purpose flour	45 mL
1	large egg, lightly beaten	1
	Salt and freshly ground black pepper	
	Nonstick baking spray	
4 tsp	vegetable oil or melted unsalted butter	20 mL

1. Shred potatoes into a medium bowl. Add enough ice water to submerge potatoes. Let stand for 5 minutes. Drain, then spoon potatoes onto a clean kitchen towel and roll tightly to press out excess moisture.

2. In a large bowl, combine potatoes, onion, flour and egg. Season generously with salt and pepper.

3. Spray wells with nonstick baking spray. Spoon about 2 tbsp (30 mL) potato mixture into each well. Drizzle ¼ tsp (1 mL) oil over each. Bake for 9 minutes or until bottoms are golden brown. Using a small offset spatula, carefully turn latkes over. Bake for 5 minutes or until browned and crisp. Transfer latkes to a serving plate. Repeat with the remaining potato mixture and oil. Serve hot.

Tex-Mex Potato Cakes

Potato cakes may be an all-time comfort food, but when seasoned with sausage and green chiles, they become a fantastic appetizer!

Tip

Chorizo is a spicy sausage. Mexican varieties are seasoned with chiles, while Spanish varieties rely on garlic. Either type adds wonderful flavor to these potato cakes.

4 oz	fresh chorizo or other pork sausage (bulk or casings removed)	125 g
½ cup	shredded pepper Jack cheese	125 mL
3 tbsp	all-purpose flour	45 mL
2 tbsp	canned chopped mild green chiles	30 mL
1	large egg, at room temperature	1
1½ cups	prepared mashed potatoes	375 mL
2 tbsp	unsalted butter, softened	30 mL
	Salt and freshly ground black pepper	
	Nonstick baking spray	

1. In a small skillet, over medium-high heat, cook sausage, breaking it up with the back of a spoon, for 8 to 10 minutes or until cooked through. Drain off fat.

2. In a large bowl, combine sausage, cheese, flour, chile pepper, egg, mashed potatoes and butter. Season to taste with salt and pepper.

3. Spray wells with nonstick baking spray. Spoon about 2 tbsp (30 mL) potato mixture into each well. Bake for 8 minutes. Using a small offset spatula, carefully turn cakes over. Bake for 5 minutes or until golden brown. Transfer cakes to a wire rack to cool slightly. Repeat with the remaining potato mixture. Serve warm.

Bayou Cakes with Rémoulade

A fun little flavor twist from the back bayous of Louisiana gives these crab cakes an edge. We both love the foods of New Orleans and can't help but give a nod to that cuisine every chance we get.

Tips

Panko crumbs are larger than typical bread crumbs, so they give these crab cakes a crispy texture. They are often shelved with the Asian foods or near the fish counter. If you can't find panko, you can substitute dry bread crumbs.

If you can't find cooked fresh crabmeat, you can substitute 2 cans (each 6 oz/175 g) backfin (lump) crabmeat.

Variations

Substitute Cajun seasoning or a seafood seasoning blend for the Creole seasoning.

Substitute 2 cans (each 4½ oz/140 g) chicken, drained, for the crab.

¼ cup	finely chopped green onions	60 mL
2 tbsp	chopped fresh parsley	30 mL
½ tsp	Creole seasoning	2 mL
1	large egg, lightly beaten	1
1 tsp	Dijon mustard	5 mL
1 tsp	Worcestershire sauce	5 mL
2 to 3	drops hot pepper sauce, or to taste	2 to 3
	Salt and freshly ground black pepper	
8 oz	cooked fresh crabmeat	250 g
¾ cup	panko, divided	175 mL
2 tbsp	vegetable oil	30 mL
	Rémoulade (see recipe, opposite)	

1. In a large bowl, combine green onions, parsley, Creole seasoning, egg, mustard, Worcestershire sauce and hot pepper sauce. Season to taste with salt and pepper. Stir in crabmeat and ¼ cup (60 mL) of the panko.

2. Spread the remaining panko in a shallow dish. Using wet hands, shape 1½ tbsp (22 mL) crab mixture into a 2-inch (5 cm) disk. Coat both sides in panko crumbs. Repeat with the remaining crab mixture.

3. Brush wells with oil. Place one crab cake in each well. Bake for 8 minutes. Using the fork tool, carefully turn each cake over. Bake for 5 minutes or until golden brown. Transfer cakes to a wire rack to cool slightly. Repeat with the remaining crab cakes. Serve warm, with Rémoulade.

Rémoulade

This creamy mayonnaise sauce makes the perfect accompaniment to Bayou Cakes (opposite), and is also wonderful with grilled seafood or chicken.

Variation
Add 2 tbsp (30 mL) chopped drained sweet pickles.

1 tbsp	drained capers	15 mL
1 tbsp	minced fresh parsley	15 mL
⅔ cup	mayonnaise	150 mL
2 tsp	Dijon mustard	10 mL
1 tsp	freshly squeezed lemon juice	5 mL
2 to 3	drops hot pepper sauce	2 to 3
	Salt and freshly ground black pepper	

1. In a medium bowl, combine capers, parsley, mayonnaise, mustard, lemon juice and hot pepper sauce to taste. Season to taste with salt and pepper.

Bacon Blue Cheese Potato Bites

Makes 16 potato bites

These appetizers have just the right amount of pungent blue cheese flavor. Don't skimp on the quality of blue cheese.

Variation
Substitute ½ cup (125 mL) shredded Cheddar cheese for the blue cheese.

1½ cups	prepared mashed potatoes	375 mL
2 oz	blue cheese, crumbled	60 g
½ tsp	salt	2 mL
¼ tsp	coarsely ground black pepper	1 mL
1	large egg, lightly beaten	1
2 tbsp	unsalted butter, melted	30 mL
5	slices bacon, cooked crisp and crumbled	5
	Nonstick baking spray	

1. In a medium bowl, combine mashed potatoes, cheese, salt, pepper, egg and butter. Stir in bacon.

2. Spray wells with nonstick baking spray. Spoon about 1½ tbsp (22 mL) potato mixture into each well. Bake for 5 minutes. Using a small offset spatula, carefully turn potato bites over. Bake for 5 to 7 minutes or until potato bites are hot in the center and edges are golden brown. Transfer potato bites to a serving plate. Repeat with the remaining potato mixture. Serve hot.

Traditional Midwestern Dressing Cakes

Roxanne's mother, a superb cook, nurtured Roxanne's love of cooking from an early age. Roxanne has been trying for years to replicate her mom's dressing recipe. The flavor here comes awfully close — delicious dressing in two-bite cake form!

Variation

Add 2 mushrooms, chopped, with the onion.

2½ cups	herb seasoning stuffing mix	625 mL
⅓ cup	unsalted butter	75 mL
¾ cup	finely chopped onion	175 mL
½ cup	diced celery	125 mL
1 tsp	rubbed dried sage	5 mL
1 tsp	poultry seasoning	5 mL
¼ tsp	salt	1 mL
¼ tsp	freshly ground black pepper	1 mL
2	large eggs, lightly beaten	2
1 cup	ready-to-use chicken broth	250 mL
	Nonstick baking spray	

1. Place stuffing mix in a large bowl. Set aside.

2. In a small skillet, melt butter over medium-high heat. Add onion and celery; cook, stirring often, for 4 to 5 minutes or until onion is tender.

3. To the stuffing mix, add onion mixture, sage, poultry seasoning, salt, pepper, eggs and broth, gently tossing to combine. If mixture seems too liquid, let stand for 5 minutes.

4. Spray wells with nonstick baking spray. Spoon a heaping 1½ tbsp (22 mL) stuffing mixture into each well. Using the back of a spoon, pack stuffing into wells. Bake for 8 to 10 minutes or until edges begin to crisp. Transfer cakes to a serving platter. Repeat with the remaining stuffing mixture. Serve warm.

Cornbread Dressing Cakes

Dressing or stuffing? Whatever you call it, these little cakes — crusty on the edges and moist in the center — are a natural choice when you're serving a crowd at Thanksgiving or any fall gathering.

Tip

Once evenly crumbled, 10 Grandma's Old-Fashioned Corn Muffins will make about 3 cups (750 mL).

1/4 cup	unsalted butter	60 mL
1 cup	finely chopped onion	250 mL
1/2 cup	finely chopped celery	125 mL
10	Grandma's Old-Fashioned Corn Muffins (page 124), cooled and crumbled	10
2 tbsp	minced fresh parsley	30 mL
1 tbsp	rubbed dried sage	15 mL
1/2 tsp	dried thyme	2 mL
1/2 tsp	salt	2 mL
1/4 tsp	freshly ground black pepper	1 mL
2	large eggs, lightly beaten	2
3/4 cup	ready-to-use chicken broth	175 mL
1/4 cup	unsalted butter, melted	60 mL

1. In a large skillet, melt 1/4 cup (60 mL) butter over medium heat. Add onion and celery; cook, stirring often, until very tender. Remove from heat and stir in muffin crumbs, parsley, sage, thyme, salt and pepper. Stir in eggs and broth.

2. Brush wells with melted butter. Spoon about 1 1/2 tbsp (22 mL) cornbread mixture into each well. Lightly brush tops with melted butter. Bake for 6 to 8 minutes or until edges are browned and crisp. Transfer cakes to a wire rack to cool slightly. Repeat with the remaining cornbread mixture. Serve warm.

Buffalo Chicken Cups

**Makes
20 to 22 wonton
cups**

Buffalo chicken dip is so popular, and now it's even better. Cook the dip and the wonton wrappers together in tasty bundles, then watch them fly off the table. No wings required!

Tips

Spicy wing sauces vary in heat level. If you're using a sauce you're not familiar with, add 3 to 4 tsp (15 to 20 mL) first, taste, then add additional sauce as desired.

If you prefer, you can substitute ½ cup (125 mL) finely chopped cooked chicken for the canned chicken.

Feeding a crowd? Make a double batch of this recipe.

Variation

Substitute tortilla cups for the wonton cups. Follow the instructions on page 194 for forming tortilla cups, but do not bake them. Once you've filled them with the chicken mixture, bake for 9 to 10 minutes or until tortilla cups are crisp and filling is hot.

20 to 22	wonton wrappers (about 3½ inches/8.5 cm square)	20 to 22
2 oz	cream cheese, softened	60 g
2 tbsp	bottled Buffalo or spicy wing sauce	30 mL
2 tbsp	ranch dressing	30 mL
½ cup	shredded Cheddar cheese	125 mL
1 tbsp	crumbled blue cheese	15 mL
1	can (4½ oz/140 g) chicken, drained	1
2 tbsp	finely chopped celery	30 mL
	Minced green onions	

1. Place 1 wonton wrapper on top of each well and gently press down into well with the pie forming tool, making a cup.

2. In a medium bowl, combine cream cheese, wing sauce and ranch dressing, stirring until smooth. Stir in Cheddar and blue cheese. Stir in chicken and celery.

3. Spoon about 1 tbsp (15 mL) filling into each wonton cup. Bake for 7 to 9 minutes or until wonton cups are toasted and crisp and filling is hot. Carefully transfer wonton cups to a wire rack to cool slightly. Repeat with the remaining wonton wrappers and filling. Serve warm, garnished with green onions.

Phyllo Stuffed with Chicken and Cheese

**Makes
9 to 10 packets**

Crisp phyllo surrounds
a cheesy chicken filling
to make the ultimate
elegant appetizer.

Tips

Different brands of phyllo
come in different-size
sheets. We used sheets
that are 14 by 9 inches
(35 by 23 cm). Some
sheets are larger (17 by
12 inches/43 by 30 cm or
18 by 14 inches/45 by
35 cm), so use 2½, cut in
half crosswise (you'll still
need to make the cut at
the end of step 3).

Instead of making packets,
you can spoon the filling
into phyllo cups. Form
8 sheets of phyllo dough
into cups as directed on
page 45. Spoon about
2 tbsp (30 mL) filling into
each phyllo cup. Bake for
10 to 12 minutes or until
cups are crisp and filling
is hot. Carefully transfer
cups to a wire rack to cool
slightly.

2 tsp	vegetable oil	10 mL
1 cup	chopped spinach	250 mL
¼ cup	chopped onion	60 mL
1 cup	chopped cooked chicken	250 mL
2 oz	cream cheese, softened	60 g
¼ cup	shredded Cheddar cheese	60 mL
3 tbsp	crumbled feta cheese	45 mL
5	sheets frozen phyllo dough, thawed	5
	Nonstick baking spray	

1. In a small skillet, heat oil over medium-high heat. Add spinach and onion; cook, stirring often, for 3 to 4 minutes or until onion is tender.

2. In a medium bowl, combine onion mixture, chicken, cream cheese, Cheddar and feta.

3. Place 1 sheet of phyllo on a cutting board. (Immediately cover the remaining sheets with plastic wrap and then a lightly dampened towel, keeping them covered to prevent them from drying out.) Cut phyllo sheet in half crosswise.

4. Fold 1 half-sheet in half crosswise. Mound 1 to 1½ tbsp (15 to 22 mL) filling in the center. Fold in longer sides, then shorter sides, enclosing the filling and making a packet that will fit in a well. Repeat with 7 more phyllo sheets.

5. Spray wells with nonstick baking spray. Place a packet in each well, pushing it down lightly. Spray tops of packets with baking spray. Bake for 5 to 6 minutes or until golden brown on the bottom. Using a small offset spatula, carefully turn packets over. Bake for 5 to 6 minutes or until golden brown. Carefully transfer packets to a wire rack to cool slightly. Repeat with the remaining phyllo sheets and filling. Serve warm.

Chilipanzingas

**Makes
10 to 11 hand
pies**

You don't have to be from Texas to enjoy their classic ham empanadas. Cheesy and with a spicy kick, these are perfect to serve at your next tailgate party, game night or any casual gathering.

Tip

The heat of a jalapeño pepper is mainly in the veins and seeds, so seeding them reduces the heat slightly. If you like heat, leave them in. To avoid skin irritation when cutting a jalapeño, wear plastic gloves or wash your hands well after handling.

Crusts

	Favorite Buttery Pie Crust (page 38) or store-bought refrigerated pie crust (see tip, page 209) Puff pastry (see tip, page 147)	

Filling

1 tbsp	vegetable oil	15 mL
½	onion, finely chopped	½
½	jalapeño pepper, seeded and minced	½
½ cup	chopped cooked ham	125 mL
1½ tsp	chili powder	7 mL
½ tsp	ground cumin	2 mL
	Salt and freshly ground black pepper	
1 cup	shredded Cheddar-Jack or Colby-Jack cheese	250 mL

1. *Crusts:* Use the large circle of the crust cutting tool to cut 10 to 11 bottom crusts from the pie crust, rerolling scraps as necessary. Place 8 crusts evenly on top of wells and gently press into wells with the pie forming tool. Cover the remaining crusts with plastic wrap and set aside.

2. On a lightly floured surface, roll out puff pastry to about ⅛ inch (3 mm) thick, pressing any perforated seams together. Use the small circle of the crust cutting tool to cut 10 to 11 top crusts. Cover with plastic wrap and set aside.

3. *Filling:* In a small skillet, heat oil over medium-high heat. Add onion and jalapeño; cook, stirring often, for 4 to 5 minutes or until onion is tender. Stir in ham, chili powder, cumin, and salt and pepper to taste; cook, stirring often, for 1 minute or until ham is heated through. Remove from heat and stir in cheese.

4. Spoon about 1½ tbsp (22 mL) filling into each bottom crust; do not overfill. Place a top crust directly over the center of each filled shell.

5. Bake for 10 to 12 minutes or until crusts are browned and crisp. Transfer pies to a wire rack to cool slightly. Let appliance cool for 5 minutes. Repeat with the remaining crusts and filling. Serve warm.

Bacon Pecan Tassies

These miniature delights are sweet and salty, rich and wonderful.

Tip

If using a store-bought refrigerated pie crust, let come to room temperature, then unroll according to package directions and proceed with the recipe. You can cut 14 Babycakes™ single crusts from one packaged pie crust (half a 14-oz/400 g package) by rerolling the scraps.

Crusts

	Cream Cheese Pastry (page 92) or store-bought refrigerated pie crust (see tip, at left)	

Filling

½ cup	packed brown sugar	125 mL
1 tbsp	all-purpose flour	15 mL
1	large egg, at room temperature	1
1 tbsp	unsalted butter, melted	15 mL
2	slices bacon, cooked crisp and crumbled	2
½ cup	chopped pecans, toasted (see tip, page 214)	125 mL

1. *Crusts:* Use the large circle of the crust cutting tool to cut 8 crusts from the pie crust. Place crusts evenly on top of wells and gently press into wells with the pie forming tool. If desired, crimp the edges.

2. *Filling:* In a medium bowl, whisk together brown sugar, flour, egg and butter. Stir in bacon and pecans.

3. Spoon 1½ to 2 tbsp (22 to 30 mL) filling into each crust. Bake for 10 to 12 minutes or until filling is set and crusts are golden brown. Transfer pies to a wire rack to cool slightly. Serve warm.

Beef Wellington Bites

● ●

**Makes
14 to 16 hand
pies**

Few recipes have
withstood the test
of time like beef
Wellington, which
originated in the 1800s.
Many feel it is the
unsurpassed "king" of
fine dining. That classic
dish is the inspiration
for these appetizers.
We think you — and
your guests — will
enjoy the tender, juicy
beef tenderloin and
mushrooms encased in
warm, crisp pastry.

Tips

You can substitute ready-
to-use beef broth for the
sherry, if you prefer.

If you don't have a shallot
on hand, substitute 2 tbsp
(30 mL) finely chopped
onion.

Crusts

	Favorite Buttery Pie Crust (page 38) or store-bought refrigerated pie crust (see tip, page 209) Puff pastry (see tip, page 147)	

Filling

2 tbsp	unsalted butter	30 mL
1	shallot, finely chopped (about 3 tbsp/45 mL)	1
1	clove garlic, minced	1
1 cup	chopped mushrooms	250 mL
8 oz	beef tenderloin, finely chopped	250 g
1 tbsp	dry sherry	15 mL
	Salt and freshly ground black pepper	
	Sherry Cream Sauce (see recipe, opposite)	

1. *Crusts:* Use the large circle of the crust cutting tool to cut 14 to 16 bottom crusts from the pie crust, rerolling scraps as necessary. Place 8 crusts evenly on top of wells and gently press into wells with the pie forming tool. Cover the remaining crusts with plastic wrap and set aside.

2. On a lightly floured surface, roll out puff pastry to about $\frac{1}{8}$ inch (3 mm) thick, pressing any perforated seams together. Use the small circle of the crust cutting tool to cut 14 to 16 top crusts. Cover with plastic wrap and set aside.

3. *Filling:* In a medium skillet, melt butter over medium-high heat. Add shallot and garlic; cook, stirring, for 1 minute. Add mushrooms and cook, stirring often, for 5 to 8 minutes or until moisture evaporates and mushrooms are tender. Add beef and cook, stirring often, for 2 to 3 minutes or until browned on all sides. Stir in sherry. Season to taste with salt and pepper.

4. Spoon about 2 tbsp (30 mL) filling into each bottom crust; do not overfill. Place a top crust directly over the center of each filled shell.

5. Bake for 10 to 12 minutes or until crusts are browned and crisp. Transfer pies to a wire rack to cool slightly. Let appliance cool for 5 minutes. Repeat with the remaining crusts and filling. Serve warm, with Sherry Cream Sauce.

This sauce adds the
finishing touch to Beef
Wellington Bites. If any
happens to be left over,
pair it with beef steak
or roast pork.

Tip

You can replace the sherry
with an additional 2 tbsp
(30 mL) beef broth, if you
prefer.

Sherry Cream Sauce

2 tbsp	unsalted butter	30 mL
2	cloves garlic, finely chopped	2
1	shallot, finely chopped	1
2 tbsp	all-purpose flour	30 mL
⅔ cup	ready-to-use beef broth	150 mL
2 tbsp	dry sherry	30 mL
1 tsp	Worcestershire sauce	5 mL
	Salt and fresh ground black pepper	
1 tbsp	heavy or whipping (35%) cream	15 mL

1. In a small saucepan, melt butter over medium heat. Add garlic and shallot; cook, stirring often, for 1 to 2 minutes or until shallot is tender. Stir in flour until smooth. Cook, stirring constantly, for 1 minute.

2. Gradually stir in broth, sherry and Worcestershire sauce until smooth. Bring to a boil, stirring constantly. Remove from heat and season to taste with salt and pepper. Stir in cream. Serve hot.

Parmesan and Bacon Tarts

Parmesan, bacon and garlic combine in these bite-size pies, making stellar appetizers that will become an instant classic.

Tip

Instead of the fresh basil, you could drizzle ½ tsp (2 mL) basil pesto over each tart just before serving.

Crusts

	Favorite Buttery Pie Crust (page 38), Cream Cheese Pastry (page 92) or store-bought refrigerated pie crust (see tip, page 209)	

Filling

1	large egg, at room temperature	1
⅓ cup	half-and-half (10%) cream	75 mL
⅛ tsp	garlic powder	0.5 mL
	Salt and freshly ground black pepper	
3	drops hot pepper sauce	3
3	slices bacon, cooked crisp and crumbled	3
⅓ cup	freshly grated Parmesan cheese	75 mL
8 tsp	minced fresh basil or flat-leaf (Italian) parsley	40 mL

1. *Crusts:* Use the large circle of the crust cutting tool to cut 8 crusts from the pie crust. Place crusts evenly on top of wells and gently press into wells with the pie forming tool. If desired, crimp the edges.

2. *Filling:* In a small bowl, whisk together egg and cream. Stir in garlic powder, salt and pepper to taste and hot pepper sauce.

3. Spoon bacon into crusts, dividing evenly. Spoon about 1 tbsp (15 mL) egg mixture into each crust. Sprinkle each with about 2 tsp (10 mL) Parmesan. Bake for 8 to 10 minutes or until filling is set and crusts are golden brown. Transfer tarts to a wire rack to cool slightly. Garnish with basil and serve warm.

Treats for Parties and Special Occasions

Hummingbird Cupcakes   BIRTHDAY

When Kathy
was growing up,
hummingbird cake
was her dad's favorite,
and no birthday was
complete without
it. These cupcakes
are a tribute to that
wonderful tradition.

Tips

Toasting pecans intensifies
their flavor. Spread chopped
pecans in a single layer on a
baking sheet. Bake at 350°F
(180°C) for 5 to 7 minutes
or until lightly browned. Let
cool, then measure.

Use the remaining crushed
pineapple and pineapple
juice in a fruit or gelatin
salad, or on top of pancakes
or waffles.

• Paper liners (optional)

1	can (8 oz/227 mL) crushed pineapple, with juice	1
1½ cups	all-purpose flour	375 mL
⅔ cup	granulated sugar	150 mL
⅓ cup	packed brown sugar	75 mL
½ tsp	baking soda	2 mL
½ tsp	salt	2 mL
½ tsp	ground cinnamon	2 mL
¼ tsp	ground nutmeg	1 mL
1	large egg, at room temperature, lightly beaten	1
1	large egg yolk, at room temperature, lightly beaten	1
½ cup	vegetable oil	125 mL
1 cup	chopped pecans, toasted (see tip, at left), divided	250 mL
1 cup	chopped banana	250 mL
1 tsp	vanilla extract	5 mL
	Cream Cheese Frosting (page 114)	

1. Drain pineapple well, reserving juice. Measure out ⅓ cup (75 mL) fruit and 3 tbsp (45 mL) juice, reserving the rest for another use (see tip, at left). Set aside.

2. In a large bowl, whisk together flour, granulated sugar, brown sugar, baking soda, salt, cinnamon and nutmeg. Stir in egg, egg yolk and oil until blended. Stir in pineapple, pineapple juice, half the pecans, banana and vanilla.

3. If desired, place paper liners in wells. Fill each well with about 1½ tbsp (22 mL) batter. Bake for 6 to 8 minutes or until a tester inserted in the center of a cupcake comes out clean. Transfer cupcakes to a wire rack to cool. Repeat with the remaining batter.

4. Frost with Cream Cheese Frosting and garnish with the remaining pecans.

Clowning Around Cupcakes

**Makes
18 to 20 cupcakes**

When planning a celebration for a special child, everything has to be perfect. These cupcakes are just the right size for little hands, and nothing could be cuter or easier to prepare.

Tip

You can also use orange, blue or green food coloring to tint the frosting for the hair, or make several of each color. Another alternative for the hair is to pinch off small swatches of pink cotton candy and arrange them on the cupcakes just before serving.

If you want to add hats, shape small pieces of colored fondant into pointed hats, or add a white-striped kiss-shaped chocolate to each cupcake.

• **2 pastry bags, each fitted with a fine writing tip**

18 to 20	Wedding Cake Cupcakes (page 218)	18 to 20
1 cup	Vanilla Buttercream Frosting (page 105), divided	250 mL
36 to 40	star-shaped sprinkles	36 to 40
18 to 20	miniature red candy-coated chocolate candies	18 to 20
	Red food coloring	
	Yellow food coloring	

1. Using a small offset spatula, frost cupcakes with $\frac{1}{4}$ cup (60 mL) of the Vanilla Buttercream Frosting, making a smooth surface.

2. Place 2 star-shaped sprinkles on each cupcake for the eyes. Add a mini red candy for the nose.

3. Transfer $\frac{1}{4}$ cup (60 mL) frosting to a small bowl. Stir in enough red food coloring to tint it bright red. Fill a pastry bag with red frosting and pipe a smiling mouth on each cupcake.

4. Stir enough yellow food coloring into the remaining frosting to tint it bright yellow. Fill another pastry bag with yellow frosting and pipe tight swirls on each cupcake for the hair.

Hawaiian Holiday Cupcakes

Makes 31 to 33 cupcakes

Wish bon voyage to your favorite travelers — or welcome them home — with these cupcakes. Even if a vacation is in your long-range plans or is merely a dream, a tropical-themed party may be just the fun you need on an otherwise dreary day. Once you taste these cupcakes, no luau will be complete without them.

Tip

Toasting macadamia nuts intensifies their flavor. Spread macadamia nuts in a single layer on a baking sheet. Bake at 350°F (180°C) for 5 to 7 minutes or until lightly browned. Let cool, then measure.

Variation

Substitute chopped walnuts for the macadamia nuts.

- Paper liners (optional)

1	can (8 oz/227 mL) crushed pineapple, with juice	1
2 cups	yellow cake mix	500 mL
3½ tbsp	vanilla instant pudding mix (half of a 3.4 oz/96 g box)	52 mL
2	large eggs, at room temperature	2
¼ cup	vegetable oil	60 mL
½ cup	sweetened flaked coconut	125 mL
¼ cup	chopped macadamia nuts, toasted (see tip, at left)	60 mL
	Cream Cheese Frosting (page 114)	
	Additional sweetened flaked coconut, toasted (see tip, page 80)	
	Additional toasted chopped macadamia nuts	

1. Drain pineapple well, reserving juice. Measure out ⅔ cup (150 mL) juice. Set both aside.

2. In a large bowl, whisk together cake mix and pudding mix. Using an electric mixer on low speed, beat in pineapple juice, eggs and oil for 30 seconds or until moistened. Beat on medium speed for 2 minutes. Stir in pineapple, coconut and macadamia nuts.

3. If desired, place paper liners in wells. Fill each well with about 1½ tbsp (22 mL) batter. Bake for 6 to 8 minutes or until a tester inserted in the center of a cupcake comes out clean. Transfer cupcakes to a wire rack to cool. Repeat with the remaining batter.

4. Frost with Cream Cheese Frosting and garnish with toasted coconut and macadamia nuts.

Petit Four Cupcakes

Makes 25 to 27 cupcakes

Petits fours are the standard when it comes to elegant entertaining. Let the Babycakes™ Cupcake Maker bake the treats in the perfect size, then cover them with classic poured fondant frosting.

Tips

Royal icing flowers and sugar flowers are available at cake decorating shops and hobby stores.

If you don't have a double boiler, combine the confectioners' sugar, water and syrup in a heat-proof bowl and place the bowl over a pan of simmering water.

Ideally, the frosting should be heated to about 100°F (38°F). If it is too hot or too cool, it becomes too thick or too thin to flow easily. In addition, if too cool, the frosting will dry to a dull matte finish instead of a pretty sheen. Reheat the frosting as necessary.

Petits fours will hold beautifully for several hours, but should be served the day they are made. At room temperature, the frosting dries to a sheen. Avoid sealing them in an airtight container, as the frosting will become sticky.

- 1⅝-inch (4.25 cm) round cookie cutter
- Double boiler (see tip, at left)

	Golden Yellow Cupcake batter (page 30), prepared through step 2	
3 tbsp	seedless raspberry preserves, warmed	45 mL
4½ cups	confectioners' (icing) sugar	1.125 L
6 tbsp	water	90 mL
1½ tbsp	white corn syrup	22 mL
½ tsp	almond extract	2 mL
¼ tsp	vanilla extract	1 mL
2 to 3	drops red food coloring	2 to 3
25 to 27	small royal icing or sugar flowers (about ¼ inch/0.5 cm diameter)	25 to 27

1. Fill each well with about 1 tbsp (15 mL) batter (do not use paper liners). Bake for 5 to 7 minutes or until a tester inserted in the center of a cupcake comes out clean. Transfer cupcakes to a wire rack to cool completely. Repeat with the remaining batter.

2. Place cooled cupcakes upside down on a work surface. Using the cookie cutter, trim each cupcake slightly so that the sides are straight and no part of the cupcake is wider than another.

3. Using a serrated knife, cut cupcakes in half horizontally. Spread ¼ tsp (1 mL) preserves over each bottom half. Replace tops. Place top side down on a wire rack set over a baking sheet.

4. In the top of a double boiler, combine confectioners' sugar, water and corn syrup. Heat over simmering water, stirring frequently, for about 7 minutes or until just warm. Stir in almond extract and vanilla. Stir in enough food coloring to tint frosting light pink.

5. Using a gentle, circular motion, drizzle 1 to 1½ tbsp (15 to 22 mL) warm frosting over each cupcake, covering the top and sides completely and quickly, so that the frosting dries to a smooth finish. (If necessary, use the tip of a small offset spatula to help cover the sides.)

6. Immediately place a flower in the center of each cupcake. Let frosting dry completely before serving.

Wedding Cake Cupcakes

**Makes
18 to 20 cupcakes**

If you really like wedding cake, it is sometimes hard to wait for the next big celebration. Wait no more! These cupcakes are for you. And, of course, they're perfect when you're planning a wedding, a shower or another elegant event. For that true "wedding cake flavor," swirl high with Vanilla Buttercream Frosting (page 105).

Tips

No buttermilk on hand? Stir 1½ tsp (7 mL) lemon juice or white vinegar into ½ cup (125 mL) milk. Let stand for 5 to 10 minutes or until thickened. Proceed with the recipe.

Shops that specialize in cake decorating often sell special wedding flavor extract. Or look for other special flavorings, such as crème bouquet or birthday cake. Use in place of the vanilla in this recipe, or follow package directions. Many of these extracts are concentrated, so don't add too much.

- Paper liners (optional)

2 cups	white cake mix	500 mL
2	large egg whites, at room temperature	2
1	large egg, at room temperature	1
½ cup	buttermilk	125 mL
¼ cup	vegetable oil	60 mL
½ tsp	vanilla extract	2 mL

1. In a medium bowl, using an electric mixer on low speed, beat cake mix, egg whites, egg, buttermilk, oil and vanilla for 30 seconds or until moistened. Beat on medium speed for 2 minutes.

2. If desired, place paper liners in wells. Fill each well with about 1½ tbsp (22 mL) batter. Bake for 6 to 8 minutes or until a tester inserted in the center of a cupcake comes out clean. Transfer cupcakes to a wire rack to cool. Repeat with the remaining batter.

Baby Bib Cupcakes

**Makes
30 to 32 cupcakes**

Miniature cupcakes make the celebration for baby even sweeter.

- 1¾-inch (4 cm) round cutter with a scalloped or smooth edge
- ⅞-inch (2.2 cm) round cutter with a smooth edge
- Pastry bag fitted with a tiny star tip or fine writing tip

1 cup	Vanilla Buttercream Frosting (page 105), divided	250 mL
	Yellow, pink and blue food colorings	
	Brown food coloring (optional)	
30 to 32	Old-Fashioned White Cupcakes (page 34)	30 to 32
	Confectioners' (icing) sugar	
	Pink or blue fondant	

1. Place ¾ cup (175 mL) of the Vanilla Buttercream Frosting in a small bowl. Stir in 1 to 2 drops each of yellow and pink coloring to create a flesh tone. For a darker skin tone, add 1 to 2 drops of brown food coloring. Lightly frost the top of each cupcake.

2. Lightly dust a cutting board with confectioners' sugar. Place a piece of prepared fondant on the cutting board and use a rolling pin to roll it out to ⅛-inch (3 mm) thickness. Use the 1¾-inch (4 cm) cutter to cut out 30 to 32 circles, rerolling scraps.

3. Position the ⅞-inch (2.2 cm) cutter on a fondant circle so that it is half on and half off. Cut out a scoop, creating a bib shape. Repeat with the remaining fondant circles. Place a bib on each cupcake.

4. Stir enough pink, blue or yellow food coloring into the remaining frosting to tint it the desired shade. Fill the pastry bag with frosting and pipe small stars or dots along the edge of each bib. Pipe a stripe of frosting across the "neck opening" of each bib for the ties. Pipe a figure 8 in the center of each stripe for a bow. In the center of each bib, pipe the baby's initial (first name, if you know it, or last name).

Strawberry Poke Cakes

Makes 20 to 22 cupcakes

Do you remember strawberry poke cake, popular in the 1970s? We think it's worth revisiting the family favorite, this time as smaller treats. Since they are so pretty and red, Valentine's Day is the perfect time to serve them.

Variation

Substitute your favorite gelatin flavor and garnish accordingly.

• Paper liners (optional)

2 cups	vanilla cake mix	500 mL
2	large eggs, at room temperature	2
1⅔ cup	water, divided	400 mL
¼ cup	vegetable oil	60 mL
1	package (3 oz/85 g) strawberry-flavored gelatin powder	1
1 cup	whipped cream or frozen whipped topping	250 mL
10 to 11	strawberries, hulled and cut in half	10 to 11

1. In a medium bowl, using an electric mixer on low speed, beat cake mix, eggs, ⅔ cup (150 mL) of the water and oil for 30 seconds or until moistened. Beat on medium speed for 2 minutes.

2. If desired, place paper liners in wells. Fill each well with about 1½ tbsp (22 mL) batter. Bake for 6 to 8 minutes or until a tester inserted in the center of a cupcake comes out clean. Transfer cupcakes to a wire rack to cool. Repeat with the remaining batter.

3. In a small saucepan, bring the remaining water to a boil over medium-high heat. Stir in gelatin until dissolved. Refrigerate for 30 minutes.

4. Using a fork, poke 3 or 4 holes in the cupcakes. Spoon gelatin mixture over cupcakes, dividing evenly. Frost with whipped cream and garnish each with a strawberry half. Serve immediately or refrigerate in an airtight container for up to 4 hours.

King Cupcakes

Makes 22 to 24 cupcakes

Let the good times roll. We love king cake — the rich, yeast-leavened cake served during Mardi Gras in New Orleans — and used it as the inspiration for these cupcakes. Decorated in the classic colors, they'll take center stage at your Mardi Gras party. Surround the cupcakes with decorative beads and masks.

Tips

For added fun, hide a treat in one of the cupcakes, inserting it quickly into the batter after filling the wells and before baking. (Or, if the treat is plastic, cut a slit in a baked and cooled cupcake, insert the treat, then frost the cupcakes.) Traditionally, a pecan half, a coin or a small plastic doll is baked in a king cake. Whoever finds the treat is named king or queen of the party. Let your guests know there is a treat in one of the cupcakes so they take care not to swallow it.

• Paper liners (optional)		
1¼ cups	all-purpose flour	300 mL
1½ tsp	baking powder	7 mL
¼ tsp	salt	1 mL
⅛ tsp	ground nutmeg	0.5 mL
¾ cup	granulated sugar	175 mL
¼ cup	unsalted butter, softened	60 mL
½ tsp	grated lemon zest	2 mL
1	large egg, at room temperature	1
1	large egg yolk, at room temperature	1
1 tsp	vanilla extract	5 mL
⅔ cup	milk	150 mL
	Vanilla Buttercream Frosting (page 105)	
	Purple, green and yellow sanding sugar	

1. In a medium bowl, whisk together flour, baking powder, salt and nutmeg. Set aside.

2. In a large bowl, using an electric mixer on medium-high speed, beat sugar and butter for 1 to 2 minutes or until fluffy. Beat in lemon zest. Add egg and egg yolk, one at a time, beating well after each addition. Beat in vanilla. Add flour mixture alternately with milk, making three additions of flour and two of milk and beating on low speed until smooth.

3. If desired, place paper liners in wells. Fill each well with about 1½ tbsp (22 mL) batter. Bake for 6 to 8 minutes or until a tester inserted in the center of a cupcake comes out clean. Transfer cupcakes to a wire rack to cool. Repeat with the remaining batter.

4. Frost with Vanilla Buttercream Frosting. Divide cupcakes into three groups. Sprinkle the cupcakes in one group with purple sanding sugar, another group with green sugar and the final group with yellow sugar.

Variation

Sprinkle a narrow strip of each color of sanding sugar on each cupcake. To keep your stripes neat, shield the other parts of the cupcake with a piece of cardboard as you sprinkle.

Filled Key Lime Cupcakes

**Makes
18 to 20 cupcakes**

Surprise! A creamy lime filling hides inside these cupcakes, making them ideal for your St. Patrick's Day party!

Tips

Key limes are smaller, more yellow in color and more flavorful than the commonly available Persian lime. But if you can't find Key limes, it's fine to use regular lime zest and juice.

When frosting over a filling, as with the lime filling here, it is easiest and neatest to pipe the frosting, covering the filling and the cupcake.

The cake pieces you cut from the tops of these cupcakes can be reserved for other uses. Try layering the cake pieces with fresh fruit for a parfait, or crumbling them over ice cream. Freeze leftover cake pieces in a freezer bag for up to 2 months.

Cupcakes

	Wedding Cake Cupcake batter (page 218)	
1/2 tsp	grated Key lime zest (see tip, at left)	2 mL

Filling

1/2 cup	sweetened condensed milk	125 mL
2 tsp	grated Key lime zest	10 mL
2 tbsp	freshly squeezed Key lime juice	30 mL
2 to 3	drops green food coloring	2 to 3

Topping

1/2 cup	heavy or whipping (35%) cream	125 mL
1 tbsp	confectioners' (icing) sugar	15 mL
	Graham wafer crumbs	
	Key lime zest curls (see page 20)	

1. *Cupcakes:* Prepare Wedding Cake Cupcake batter as directed, beating in lime zest with the other ingredients. Bake as directed and let cool completely.

2. *Filling:* In a medium bowl, whisk together milk, lime zest, lime juice and food coloring. Cover and refrigerate for 1 hour or until thick.

3. Using a serrated knife, cut a 1/2-inch (1 cm) circle out of the top of each cupcake. Fill each circle with about 1/2 tsp (2 mL) filling (see tips, at left).

4. *Topping:* In a chilled small bowl, using an electric mixer on medium-high speed, beat cream until frothy. Beat in confectioners' sugar until stiff peaks form. Pipe or dollop on top of each cupcake, covering the filling. Garnish with graham wafer crumbs and lime zest curls.

Orange Marmalade Cupcakes

Makes 23 to 25 cupcakes

Make Mom's Day special with these delightful orange marmalade cupcakes. We are both avid fans of Jan Karon's series of books about the town of Mitford. (Maybe Mom is too?) At every special event in that delightful storybook town, a decadent orange marmalade cake takes center stage. We think our cupcake versions are the perfect treat to serve on Mother's Day.

Tips

No buttermilk on hand? Stir 1½ tsp (7 mL) lemon juice or white vinegar into ½ cup (125 mL) milk. Let stand for 5 to 10 minutes or until thickened. Proceed with the recipe.

If your marmalade includes any large pieces of rind, chop them before melting the marmalade.

- Paper liners (optional)
- Pastry bag fitted with a fine writing tip

1⅓ cups	all-purpose flour	325 mL
½ tsp	baking powder	2 mL
½ tsp	baking soda	2 mL
¼ tsp	salt	1 mL
1 cup	granulated sugar	250 mL
½ cup	unsalted butter, softened	125 mL
1	large egg, at room temperature	1
1	large egg yolk, at room temperature	1
	Grated zest of 1 orange	
1 tsp	vanilla extract	5 mL
½ tsp	orange extract	2 mL
½ cup	buttermilk	125 mL
	Orange Frosting (page 108)	
⅓ cup	orange marmalade (see tip, at left)	75 mL

1. In a small bowl, whisk together flour, baking powder, baking soda and salt. Set aside.

2. In a large bowl, using an electric mixer on medium-high speed, beat sugar and butter for 1 to 2 minutes or until fluffy. Add egg and egg yolk, one at a time, beating well after each addition. Beat in orange zest, vanilla and orange extract. Add flour mixture alternately with buttermilk, making three additions of flour and two of buttermilk and beating on low speed until smooth.

4. If desired, place paper liners in wells. Fill each well with about 1½ tbsp (22 mL) batter. Bake for 6 to 8 minutes or until a tester inserted in the center of a cupcake comes out clean. Transfer cupcakes to a wire rack to cool. Repeat with the remaining batter.

5. Fill the pastry bag with Orange Frosting and pipe a ring around the outer edge of each cupcake.

6. Place orange marmalade in a small microwave-safe glass bowl. Microwave on High for 30 seconds or until slightly melted. Stir well. Using the tip of a kitchen teaspoon, spoon about ½ tsp (2 mL) orange marmalade on top of each cupcake, inside the frosting ring.

Maple Bacon Cupcakes

FATHER'S DAY

• •

**Makes
13 to 15 cupcakes**

We are both Midwest
girls, born and raised.
Bacon played a big
part in our culinary
upbringing, and many
fond food memories
are tied to its aroma,
flavor and texture. Our
dads were bacon fans,
too, so adding bacon to
cupcakes is a natural
way for us to celebrate
Dad's Day.

• •

Tips

No buttermilk on hand? Stir
¾ tsp (3 mL) lemon juice or
white vinegar into ¼ cup
(60 mL) milk. Let stand for
5 to 10 minutes or until
thickened. Proceed with
the recipe.

If you prefer, you can leave
the bacon garnish off
and simply enjoy maple
cupcakes.

Be sure to store these
cupcakes in the refrigerator.

• Paper liners (optional)

¾ cup	cake flour	175 mL
¾ tsp	baking powder	3 mL
¼ tsp	salt	1 mL
⅓ cup	granulated sugar	75 mL
¼ cup	unsalted butter, softened	60 mL
1	large egg, at room temperature	1
1 tsp	vanilla extract	5 mL
¼ cup	buttermilk	60 mL
	Maple Frosting (page 112)	
6	slices bacon, cooked crisp and broken into 1-inch (2.5 cm) pieces	6

1. In a small bowl, whisk together flour, baking powder and salt. Set aside.

2. In a medium bowl, using an electric mixer on medium-high speed, beat sugar and butter for 1 to 2 minutes or until fluffy. Beat in egg and vanilla. Add flour mixture alternately with buttermilk, making three additions of flour and two of buttermilk and beating on low speed until smooth.

3. If desired, place paper liners in wells. Fill each well with about 1½ tbsp (22 mL) batter. Bake for 5 to 7 minutes or until a tester inserted in the center of a cupcake comes out clean. Transfer cupcakes to a wire rack to cool. Repeat with the remaining batter.

4. Frost with Maple Frosting and garnish with bacon.

All-American Flag

**Makes
35 servings**

This easy, festive flag dessert is perfect for any patriotic American gathering — a Fourth of July party, for sure, but how about a Memorial Day picnic? Pick your favorite cupcake flavor — chocolate, white, yellow — as a base, or make a variety of flavors.

Tips

Large, long strawberries will work better in this design than round ones.

If you want to host a patriotic party for another nation — for Canada Day, for example, or to celebrate a World Cup win — use this basic idea as your template, choosing garnishes in the colors of the nation's flag and arranging them appropriately.

35	cupcakes	35
	Vanilla Buttercream Frosting (page 105) or whipped cream	
24	blueberries	24
8	strawberries, cut into quarters	8

1. Frost cupcakes with Vanilla Buttercream Frosting. On a decorative tray, tightly arrange cupcakes in five rows of 7 cupcakes. Arrange blueberries on the 6 cupcakes in the top left corner (3 in the first row and 3 in the second row).

2. Arrange one strawberry quarter, cut side down, on each of the remaining cupcakes, positioning the berries so they are parallel to the long side of the flag.

Toasted Pecan and Cranberry Muffins

**Makes
30 to 32 muffins**

No fall celebration would be complete without cranberries and pecans. Start the holiday off right with freshly baked muffins. Your out-of-town guests and family will love them.

Tips

Fresh cranberries are usually available only in the late fall and early winter. Buy extra when you see them and freeze them to enjoy all year long.

Toasting pecans intensifies their flavor. Spread chopped pecans in a single layer on a baking sheet. Bake at 350°F (180°C) for 5 to 7 minutes or until lightly browned. Let cool, then measure.

- Food processor
- Paper liners (optional)

Cranberry-Pecan Mixture

1 cup	fresh or frozen cranberries (partially thawed and drained if frozen)	250 mL
½ cup	chopped pecans, toasted (see tip, at left)	125 mL
1 tbsp	granulated sugar	15 mL
1 tbsp	all-purpose flour	15 mL
	Grated zest of 1 orange	

Muffins

2 cups	all-purpose flour	500 mL
1¼ tsp	baking powder	6 mL
½ tsp	baking soda	2 mL
¼ tsp	ground cinnamon	1 mL
¼ tsp	salt	1 mL
1 cup	granulated sugar	250 mL
½ cup	unsalted butter, softened	125 mL
2	large eggs, at room temperature	2
1 tsp	vanilla extract	5 mL
¾ cup	sour cream	175 mL
¼ cup	buttermilk	60 mL

Orange Glaze

1½ cups	confectioners' (icing) sugar	375 mL
2 tbsp	unsalted butter, melted	30 mL
2 to 4 tbsp	freshly squeezed orange juice	30 to 60 mL

1. *Cranberry-Pecan Mixture:* In food processor, combine cranberries, pecans, sugar, flour and orange zest; pulse until chopped (do not overprocess or purée). Set aside.

2. *Muffins:* In a small bowl, combine flour, baking powder, baking soda, cinnamon and salt. Set aside.

Tip

No buttermilk on hand? Stir ¾ tsp (3 mL) lemon juice or white vinegar into ¼ cup (60 mL) milk. Let stand for 5 to 10 minutes or until thickened. Proceed with the recipe.

3. In a large bowl, using an electric mixer on medium-high speed, beat sugar and butter for 1 to 2 minutes or until fluffy. Add eggs, one at a time, beating well after each addition. Beat in vanilla. Beat in sour cream and buttermilk. Reduce mixer speed to low and beat in flour mixture until just moistened. Stir in cranberry-pecan mixture.

4. If desired, place paper liners in wells. Fill each well with about 1½ tbsp (22 mL) batter. Bake for 6 to 8 minutes or until a tester inserted in the center of a muffin comes out clean. Transfer muffins to a wire rack to cool slightly. Repeat with the remaining batter.

5. *Glaze:* In a small bowl, combine confectioners' sugar, butter and 2 tbsp (30 mL) of the orange juice. Stir in additional orange juice as needed to reach a glaze consistency. Drizzle over cooled muffins.

Santa's Reindeer Cupcakes

**Makes
35 to 37 cupcakes**

Begin with a batch of great chocolate cupcakes, add some simple decorations and let the holiday party begin.

• 2 pastry bags, each fitted with a fine writing tip

35 to 37	All-American Chocolate Cupcakes (page 32) Vanilla Buttercream Frosting (page 105) Classic Chocolate Buttercream Frosting (page 106)	35 to 37
35 to 37	miniature semisweet chocolate chips or miniature red candy-coated chocolate candies	35 to 37
35 to 37	small pretzel twists, broken in half	35 to 37

1. Using a small offset spatula, frost the top of each cupcake with Vanilla Buttercream Frosting, making a smooth surface. Reserve the remaining frosting.

2. Fill a pastry bag with Classic Chocolate Buttercream Frosting. Pipe a figure 8, about $1\frac{1}{2}$ inches (4 cm) long and 1 inch (2.5 cm) wide, in the center of each cupcake. Fill in the figure 8 so that it is solid chocolate.

3. Fill another pastry bag with the remaining vanilla frosting and pipe eyes within the top circle of each figure 8.

4. Use the chocolate frosting to pipe tiny pupils in the center of each eye.

5. For the nose, place a chocolate chip just below the center point of each figure 8.

6. Position pretzel halves as antlers on each cupcake.

Candy Cane Cupcakes

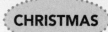
CHRISTMAS

**Makes
16 cupcakes**

Chocolate and
peppermint make a
beautiful and tasty
combination for the
holidays.

Tip
You can substitute crushed
chocolate mints or your
favorite peppermint candies
for the candy canes.

• Paper liners (optional)

1½ cups	devil's food cake mix	375 mL
4 tsp	unsweetened cocoa powder	20 mL
2	large eggs, at room temperature	2
¼ cup	vegetable oil	60 mL
¼ cup	water	60 mL
	White Chocolate Peppermint Frosting (variation, page 109)	
⅔ cup	crushed peppermint-flavored candy canes	150 mL

1. In a large bowl, using an electric mixer on low speed, beat cake mix, cocoa, eggs, oil and water for 30 seconds or until moistened. Beat on medium speed for 2 minutes.

2. If desired, place paper liners in wells. Fill each well with about 1½ tbsp (22 mL) batter. Bake for 6 to 8 minutes or until a tester inserted in the center of a cupcake comes out clean. Transfer cupcakes to a wire rack to cool. Repeat with the remaining batter.

3. Frost generously with White Chocolate Peppermint Frosting. Immediately sprinkle each cupcake with about 2 tsp (10 mL) crushed candy canes.

Brownie Ornaments

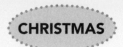

**Makes
16 to 18 brownies**

These brownie "ornaments" are the perfect treat to enjoy while decorating the holiday tree.

Tip

Tint the frosting any color you like, or make brownie ornaments in several different colors. But be sure to leave about ½ cup (125 mL) of the frosting white, for the decorative stripes.

• Pastry bag fitted with a fine writing tip

1 cup	Vanilla Buttercream Frosting (page 105), divided	250 mL
	Red food coloring	
16 to 18	Traditional Brownie Bites (page 67)	16 to 18
16 to 18	2-inch (5 cm) pieces black shoestring licorice	16 to 18
16 to 18	miniature marshmallows	16 to 18
80 to 108	miniature candy-coated chocolate candies (about 1 oz/30 g)	80 to 108

1. Fill the pastry bag with half the Vanilla Buttercream Frosting and set aside. Stir enough food coloring into the remaining frosting to tint it bright red.

2. Using a small offset spatula, frost brownies with red frosting, making a smooth surface.

3. Fold a licorice piece into a loose loop and insert both ends into the top of a marshmallow. Use a small dab of white frosting to secure the marshmallow at the top edge of a brownie, so it resembles the top of an ornament.

4. Pipe a strip of white frosting across the brownie, just above the center. Pipe another strip immediately below the first one. Continue piping strips until you have created a stripe about ¼ inch (0.5 cm) wide that runs across the center of the brownie. Arrange 5 or 6 candies along the stripe.

5. Repeat steps 3 and 4 with the remaining ingredients.

Internet Support and Mail Order Sources

The Electrified Cooks, LLC: www.electrifiedcooks.com

Kathy and Roxanne's blog, filled with recipes, tips, classes and more: www.pluggedintocooking.com

Select Brands: www.selectbrands.com

The Select Brands Babycakes™ site: www.thebabycakesshop.com

Cake Decorating Supplies

Beryl's: www.beryls.com

Fancy Flours: www.fancyflours.com

N.Y. Cake: www.nycake.com

Sweet! Baking & Candy Making Supply: www.sweetbakingsupply.com

Wilton: www.wilton.com

Kitchen Utensils, Kitchen Equipment, Spices, Serving Platters and Packaging

Bridge Kitchenware: www.bridgekitchenware.com

Crate & Barrel: www.crateandbarrel.com

Golda's Kitchen: www.goldaskitchen.com

Sur la Table: www.surlatable.com

Williams-Sonoma: www.williams-sonoma.com

Flours, Sugars, Spices, Extracts and Premium Ingredients

C & H Pure Cane Sugar: www.chsugar.com

Hudson Cream Flour: www.hudsoncream.com

King Arthur Flour: www.kingarthurflour.com

Land O'Lakes: www.landolakes.com

Penzeys Spices: www.penzeys.com

Sarabeth's Kitchen: www.sarabeth.com (we adore her preserves)

Library and Archives Canada Cataloguing in Publication

Moore, Kathy, 1954-
    The big book of babycakes cupcake maker recipes : homemade bite-sized fun! /
Kathy Moore, Roxanne Wyss.

Includes index.
ISBN 978-0-7788-0417-8

    1. Cupcakes. 2. Cookbooks. I. Wyss, Roxanne II. Title.

TX771.M65 2012   641.86'53   C2012-902804-5

Index